Zeitschrift für Ethnologie

Band 138, 2013

REIMER

Zeitschrift für Ethnologie, Band 138, 2013

Herausgegeben im Auftrag
der Deutschen Gesellschaft für Völkerkunde
und der Berliner Gesellschaft für Anthropologie, Ethnologie und Urgeschichte von

Peter Finke	Ethnologisches Seminar Zürich, Andreasstr. 15, CH-8050 Zürich
Lars-Christian Koch	Ethnologisches Museum, Arnimallee 23–27, D-14195 Berlin

Redaktion:

Thomas Bierschenk	Institut für Ethnologie und Afrikastudien, Forum Universitatis 6, D-55099 Mainz
Mareile Flitsch	Völkerkundemuseum der Universität Zürich, Pelikanstr. 40, CH-8001 Zürich
Ernst Halbmayer	Fachgebiet Kultur- und Sozialanthropologie, Kugelgasse 10, D-35032 Marburg
Carola Lentz	Institut für Ethnologie und Afrikastudien, Forum Universitatis 6, D-55099 Mainz
Markus Schindlbeck	Ethnologisches Museum, Arnimallee 23–27, D-14195 Berlin
Martin Sökefeld	Institut für Ethnologie, Oettingenstr. 67, D-80538 München

Wissenschaftlicher Beirat/Advisory Editorial Board: Thomas Hylland Eriksen (Oslo), Michael Carrithers (Durham/UK), Chris Gregory (Canberra), Brigitta Hauser-Schäublin (Göttingen), Nefissa Naguib (Bergen), Joanna Pfaff-Czarnecka (Bielefeld), Josephus Platenkamp (Münster), Peter Probst (Boston), David Shankland (London und Bristol), Sabine Strasser (Bern), Peter Schweitzer (Wien)

Buchbesprechungen:

Thomas Hüsken	Ethnologisches Seminar, Universität Luzern, Frohburgstrasse 3, CH-6002 Luzern

Guidelines for Contributors

1. All manuscripts should be submitted to the editorial assistant of the journal (christopher.kelley@uzh.ch), Ethnologisches Seminar Zürich, Andreasstr. 15, CH-8050 Zürich.
2. The editors welcome original articles up to 8.000 words, reviews up to 1000 words, in German or English. The submitted articles should not be under consideration elsewhere.
3. Articles should be formatted as $1\,^1/_2$ space with a 3 cm margin on all sides. Submissions should be by email attachment in MS Word format. Avoid underlining as far as possible. Foreign words should be italicized. Articles should be accompanied by English abstracts of not more than 200 words.
4. References within the text should be cited in the following form: (Best 1924:184). Footnotes should be kept to a minimum and they must be numbered consecutively throughout the text. Any figure captions should be on a separate sheet. On a further sheet complete references to all works cited must be listed, arranged in alphabetical and calendrical order, as in the following examples:
- Best, Elsdon 1924: *The Maori*, Vol. 1. Wellington: Polynesian Society.
- Firth, Raymond 1936: *We, the Tikopia.* London: George Allen and Unwin.
- Firth, Raymond 1940: The analysis of *mana*: An empirical approach. *Journal of the Polynesian Society* 49:483–510.
- Howard, Alan; Kirckpatrick, John 1989: Social organization. In: A. Howard and R. Borofsky (eds.), *Developments in Polynesian Ethnology.* Honolulu: University of Hawaii Press, pp. 47–94.

Tables, maps and illustrations should be on separate page, numbered and with headings. Indicate in the text where they should appear.

5. All articles are submitted to referees. Responsibility for opinions published remains with the authors.
6. When articles have been accepted in their final form, they should be submitted for publication as email attachment or on a CD. Please keep formatting and the use of tabs and spaces to a minimum. Authors will receive proofs for correction, which have to be returned within ten days of receipt to the publisher. Authors of articles receive 30, reviewers 13 free offprints.

We can't pay regard to subsequent text corrections, deviating from manuscript, except the author is willing to bear the additional expenditure.

Inhalt

Chemeta, David: Deutsche Identität, Kultur und Sprache im deutschen Rap 37
Féaux de la Croix, Jeanne: Grounding Mobile Ideas: Kyrgyzstani NGO-leaders and the Notion of 'Knowledge Transfer' as a Source of Social Cohesion 217
Finke, Peter und Lars-Christian Koch: Mitteilungen der Herausgeber 1
Finke, Peter, Rita Sanders and Russell Zanca: Mobility and Identity in Central Asia: An Introduction 129
Finke, Peter: Historical Homelands and Transnational Ties: the Case of the Mongolian Kazaks 175
Ilkhamov, Alisher: Labour Migration and the Ritual Economy of the Uzbek Extended Family 259
Isabaeva, Eliza: Migration into the "Illegality" and Coping with Difficulties in a Squatter Settlement in Bishkek 139
Joniak-Lüthi, Agnieszka: Han Migration to Xinjiang Uyghur Autonomous Region: Between State Schemes and Migrants' Strategies 155
Köhler, Florian: Kaakol und Eletel: Zur kulturellen Biografie zweier Objekte der Wodaabe-Frauen in Niger 55
Sanders, Rita: Deutsche im ländlichen Kasachstan: Das Streben nach besseren Lebensumständen und die Rolle von Ethnizität 195
Schiffauer, Leonie: The Mobile Phone in Siberia: The Impact of a New Communication Technology on the Everyday Culture of a Postsocialist Society ... 23
Schlehe, Judith, Melanie V. Nertz and Vissia Ita Yulianto: Re-imagining 'the West' and performing 'Indonesian modernities': Muslims, Christians and paranormal practitioners 3
Schröder, Philipp: Ainuras Amerikanische Karriere – Räumliche und soziale Mobilität einer jungen Kirgisin 235
Zanca, Russell: Asianizing Russia after 'The Friendship among Peoples' 285

Miszellen der Ethnologiegeschichte

Marschall, Wolfgang: Ein Freund Deutschlands schreibt einem deutschen Emeritus   85

Nachrufe

Krüger, Franz: Rüdiger Schott (1927–2012) 99
Beyer, Judith und Markus Weilenmann: Franz von Benda-Beckmann (1941–2013) 105

Ausstellungsbesprechungen

Högner, Bärbel: „Probebühne 1" des Humboldt Lab Dahlem, Museen Dahlem, Berlin,
    14. 3. – 12. 5. 2013 111

Buchbesprechungen

Beer, Bettina und Hans Fischer (Hg.) (2012): *Ethnologie. Einführung und Überblick*
    (Hans P. Hahn) 117
Bierschenk, Thomas, Matthias Krings und Carola Lentz (Hg.): *Ethnologie im 21. Jahrhundert*
    (Peter Geschiere) 295
Bonz, Jochen: *Subjekte des Tracks. Ethnographie einer postmodernen/anderen Subkultur*
    (Aimar Ventsel) 296
Dennaoui, Youssef: *Sinn und Macht in der globalen Moderne* (Eva Kalny) 118
Göpfert, Mirco und Andrea Noll: *Disziplin und Kreativität an ghanaischen Internatsschulen*
    (Sarah Fichtner) 298
Heidemann, Frank: *Ethnologie. Eine Einführung* (Werner M. Egli) 121
Kapferer, Bruce (ed.): *Legends of People, Myths of State. Violence, Intolerance, and Political Culture in
    Sri Lanka and Australia* and Hobart, Angela and Bruce Kapferer (eds.): *Contesting the State:
    The Dynamics of Resistance and Control* (Aleksandar Bošković) 301

Web-Besprechungen

Drotbohm, Heike: *Rezension: http://www.germananthropology.com/* 125
Verne, Markus: *Rezension: http://www.germananthropology.com/* 126

Gebr. Mann Verlag
Dietrich Reimer Verlag
Deutscher Verlag
für Kunstwissenschaft
Berliner Straße 53
10713 Berlin
DEUTSCHLAND

Bitte als
Postkarte
frankieren

Informieren Sie mich bitte künftig und unverbindlich über die Neuerscheinungen der Verlage Gebr. Mann / Dietrich Reimer / Deutscher Verlag für Kunstwissenschaft.
Ich interessiere mich vor allem für:

☐ Kunst/Kunstwissenschaft ☐ Numismatik
☐ Architektur ☐ Ethnologie
☐ Archäologie/Orientalistik ☐ Linguistik/Afrikanistik

☐ Bitte senden Sie den kostenlosen E-Mail-Newsletter.
E-Mail-Adresse: _____

Absender: Datum: _____

Name _____ Vorname _____

Straße und Hausnummer _____

PLZ _____ Ort _____

Diese Karte entnahm ich dem Buch _____

Ich bin damit einverstanden, daß diese Angaben gespeichert und automatisch verarbeitet werden.

Mobility and Identity in Central Asia: An Introduction

Peter Finke
Ethnologisches Seminar, Universität Zürich, Andreasstrasse 15, CH-8050 Zürich

Rita Sanders
Emser Str. 19, D-12051 Berlin

Russell Zanca
Department of Anthropology, Northeastern Illinois University, 5500 N. St. Louis Avenue, Chicago, USA-IL 60646

Since social and cultural change long has been construed axiomatically in anthropology, this became a concern *a fortiori* in socialism's wake with the overwhelming technological and political incursions as well as economic investments of the west, usually subsumed under the term globalization. As social scientists we are so well attuned to the discourse around this term that we often find ourselves invoking it in ways already banal. Nevertheless, globalizing processes obviously have a major impact on the lives of people among whom we conduct fieldwork. This is particularly true for those societies labelled as socialist until about twenty years ago, and one might well say that their switch to a market economy or capitalist system may serve as a more than paradigmatic case for what we call globalization.

Few topics seem to embody globalization in Central Asia and elsewhere quite so significantly as mobility does. And while change is not always connected to the movement of people, goods and ideas, we think that in Central Asia – and many other parts of the former socialist world – a variety of types of migration and mobility that, both physical and psychological, link change, movement and identity strongly. With this concept in mind, we convened a workshop on this topic at the *Völkerkundemuseum* in Zurich during May of 2012. We deliberately decided to keep the concept of mobility broad to include such diverse phenomena as labour migration, the repatriation of people to newly sovereign nation-states, the enduring (although possibly evanescent) place of European minorities in the region as well as the changing inter-ethnic relations among incoming settler migrants of the dominating culture, such as the Han Chinese in Xinjiang, or the ways in which western NGOs, perhaps inadvertently, attempt to change workplace organization and social structure.

In providing a consideration of what we mean by mobility above, we imply that its connection with identity is all too obvious. The latter notion has been so emphasized throughout the 20th century, in Soviet and Chinese cases in particular with regard to formalized ethnicity, that we often neglect myriad forms of identity beyond that. Thus, in this issue we will make persuasive cases for the connectedness of mobility and identity that demonstrate their changeable natures with regard to social belonging, gender norms, religion or rural/urban and professional/non-professional dichotomies. We think that the upheavals, stresses, risks, and opportunities to which mobility gives rise in the post-socialist Central Asian contexts also force people to reassess who and what they are as well as what they hope to achieve in a world unmoored from what it propounded to be just 20 or so years ago. This also bolsters the continued importance and necessity for anthropologists to concern themselves with social and cultural change more as a constant of human dynamism as opposed to something that punctuates ordinarily staid conduct and behaviour among people in societies.

Mobility and migration in Central Asia

Increased levels of migration are, of course, not new to people in Central Asia, and in most cases had far reaching effects on their livelihoods, often not for the better. One might even say that the region is a paradigmatic case of human mobility, epitomized by succeeding waves of mass migration out of and into the region. During Soviet times, an additional aspect came to the forefront, namely politically provoked migration and forced resettlements. Central Asians were notorious for resisting pressure from Moscow or Peking to start a new life as industrial workers in places where their labour was needed. In turn, however, the region became a destination for large-scale resettlement programs within and beyond. Part of this was the need to attract mountain and steppe settlers to join work on the enlarged cotton fields. Other migrants came from more far-away regions, including millions of European settlers and the deported peoples during World War II.

With the demise of socialism life again has changed fundamentally for people in the region. The majority experienced a rapid decline of living standards, at least for much of the 1990s, and in some places beyond. The reasons for that have been debated for almost twenty years now and so have potential ways out of this misery. For people on the ground, these remained largely academic disputes with little relation to their own situation. Different types of mobility, described in the contributions to this volume, for many seemed a possible way to make ends meet. Among the first were labour migrants from Kyrgyzstan in Kazakstan. On a smaller scale were daily commuters as in the case of Uzbek labourers on the agricultural fields of southern Kyrgyzstan (Sancak 2012). Petty trade may be considered as another type of mobility, and it ranked highly among the survival strategies for many households in the region, particularly during the 1990s. Others sought refuge in studying abroad and engaging with international organizations of various kinds (see Schröder, this volume).

Apart from these push factors, there were pull factors that made themselves ever more perceptible in the course of the first decade of the new millennium. With the booming economies in Russia and Kazakstan, an increased need for cheap labour arose, especially in the construction sector. Primarily attracted by this were the crisis-stricken countries of Tajikistan, Uzbekistan and Kyrgyzstan. How sustainable these booms may prove to be is a matter of debate as both ultimately rest on resource extraction, namely oil and gas, prone to the Dutch disease. Be that as it may, for the time being both Russia and Kazakstan, as the main destinations for migration-willing Central Asians, promise millions of impoverished families at least a temporary hope.[1]

National politics, obviously, play a prominent role in this. One is tempted to say that Russia in particular takes an opportunistic stake, enabling and fostering immigration as it helps to bolster its economic growth while at the same time condoning many of the nasty epiphenomena, such as increasing racist attacks on the migrants. Kazakstan has a slightly different take on this, but, apparently, is also not very preeminent in preventing exploitative relationships in regard to migrants. At the same time, the latter has the most active, if not the only, policy of encouraging its so-called diasporas to join the alleged fatherland (see Finke, this volume).

Another aspect of state politics is state relations with internal diversity and mobility, be that ethnic, regional or social. Many of the current migration movements are, in fact, internal and primarily affect the urban centres like Almaty, Bishkek or Tashkent. In their new settlements the rural migrants often face real discrimination and exploitation, in many places fostered by a continuation of the old Soviet registration system, the *propiska* (Turaeva 2010; Isabaeva, this volume). Internal migrants may thus also become an issue in national identity construction, as do those going to or coming from abroad.

Social impacts of mobility: integration, transnational ties and institutional change

After migrating abroad, the arrivals often face a difficult stay at their new "home", which may not be considered theirs by both themselves and by their hosts. This is certainly not a specific phenomenon in the post-Soviet sphere and is widely described for classic immigration societies in North America and Western Europe. What is remarkable is the fact that the places of migratory origin, the independent Central Asian countries, were part of the same state, namely the Soviet Union, as are the two major

---

[1] For recent overviews of migration movements in post-Soviet Central Asia see Marat (2009), Reeves (2011) and Laruelle (2013).

destination countries, Russia and Kazakstan. To this day, furthermore, the Soviet Union remains a polity that many still long for.

The hostility towards people from Central Asia and the Caucasus in Russia is, of course, not new, but has reached unprecedented heights in recent years. An interesting contrast is the situation in Xinjiang where the immigrants described by Joniak-Lüthi (this volume) form part of the dominating Han population, which is strategically used also as an agent of 'internal colonialism,' as one might say following the terminology of Hechter (1975). In the case of China, the migrants often succeed in having a better standard of living than the local population, not to the amusement of the latter. On the other hand, co-ethnicity is no guarantee for a successful integration of migrants either, as the case of the Kazak diaspora illustrates (Finke, this volume).

As mentioned above, many of the migrants face discrimination and exploitation during the migration process and at their destinations. These may take very different forms. Reports indicate that some are kept in slave-like conditions when their passports are taken away and they have to work more or less for free. The illegal status of many of the migrants obviously facilitates such practices. However, exploitation may also affect internal migrants as the *propiska* regime in some way corresponds to the status of being an illegal resident, something against which those concerned vociferously protest (Isabaeva, this volume).

Other cases of mobility, such as the one described by Schröder (this volume), are intentionally planned by the individuals concerned and designed in order to enable its practitioners a more prosperous future. A temporary stay abroad can become a platform to build a career on, especially if connected with expertise in foreign languages or other skills rare at their place of origin. It also introduces new concepts and lifestyles with which not everyone back home is necessarily happy. The same may be said about internal migrants who, after a move to town, may end up in a setting with different cultural understandings of proper behaviour. This, in turn, may induce a change of social norms at the place of origin.

In more recent literature on migration, great concern is given to the development of transnational ties between the countries of origin and destination. Although maybe not quite as new an idea as some of its adherents try to make us believe, the phenomenon has not been given high prominence in earlier work. What is important to note is that this is primarily a question of empirical validity. That is to say, the existence of transnational ties cannot be taken for granted but need to be shown. And its strength depends on the needs and possibilities of the people concerned. One aspect of this is new technologies that make these connections easier and cheaper, even for those who are less privileged. In the case of Central Asian migrants, the fact that the former Soviet realm is still a related one is significant also in respect to cheap mobile phone rates. And, as shown by Ilkhamov (this volume), for many of those working in Russia their homes back in Uzbekistan or Tajikistan are not only important as emotional rescue but constitute the places to invest the earned money for economic and social purposes, too.

Identities in Central Asia

The body of literature on the 'nationality question' in the former Soviet Union and its successor states is dominated by political scientists who investigate societies' transition process (e. g. Akiner 2005; Chinn & Kaiser 1996; Dave 2007; Gumppenberg 2004; Olcott 2002; Slezkine 1994; Smith 1996). Most studies touch on the notion of identity, but its formation is conceptualized – at least implicitly – predominantly as a 'top down process' and conceived of as identity politics. Moreover, the concept of nationality is often seen as an unchallenged take-over from Soviet times. Till the end of the 1990s, many studies, thus, tended to predict ethnic turmoil and large-scale uprisings in all of the Union's successor states. In this vein, many of those analyses conceived ethnicity itself as a cause for potential conflicts, and, thus, arguing that once the Soviet Union as an oppressive force had faded away, ethnic differences would now trigger various kinds of (ethnic) conflicts. Indeed, the Andijan incident in Uzbekistan in 2005, the Tulip Revolution of March 2005 and further uprisings in Kyrgyzstan in 2010 have demonstrated that people may violently protest against unpopular policies and corruption. Furthermore, the latest conflict also involved an ethnic dimension when Uzbeks were the principal victims in Southern Kyrgyzstan. Nonetheless, it is less the Soviet heritage of nationality concept, but economic instability, energy insecurity and elite's control of resources that trigger people's protest.

Moreover, national identities are seen as major influence on migratory processes. In particular, the massive outflow of Russians and Germans from all Central Asian countries is interpreted against the light of national discrimination and people's wish to return to one's 'homeland'. Consequently, that ethnic turmoil did not emerge in Kazakstan is often explained by the fact that those displaced non-Kazaks opted for emigration instead of fighting for more minority rights within the country (e. g. Dave 2007:139; Masanov 1999). Others (e. g. Davis & Sabol 1998; Yessenova 1996), however, argue that it was not feelings of ethnically-based exclusion but disastrous economic conditions during the 1990s that caused many to decide to leave the country. On the other hand, a move to another country, be that as a labour migrant or as an ethnic repatriant, may cause fundamental discomfort and a reorientation of one's social belonging.

In anthropology, the formation of new Central Asian nation-states and its effects on ethnic boundary drawing have not attracted much academic attention (exceptions are Schöberlein 1994). But studies on the issue of ethnic identity have questioned broad statements on the topic and instead pointed to national and regional variation. For instance, a major distinction has to be drawn between previously nomadic communities and those that refer to a sedentary mode of organizing society. Thus, Uzbeks and Tajiks tend to grasp ethnic identities by means of territorial belonging, which has also resulted in different localized versions of Uzbek identity, Kazaks and Kyrgyz, conversely, stress genealogical aspects when delineating ethnic group membership (Finke 2014).

These diverse conceptions of ethnic belonging also have an impact on dealings with co-ethnics living outside the country, both in public and by state policies. For instance, Kazaks living abroad have been invited by the state's president Nazarbayev to settle in Kazakstan. Though the living together of migrants and locals is not always harmonious, the policy itself is rarely contested (Finke & Sancak 2005). In Uzbekistan, by contrast, the repatriation of Uzbeks living outside of the country has never been an issue. Moreover, the size and status of the titular nationality differ substantially in the Central Asian states and, accordingly, this varies relative to the way the multi-ethnic takeover has been handled since Soviet times. Kazakstan was the only Central Asian republic in which the titular group made up less than 50 per cent of the population when the state was founded. The demographic situation reversed substantially till the late 1990s; nonetheless, the president likes to recast himself as promoter of ethnic diversity. This is a contrast to Uzbekistan, where 'internationalism' has never been as celebrated as in Kazakstan, and where the titular group has always been unchallenged because of its numerical strength.

Overview of the issue

The Zurich Workshop referenced above brought together a number of scholars working on migration and mobility issues pertaining to Central Asians both within and outside of the region as they relate to identity and social relations. While the essay topics may appear disparate at first glance, we think that many of the subjects and situations discussed link and integrate them in ways that become apparent through careful reading. All of the scholars attempt to describe and explain changes within Central Asian societies and cultures that have shaken and ruptured so-called norms in behaviour and thought that certainly seemed more stable.

As will become obvious, the papers in this volume come in pairs, each highlighting a specific type of mobility. It starts with two contributions on internal migration. Eliza Isabaeva investigates Kyrgyz who, mainly originating from rural areas, have squatted in one of the capital Bishkek's informal settlements on the edge of the city. She demonstrates how people have managed to effectively organize themselves in order to gradually legalize their stay. Thus, they successfully utilized a momentum of political uprising in 2010 to fight for access to the water supply and electricity, and keep on challenging local politicians. As a result, living conditions have improved markedly during the last year. Nevertheless, the migrants' previous expectations of urbanity and their image as illegal settlers have its effect: people often refrain from telling those back home in the village of their life in Bishkek.

Joniak-Luthi provides a contribution about Xinjiang and ethnic relations in China that we rarely consider – namely, immigration into Xinjiang and living among Uyghurs from a Han perspective. This has, first, to take into consideration the different periods of Han immigration since the Communist takeover, but also variations in terms of place of origin, professions as well as area of settlement within Xinjiang. Joniak-Luthi thus can demonstrate – qualitatively and quantitatively – changing inter-ethnic relations, in particular those that have occurred since China's turn toward capitalism in the 1980s. Another crucial event for Han-Uyghur relations have been the independence for Turkic Muslim Central Asians of the former U.S.S.R. Without specifically engaging in discussion of Uyghur liberation movements or an anti-Chinese Uyghur worldview, the author demonstrates the importance of understanding the subtleties and complexities of the relations that render any simple prediction of Xinjiang's political future tendentious at best.

The second pair turns attention to a very distinct type of migratory process, namely the repatriation of diaspora groups. Peter Finke explores the case of Kazak migrants from Mongolia, analysing both the changing motives for staying or moving as well as patterns of integration into Kazakstani society. Striking in this case is that for most of those who left Mongolia and the relatives back home persist as major points of reference and transnational relationships compensate for a lack of institutional embedding into Kazakstani society. While today approximately half of the community has resettled, the situation is far from being settled. The future development will most importantly depend on the expected economic opportunities in both countries, which is in turn affected by the number of migrants. One's decision and its outcome is thus to a large degree affected by those of others, which does not make things easier.

Rita Sanders investigates migrants' decision-making about staying or moving for the case of Kazakstani Germans. Considering both internal and international migration, she examines different migration plans and explores why some fail and others do not. In particular, the rapidly changing economic, legislative and social circumstances in Kazakstan and Germany complicate people's plans, in particular if they have opted for a longer planning horizon. Some of Kazakstani Germans – and these are in the focus of this paper – do not intend to leave their homes in rural Kazakstan and have created their own small cosmos in which they try to adhere to continuity. Thus, people are not only differently successful in realizing their plans, but have, in the first instance, very different plans and ideas about their future life.

The articles by Jeanne Féaux de la Croix and Philipp Schröder deal in different ways with the impacts of international organizations in Kyrgyzstan on individual life plans. Jeanne Féaux de la Croix addresses the issue of NGOs, laying the focus on mobile ideas rather than on people. In doing so, she questions the binary view that the categories 'local' and 'global' suggest and argues on the grounds of empirical research for regarding Kyrgyz development workers as 'in-between' – in terms of their role and their point of views. In their daily lives as NGO employees, they routinely mix up the binary pools and try to make sense of them by following what they call the 'third way' towards a thriving future. Thus, Jeanne Féaux de la Croix concludes that the work of international organizations is less extraneous to Kyrgyz society than otherwise often assumed.

Philipp Schröder examines social and spatial mobility in Kyrgyzstan from another viewpoint and demonstrates the effects of the US's civil society engagement. He depicts one particular case of a young female from the countryside whose professional career involves several migration steps, internal as well as international ones. Back in Bishkek, she establishes a social network of similar minded friends and colleagues who often work like her in international organizations. This network around her 'US-identity' is counterbalanced by the close ties to her kin group, which are equally important to her. But, rather exceptional for a young Kyrgyz female, she is able to resist her family's expectation in regard to a speedy marriage because of her 'international' salary and the benefits she can thus provide.

The final pair regards the impact that mobility has both on sending and receiving societies. Alisher Ilkhamov explores an important, though often neglected, aspect of labour migration, namely the change of social institutions at home. His article focuses on life cycle rites of those who stayed behind in Uzbekistan, but who profit from their relatives' income in Russia. He argues that the migrants' experiences from abroad have only limited effect in terms of bringing modernity to rural Uzbekistan. On the contrary, the fact that people today rely more on remittances from abroad than on the financial help of local extended family members has strengthened the role of the elders – who are in charge of redistributing the money from Russia – and has ultimately promoted conservatism along with increasing social stratification.

Russell Zanca closes the volume with an overview of recent publications in the field of labour migration from the Central Asian states and what has proceeded as a result in Russia for both migrants and citizens of the Russian Federation. Zanca looks to the ethnography of labour migration, as a means to consider what causes and sustains relative degrees of accommodation and/or divisiveness because of the very presence of migrants.

References

Abashin, S. 2007: *Natsionalizmy v Crednej Azii. V Poiskakh Identichnosti*. Sankt-Peterburg: Aletejya.
Akiner, S. 2005: Towards a Typology of Diasporas in Kazakhstan. In: T. Atabaki and S. Mehendale (eds.), *Central Asia and the Caucasus: Transnationalism and Diaspora*. London: Routledge, pp. 21–65.
Brubaker, R. 1999: *Nationalism Reframed. Nationhood and the National Question in the New Europe*. Cambridge: Cambridge University Press.
Brubaker, R. 2004: *Ethnicity without Groups*. Cambridge: Harvard University Press.
Chinn, J.; Kaiser, R. 1996: *Russians as the New Minority. Ethnicity and Nationalism in the Soviet Successor States*. Boulder: Westview.
Dave, B. 2007: *Kazakhstan. Ethnicity, Language and Power*. London: Routledge.
Davis, S.; Sabol, S. 1998: The Importance of Being Ethnic: Minorities in Post-Soviet States – the Case of Russians in Kazakhstan. *Nationalities Papers* 26:473–491.
Finke, P. 2014: *Variations on Uzbek Identity. Strategic Choices, Cognitive Schemas and Political Constraints in Identification Processes*. New York, Oxford: Berghahn Books.
Finke, P.; Sancak, M. 2005: Migration and Risk Taking. A Case Study from Kazakhstan. In: L. Trager (ed.), *Migration and Economy: Global and Local Dynamics*. Walnut Creek: AltaMira Press, pp. 127–162.

Gumppenberg, M.-C. 2004: Nation- and State-Building in Kazakhstan between Ethnic and Social Conflict. In: G. Rasuly-Paleczek and J. Katschnig (eds.), *Central Asia on Display: Proceedings of the VII. Conference of the European Society for Central Asian Studies*. Wien: Lit, pp. 77–82.

Laruelle, M. (ed.) 2013: *Migration and Social Upheaval as the Face of Globalization in Central Asia*. London: Brill.

Marat, E. 2009: *Labor migration in Central Asia: Implications of the global economic crisis*. Silk Road Studies Program: Institute for Security and Development Policy.

Masanov, N. 1999: Migratsionnye metamorfozy Kazakhstana. In: N. Kosmarskaya, A. Vyatkin and S. A. Panarin (eds.), *V dvizhenii dobrovol'nom i vynuzhdennom*. Moscow: Natalic.

Olcott, M.B. 2002: *Kazakhstan. Unfulfilled Promise*. Washington: Carnegie Endowment for International Peace.

Reeves, M. (ed.) 2011: Movement, Power and Place in and beyond Central Asia. *Special issue of Central Asian Survey* 30(3–4).

Schoeberlein, J. S. 1994: *Identity in Central Asia. Construction and Contention in the Conceptions of "Ozbek", "Tajik", "Muslim", "Samarkandi" and Other Groups*. Unpublished doctoral dissertation: Harvard University.

Slezkine, Y. 1994: The USSR as a Communal Apartment, or How a Socialist State Promoted Ethnic Particularism. *Slavic Review* 53:414–452.

Smith, G. 1996: *The Nationalities Question in the Post-Soviet States*. London: Longman.

Tishkov, V. 1997: *Ethnicity, Nationalism and Conflict in and after the Soviet Union. The Mind Aflame*. London: Sage.

Turaeva, R. 2010: *Identification, Discrimination and Communication: Khorezmian migrants in Tashkent*, PhD dissertation, Faculty of Philosophy I, Martin Luther University Halle-Wittenberg.

Yessenova, S. 1996: The Outflow of Minorities from the Post-Soviet State: The Case of Kazakhstan. *Nationalities Papers* 24:691–707.

Migration into the "Illegality" and Coping with Difficulties in a Squatter Settlement in Bishkek

Eliza Isabaeva

Ethnologisches Seminar, Universität Zürich, Andreasstrasse 15, CH-8050 Zürich

Abstract. This paper deals with internal migrants who live in a *de jure* illegal squatter settlement on the outskirts of Kyrgyzstan's capital city Bishkek. It discusses how squatter-settlement residents access basic material infrastructure such as electricity and drinking water. The author argues that the lack of interest shown by the state towards the squatter settlement has forced the inhabitants of the latter to provide for their own infrastructure. In so doing, the residents of the squatter settlement have turned themselves into "quiet encroachers": ordinary people driven by a will to survive and obtain a dignified life.
[land grabbing, squatter settlement, basic infrastructure, inclusion/exclusion, Bishkek, Kyrgyzstan]

The emergence of periphery settlements in Bishkek, Kyrgyzstan's capital city, has to be situated in the context of rising internal migration. Not only this but also, as Balihar Sanghera (2011) argues, shortage of urban housing, a fragile rural economy, an expanding urban population and a weak state capacity serve as the main causes for the rise and proliferation of the settlements in the outskirts of the city. People from villages and small provincial towns have been coming to Bishkek mainly for economic reasons such as finding employment, earning money and generating some wealth. Yet other migrants move to Bishkek searching a better life – that is, access to higher education, health care and superior living conditions. Before going into detail regarding whether migrants' expectations have been met or not, I would like to specify that this paper focuses on migrants who are residing in informal squatter settlements on the edge of Bishkek with poor or absent resources as well as social infrastructure. This distinguishes them from other internal migrants who live in the city center, microregions[1], and other formalized settlements of Bishkek. Another restriction of the paper is that it explores issues around the basic material infrastructure only – electricity and drinking water – and thus, does not consider other major issues of registration in the city and obtaining official documents for private property.

Settlements on the outskirts of Bishkek are inhabited by internal migrants, who have been living in the city for many years but did not have a house of their own.

---

[1] Frunze 1984: Encyclopedia. Microregions (russ. *mikroraiony*) are residential areas, consisting of several multi-storey apartment houses. Their construction dates back to the end of 1950s–beginning of 1960s due to a rapid growth of housing construction in the city, p. 176.

Instead, they used to rent small and poorly furnished rooms or shacks from house owners in the other formalized settlements. People refer to these small rooms as *kvartira*[2] and those who rent a *kvartira* are called *kvartiranttar*. One of the problems with renting a *kvartira* is that there is a constant fear of getting evicted by a house owner for any reason, be it a late rental payment, inappropriate behavior of tenants, new plans of a landlord, etc. Thus, *kvartira* cannot be regarded as a long-term dwelling. Morever, *kvartira* is a place where most migrants feel themselves constrained because they live under the 'watchful' eye of a landlord. The constraints include that tenants cannot host many relatives in their small rooms, their children should not make too much of noise, they should not use too much electricity by watching television until late at night, and many other rules. Therefore, the *kvartiranttar* have always wanted to have their own house, in order not to be dependent on a landlord and bring an end to insecurity, fear and having to constantly move from *kvartira* to *kvartira*.

Such difficulties notwithstanding, internal migrants continue to travel to Bishkek. In the city, the relatively expensive rent for a comfortable apartment forces needy migrants to seek low-cost living accommodation on the outskirts of Bishkek (Hirt & Stanilov 2009). Having unregulated prices on housing, rent and utilities, one even runs the risk of remaining homeless (Bayat 2000:534). Similarly, limited resources make it difficult for Bishkek to absorb the population influx. Nevertheless, the city is growing – both demographically and geographically. Demographically, according to the Bishkek Mayor's Office, the population of the city is now estimated to be 1.35 million people, which exceeds the capacity of the city's infrastructure[3]. The geographic expansion of Bishkek is due to new settlements, which emerged on the city's edge recently and mushroomed within a short time.

Currently there are 47 settlements in Bishkek with roughly 400.000 inhabitants[4], that is, 30 % of the city's population. Locals refer to these settlements as *zhany konush* in Kyrgyz and *novostroika* in Russian. There is another Russian term *zhil massiv*[5], which is widely used as well in Bishkek. When I asked one of Bishkek residents, who was an internal migrant in the city, about the difference between *novostroika* and *zhil massiv*, he answered that the latter referred to a formalized settlement with material and social infrastructure while the former does not. It is also important to note the two-fold meaning of the Russian term *novostroika* (lit. new construction), which reveals confusion among the people in Bishkek: *novostroika* can mean not only periphery settlements but also elite construction housing.

---

[2] *Kvartira* is a Russian word for an apartment. It implies an apartment in a multi-storied house. In the context of periphery settlements, *kvartira* denotes a small room or a shack that can be rented out for tenants.
[3] Kyrgyz Telegraph Agency: http://www.kyrtag.kg/?q=ru/news/35415.
[4] Kyrgyz Telegraph Agency: http://www.kyrtag.kg/?q=ru/news/18761.
[5] *Zhil massiv* is a short term for *zhiloi massiv* and stands for a housing estate.

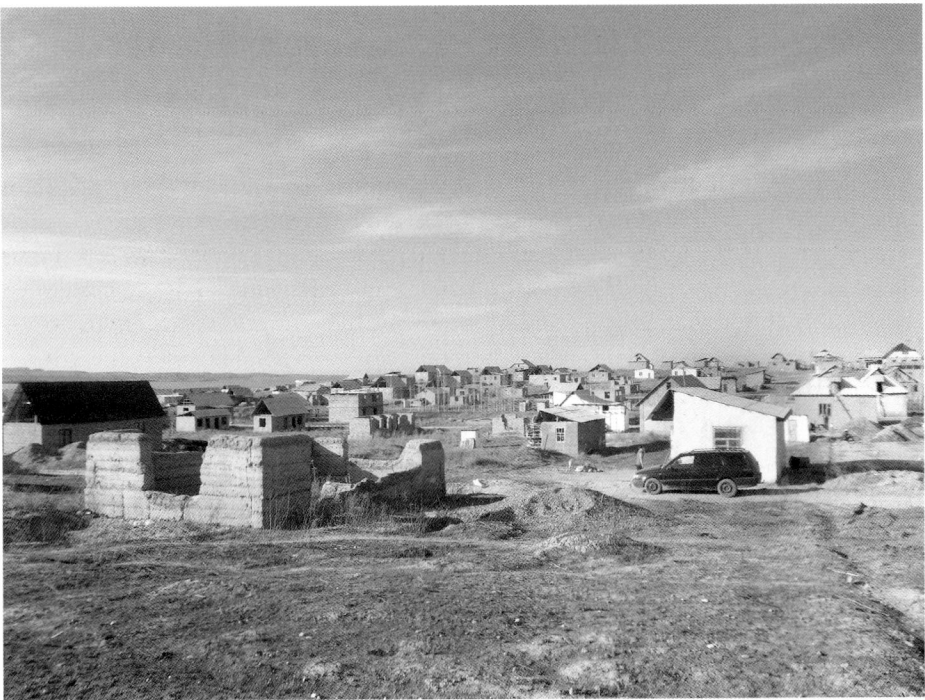

Figure 1 A part of Kyzyl Zher squatter settlement (Photo: Eliza Isabaeva)

In this paper, I would like to focus on a periphery settlement in Bishkek, which, for reasons of confidentiality, I shall call Kyzyl Zher, whose semi-legal[6] status makes it difficult for its dwellers to be fully-fledged residents of the city. However, despite numerous difficulties, Kyzyl Zher residents are eager and ready to be included into the ranks of Bishkek citizens. Their eagerness is demonstrated by how they take initiatives into their own hands instead of waiting for the state to provide services. I argue that the state's constant and continuous there-is-no-money attitude has forced people in Kyzyl Zher to help provide their own infrastructure. Moreover, such an attitude has enabled the residents of the settlement to become satisfied with fewer resources than might be expected. To be more precise, these people, even though they could exert more pressure on the state, do not do so. Conversely, they are content with the little unfinished infrastructure that they have. This attitude, however, has to do with what they had gone through before.

---

[6] I do not apply the word 'illegal' to the example of Kyzyl Zher. Instead I suggest that Kyzyl Zher came into existence already as a semi-legal settlement because if it were completely illegal, that is, against written formal rules, it would have been demolished long ago by those who claim that the settlement was illegal. Namely, illegality in respect to Kyzyl Zher is a state perspective.

Before I start discussing Kyzyl Zher's short history, the everyday life of its inhabitants and their experiences, I would like to contextualize Bishkek in the framework of a socialist city.

Frunze[7] as a Socialist City

One of the many reasons for rising internal migration in Kyrgyzstan is the collapse of the Soviet Union, which resulted in economic stagnation and deterioration due to the termination of fiscal transfers from Moscow. Consequently, people in rural areas and provincial towns became unemployed and responded with mass migration, both internal and international (Abazov 1999, Bichsel et al. 2005, Röhner 2007, Thieme 2008, Schmidt & Sagynbekova 2008, Isabaeva 2011, Reeves 2012). Since the capital city was the place where economic, political and social power was generated, most internal migrants came to Bishkek. However, Bishkek's current primacy, superiority and importance go back to Soviet times. "In the Soviet Union, cities were the cradle of progress, the place of modernity and, after the 1930s, quite distinct from a rural way of life" (Alexander et al. 2007:2). Following the path of Soviet urban development, Frunze was transformed into a modern city with a diversified economy, major scientific and educational centers, important transport and communication hubs and a diverse cultural life (Oruzbaeva 1984:7). Therefore, based on the city's standing over the years, internal migrants' quest for a better life in Bishkek seems legitimate.

The population of Frunze during Soviet times increased significantly compared to pre-Soviet times. Already in 1976, Frunze had half a million inhabitants (ibid:13). This growth was mainly due to a high birth rate, migration from rural areas and provincial towns to the capital city, and the incorporation of districts located close to Frunze (ibid:13).

During Soviet years, especially in the post-war period, Frunze experienced a boom in housing construction, as illustrated in Fig. 1 (ibid:127):

In a self-reinforcing pattern, the number of houses grew because the number of city residents grew, and more houses then attracted more residents. However, at some point, when the population of Frunze exceeded the actual number of available houses, so-called periphery settlements began to emerge (Alymbaeva 2008). In her article on urbanization in Kyrgyzstan, Alymbaeva writes about a settlement called Tököldösh consisting mainly of shacks, which appeared in the aftermath of illegal land squatting. To call Tököldösh a periphery settlement nowadays would be wrong, for the settlement is located in the center of the city, and a large part of it was demolished in order to build today's *microregion* called "Vostok-5" (ibid: 72).

---

[7] From 1926 until 1991, Bishkek's official name was Frunze. Prior 1926, the city's was known under the name of Pishpek.

Years	Total housing	Communal housing	Private housing	Average m² per pers.
1926	179	23	156	4.9
1940	568	246	322	5.4
1966	3032	1559	1473	8.0
1982	6718	4331	2252	11.6

Fig.1. Housing in Frunze: 1000 m² of usable area in a living space)

The example of Tököldösh suggests that squatting is not a new post-Soviet phenomenon in Bishkek. If it took place for the first time during the Soviet time because of lack of housing, the second major incidence was during the years 1989–1991, i. e. in the last years of the Soviet Union and shortly after its dissolution when rural migrants came to Bishkek in search of employment. The third wave of land squatting is more recent, namely in 2005, when the country underwent another critical juncture in its history, to which I turn in the next section.

The Tulip Revolution

Extending the geographic space of so-called colored revolutions, which began with the Rose Revolution in Georgia in 2003 and the Orange Revolution in Ukraine in 2004, Kyrgyzstan was the third country in the post-Soviet space and the first in the Central Asian region to experience a popular revolt. Kyrgyzstan's "revolution" occurred in the spring of 2005 and later came to be known as the Tulip Revolution. As in the first two cases, political unrest in Kyrgyzstan also led to a change in power. The former president of the country, Askar Akaev, left the country in the midst of the unrest and it took some time before the opposition bloc chose Kurmanbek Bakiev to lead the interim government (see also Marat 2008). This political turmoil and the resulting power vacuum caused chaos in Bishkek. While the city center was unceremoniously looted, the outskirts became the site of illegal land squatting. At this critical political juncture, the citizens – squatters in this case – took advantage of the chaos and fragility of state institutions to grab land and establish residence. Fragility in this case meant that for a short period, Kyrgyzstan found itself without ruling leaders because the president and prime-minister had fled the country and new, legitimate leaders had not emerged.

Although squatter settlements have gained significance in recent years in Kyrgyzstan, there has been little research on them. However, the issue is worth studying since informal settlements represent a social, economic and political challenge in the country (Sanghera 2012). John Heathershaw reports that "[…] of around 500 protests which have taken in Bishkek this year – 2012 – approximately 50 % were of a social-economic character, usually demanding the provision of basic utilities and services. Many of these protests – including some of the largest – involved groups from the new settlements on the edges of Bishkek" (2012). Furthermore, Sanghera writes that informal-settlement residents in Bishkek live in "[…] over-crowded, unhealthy conditions … lacking resident permits which limit their access to education, health care and social benefits" (2010:2). Sangera's study concludes that unless structural inequality and widespread corruption in Kyrgyzstan are addressed, the lives of people residing in informal settlements in Bishkek will not improve substantially (2011:3). Thus, he challenges the position of international donors such as the United Nations and the World Bank, who relate poverty reduction to the enhancement of poor people's legal rights (e.g., land and property rights), protection from labor exploitation and access to justice (ibid: 4). Building on Sanghera's line of thought, I suggest that the problems of squatter-settlement residents extend beyond granting them legal rights because they usually develop different strategies themselves to confront problems they face.

A shortage of housing in Bishkek by the end of 1980s and beginning of 1990s led the 'homeless' in the city either to squat land plots for constructing a house or register at a city municipality for housing. Malabaev notes that after a mass land squatting in 1989 on state and kolkhoz lands, the authorities of the city council decided to distribute 9'759 land plots (Alymbaeva 2008). Both recent land squatting of 2005 and 2010[8] were likewise need-driven. As Sanghera correctly points out, "[…] this [political unrest] was neither a class revolt nor a demand for greater democracy, but rather an opportunity to make their daily life bearable … because many urbanized poor people have no choice but to rent small, poorly furnished rooms from slum landlords, struggling to pay exorbitant rent and often getting evicted" (op.cit. Sanghera 2010:2).

Stigmatized 'Founding Mothers' of Kyzyl Zher

Kyzyl Zher – my research site – is a massive settlement with over seven thousand official inhabitants. Unofficially, the population number is estimated to be close to ten thousand people. This is bigger than an average village in Kyrgyzstan in terms of population. The settlement is located to the north of Bishkek, close to one of the biggest Central Asian wholesale markets, the Dordoi.

Previously, the territory of Kyzyl Zher did not belong to the city of Bishkek but to the district of Chui, in which Bishkek is situated. However, the administration of Chui

---

[8] In April of 2010 Kyrgyzstan experienced a second political unrest since its independence which also led to the change in power as in 2005. 2010 April events were, as opposed to March events of 2005, violent leaving more than 80 people dead. This time people again attempted to seize the land but police had to resort to force. See: http://business.highbeam.com/407705/article-1G1–231190457/bishkek-police-clearing-suburbs-squatters.

district did not want to have Kyzyl Zher on its books because they claimed it did not have the financial means to provide the new settlement with resources and infrastructure. Thus, Kyzyl Zher has had an ambivalent position ever since its emergence, acknowledged neither by the district of Chui nor by the city of Bishkek.

Before Kyzyl Zher was squatted, a politician who had planned to build a market there took a lease on the land. However, he could not put his plan into effect, and the land was squatted in the spring of 2005 in the immediate aftermath of the Tulip Revolution. As opposed to the earlier squatting in the late 1980s and early 1990s, where there used to be a squatters' movement (e.g. *Ashar* Movement), squatting after March 2005 was done by a group of people known locally as "*top bashy*" (lit. head of a group). Different recounted stories divide these *top bashys* into several categories: those who had a connection to some high-ranking state officials and were regarded as the 'state's people'; those who were connected to the politician with a market-building project; and those who had simply heard that a land plot was squatted and joined the mass. The first two were easy to mobilize as a group: serving someone's political interest, the *top bashys* were given an opportunity to get a land piece as well as make good money from selling land. Having grabbed more than one piece of land, the *top bashys* either transferred land parcels to family members or sold them for a substantial amount of money. This is one of the reasons for frequent land conflicts in Kyzyl Zher because the same land plot sometimes was sold to several people.

Interestingly, *top bashy* is a gendered category, i.e. as a rule, these are women. A generic umbrella term for a phenomenon like *top bashy* is OBON[9]. OBON is analogous to the Russian term, OMON[10]. Equating a group of women with a special police troop, one could correlate similarities between the two[11]. OBONs (and *top bashys*) are indisputably skilled in persuading someone or, if that does not work, attacking them verbally, and if needed, physically. In Kyzyl Zher, locals, especially men, referred to *top bashys* as barking dogs (*it* but also *ovcharka*) and compared them with an angry dog, who is ready to bite if necessary. Among Kyrgyz people, being compared to a dog is very insulting. For instance, conflicting parties might criticize each other saying "*it ekensin*" (kyrg. You're a dog) diminishing one's human dignity to an animal's, which is unable to think and act reasonably and morally.

It is difficult nowadays to find the original *top bashys* in Kyzyl Zher because many of them disappeared after having made a good deal of business. Their whereabouts are largely unknown to the current residents. There are some who have stayed but they are reluctant to identify themselves as *top bashys*, knowing that their reputation in the set-

---

[9] *OBON* is an abbreviation, which stands for *Otryad Bab Osobogo Naznacheniya* (lit. Female Troop for a Special Operational Task).

[10] *OMON* stands for *Otryad Militsii Osobogo Naznacheniya* (lit. Police Troop for a Special Operational Task).

[11] For more on *OBON*, see E. Ivashenko at: http://www.fergananews.com/articles/7546 and Mavloni at: http://www.centrasia.ru/newsA.php?st=1284495180.

tlement is not spotless. I knew a woman named Aigul[12] who was a *top bashy* when Kyzyl Zher was squatted. At the time of my research (2012), she was a member of the informal, self-governing administrative body of the settlement[13]. Aigul is a very emotional person who speaks and laughs loudly, uses abusive and inappropriate vocabulary, at times treating people aggressively; she is known for resolving conflicts in Kyzyl Zher with the physical power of her fist. Although I had met with and seen Aigul several times before in the office (*kontora*) of the informal self-governance body together with her other fellow colleagues, it took me some time and effort to convince her to talk to me. When I interviewed her alone for the first time, I started by saying I was interested in the history of Kyzyl Zher.

In a surprisingly calm manner, she started recounting that the settlement was squatted in 2005 as a result of mass land squatting (*zakhvat*). According to her, there was a man who was the main *top bashy* that time. He started dividing people into groups (*top*), each consisting of around 50 people, and for each group he appointed a *top bashy*. Even more surprising for me was when Aigul said she was recruited by that main *top bashy* to work as a *top bashy*. All in all, Aigul recalled, there were around 28 *top bashys*. Their main task was group self-organization, i. e. collecting identification documents and making copies for registration. Aigul told me all the good work that *top bashys* had accomplished but she withheld comments about accusations of common Kyzyl Zher population regarding frequent land conflicts in the settlement. Unfortunately our conversation was disturbed by several people including, among others, her drunken husband. There was, however, another time when Aigul completely refused to talk. It happened during the summer in the office of the self-governance body. A group of journalism students studying at the OSCE Academy in Bishkek had to shoot a short documentary about Kyzyl Zher. When they arrived at the office, the members of the informal self-governance office, including Aigul, were present as well. The film crew explained their intention and asked whether they could talk to some squatters. Aigul's fellow colleagues pointed at her and suggested that she should talk to the students. All of a sudden, Aigul got furious and said she would not talk to them. Moreover, she said there were many squatters (*zakhvatchiki*) in Kyzyl Zher and the students should talk to them but leave her alone. She even refused to take the film crew to those squatters she had referred to. Having seen Aigul's reaction, one of the students said that Aigul should not stick to the word *zakhvatchik* but he was helpless in convincing her. To my surprise, Aigul concluded her anger saying "why should I talk to them? There is no benefit, no help from them anyways". I have analyzed Aigul's behavior on two matters: First, the term *zakhvatchik* (squatter) carries a negative connotation because, according to the criminal code of Kyrgyzstan, it implies an illicit act.

---

[12] To protect informants' anonymity, all the names throughout the paper have been changed.
[13] As a matter of fact, members of this informal self-governance body, i. e. Aigul's colleagues, directed me to her.

Furthermore, based on this state perspective, there is a societal stigma attached to the term: to be identified as or called *zakhvatchik* is shameful because this is connected with being immoral, insubordinate and backward (see also Sanghera 2011). This is probably the reason why Aigul did not want to appear in the documentary and be shown to the wider public as a squatter. Second, Aigul was not ready to cooperate with the students unless she gained something in return. She might mean this either as an individual person, who seeks some benefit for herself and her family, or as a member of the informal self-governance body, who wants help for the entire Kyzyl Zher community.

Another occasion where the stigma of being *zakhvatchik* became an issue happened to me in the early stage of my research. One of my informants had told me that he knew someone in Kyzyl Zher who was a squatter; this informant agreed to accompany me to the squatter's house. Upon arrival, we knocked on the main door and an old man appeared, opening the door and welcoming us in. In the kitchen, while the old man's daughter was serving us tea, I introduced myself and tried to explain in general terms my research intentions. Being aware of the negative connotation of the term, I avoided using it. However, my companion mentioned it and the old man's daughter's attitude changed right away. She first asked whether I was a journalist, which I denied. Then she said her father was not a squatter and prohibited him to provide any information to us. As Aigul had done, the daughter said we should talk to other squatters in Kyzyl Zher but not to bother her father anymore. In the subsequent exchange, we were kindly asked to leave the house and never come back.

The difficulties of communication that I had faced with the so-called squatters in Kyzyl Zher during my research reveal how strong the stigma of being *zakhvatchik* is. I assume it is because of the strong normative state perspective behind it. This is not to suggest that land squatting is the only illegal act in Kyrgyzstan that people commit. For instance, in the same manner one could accuse, condemn and criticize drivers in the streets of Bishkek who do not follow traffic regulations; or a policeman, doctor or teacher, who takes bribes; or high-ranking state officials who do not fulfill their obligations, etc. The difference is that squatters and the residents of informal settlements in general are a vulnerable and marginalized group of people. Despite their attempts to participate in political activities, they have been largely unable to propose their own perspective and promote their own interests to the state. Namely, the residents of Kyzyl Zher argue that as citizens (*zharan*) of Kyrgyzstan, they have a right to live wherever they want and have equal rights to access social services as others do. Based on citizenship, they could exert more pressure on the state in demanding their rights but they do not do so. Instead, they are content with the little infrastructure that the state has provided and are willing to fill the service gap at their own cost.

In order to explain such resilience of Kyzyl Zher residents, I employ Bayat's 'quiet encroachment' approach used in relation to the ordinary people (2000). "The notion of 'quiet encroachment' describes the silent, protracted but pervasive advancement of the ordinary people on the propertied and powerful in order to survive and improve their lives" (Bayat 2000:545). Quiet encroachers, for Bayat, attach little political meaning to their actions; rather, "they are driven by the force of necessity – the necessity to survive and improve a dignified life. Necessity is the notion that justifies their often unlawful acts as moral and even 'natural' ways to maintain a life with dignity" (ibid:547). Thus, one could conclude that necessity has made Kyzyl Zher residents resilient, that is, they agree to provide partially for their resources in the settlement given that they can retain their illegal houses in Kyzyl Zher and remain in Bishkek.

Kyzyl Zher residents, who are originally from different parts of Kyrgyzstan, have been left to rely on their own to survive. Struggling against everyday life difficulties in their *de jure* illegal settlement, they have internalized their problems, meaning that they take them for granted and think of them as inevitable living conditions in a poor settlement like Kyzyl Zher. However, as quiet encroachers who are determined to improve their life in Bishkek, the settlement residents find solutions to existing problems. They tap electricity, they do not yet pay taxes for using land, most of them are employed in the informal sector and thus their contribution to the formal economy is insignificant, their children go to schools even with no proper documents for residing in the city, etc. As it is seen through such informal practices, the struggles and gains of Kyzyl Zher inhabitants are largely at the cost of the state and other Bishkek residents. This is another feature of the ordinary quiet encroachers.

The Plight of Electricity and Water

Most of my informants, when asked about their life in Kyzyl Zher, answered "it is good now". This "now" triggered a question of the past – "how was it before?" The stories of the past reveal what Kyzyl Zher residents went through and the reasons why they do not exert more pressure on the state and instead are willing to aid it by partially absolving the state from its obligations. In the following, I turn to those recounted stories of the past in Kyzyl Zher.

From the time when Kyzyl Zher was squatted in 2005 until late 2011, the residents of the settlement lived without basic living necessities, that is, electricity and drinking water. To be more precise, they did not have any infrastructure provided by the state but had to organize it themselves. As a solution to the lack of drinking water, Kyzyl Zher inhabitants bought it from sellers who came to the settlement with minibuses full of water in containers. The water was sold at the price 50 tyiyns (ca. 1 US cent) per liter. So, minibus drivers had a market advantage: by transporting water, a scarce resource, to the settlement, they could demand a high price for the resource[14]. The

---

[14] Water in Kyrgyzstan is not sold by the liter. Typically, at the end of each month, people receive a bill for the water they have used. The approximate price for the water in Bishkek is 6 soms per cubic meter. 6 soms are equal to about 12 US cents. The average amount of water per person is 3–3.5 cubic

problem with electricity was more difficult to solve. The dwellers of Kyzyl Zher lit up their houses in the evenings with private generators (*dvizhok*), which were only powerful enough to light the house; and thus, people could not watch television or have a running refrigerator at home because they lacked sufficient electrical power. Often, my informants referred to themselves as 'backward' people because they were not up-to-date with the news in the country as they could not watch television. Similarly, they were also concerned for the future of their children, for whom life in Kyzyl Zher also led to 'backwardness'. Sarcastically, people also joked that the lack of electricity was a driving factor for the population increase in Kyzyl Zher because they had no choice but to go to bed early.

Since there was no central gas/electricity heating in Kyzyl Zher, houses were heated using coal, which was expensive for the locals. Therefore, only a limited number of rooms (usually one or two) were heated, where a whole family would stay until the end of winter. The entire house could only be used in warmer months. Most houses in Kyzyl Zher do not have thermo-insulation and thus, the heat generated by coal could not be kept for a long time. Cooking was done in the oven heated by coal or using gas. These measures solved the basic problem but the settlement dwellers lamented their expensive cost.

Worn down by the plight of winter as well as summer, cold and heat, and lacking basic infrastructure, Kyzyl Zher residents organized numerous demonstrations to meet with high-ranking state officials and tell them about their difficult living conditions, hoping to acquire electricity and water. Politicians' empty promises, however, could not improve the situation. The settlement residents even tried once to block the road but the state's military troops used violence to quickly disperse the demonstrators.

In April 2010, Kyrgyzstan's second president Bakiev was overthrown. In June of the same year, a so-called 'ethnic conflict' between Kyrgyz and Uzbeks took place with tragic consequences for many. The country found itself in a precarious situation once again. Additionally, increasingly frequent political protests in Bishkek posed the danger of even greater instability. During such a 'fragile' moment, Kyzyl Zher residents engaged in their next large-scale political protest. Namely, in September 2011, they blocked one of the most strategically important roads in Bishkek for several days, burning tyres in the middle of the roadway. The road's importance was not only internal but also external because it connects Kyrgyzstan with Kazakhstan and Uzbekistan. The protesters demanded the provision of basic infrastructure and the formal legalization of their settlement. Being fed up with empty promises, blocking the road seemed an effective and quick way to attract the attention of state officials to their plight. "If we had not blocked this road, we would not have gotten electricity and water even in 20 years" said one of my informants, who actively participated in the protest. Indeed,

---

meters. If Kyzyl Zher residents use 30 liters of water per day, it will cost them 450 soms at the end of each month.

the then Prime Minister, Almazbek Atambaev and the city mayor, Isa Omurkulov came to meet the protestors. Having listened to their complaints and demands, the politicians promised rapid resolution of their problems. My informant even recalled Atambaev's surprise when he saw how big Kyzyl Zher was. Later, on his political party's website, Atambaev was quoted, "I was shocked to have seen how people live in Kyzyl Zher: they have no electricity, no drinking water and the roads are in terrible condition... *Novostroika* residents are the citizens of our country and we are obliged to resolve their social problems."[15] One could speculate that Atambaev promised to legalize Kyzyl Zher and provide its dwellers with infrastructure because the state officials did not know where to resettle such a large number of people. Furthermore, Kyrgyzstan's precarious political situation provided another reason why the state reacted relatively rapidly to the demands of the protestors: Kyrgyzstan, which had long been admired by international observers as an 'island of democracy' (Anderson, 1999) has been politically unstable since 2005. Instability in Kyrgyzstan has recently come to mean that the government might be overthrown by angry masses of people. The fairly new government, not yet confident of stability and public support, probably feared being overthrown. On the other hand, "city administrations have started to legalize settlements partly to defuse political and social tensions, and partly to respond to a depressed property market" (op.cit. Sanghera 2011:3). Finally, Kyzyl Zher is a neatly organized settlement with a functioning, if legally unapproved self-governance body. Therefore, why not formalize the settlement?

'Life Is Getting Better Now'

Following Atambaev's order, Kyzyl Zher residents gained access to electricity and water by the end of December 2011. However, not every household could light their houses and some still transported water from a far distance. The city's reason for this continued lack of services, as explained to the locals of Kyzyl Zher, was the inadequate finances in the city budget. One of my informants told me that the city administration had allocated 36 million soms (ca. 80.000 $) for Kyzyl Zher: 16 million for the electrification works, 10 million for water and the remaining 10 million for paving the central road of the settlement. This sum of money was exhausted when the work was only partially complete. The locals were told to wait until the new budget would be finalized or hinted covertly to finance the rest of the work themselves.

Kyzyl Zher residents approached this problem in two different ways. First, those things that needed to be purchased (e.g. electrical pylons and cables) were purchased by the people; second, where it was possible to acquire certain things for free, the locals

---

[15] Social Democratic Party of Kyrgyzstan: http://www.sdpk.kg/party-line/meetings-with-voters/ 584--ll-----------r.

developed their own strategies. For example, those households located far from the central street of Kyzyl Zher, where all electrical pylons were placed, decided to derive their electricity from the households located closer to the central street. In exchange, the borrowers either shared the bill for the electricity at the end of the month among themselves, excluding the share of the electricity-providing household, or all households shared the payment equally. Needless to say, this has an impact on the quantity of electricity and the capacity of high-voltage substations, which frequently break down due to overload, leading to interruptions of the power supply. A Kyzyl Zher resident put it this way, "[w]hen I go back to the village, my fellow villagers get jealous saying that I live in the city. They do not know that life in the village is better than here (Kyzyl Zher) because they have unrestricted, powerful electricity and they do not have to share it with others, they can watch television, they have a running refrigerator at home." Another informant confessed, "in fact, we are ashamed to tell our relatives in the village that we live in Bishkek. Is this a city life when your living conditions are worse than in rural areas? We had a totally different image of living in the city in our heads".

Despite this disappointment with life in the city, Kyzyl Zher residents say that life in the settlement is getting better. Obviously, this is due to the basic infrastructure that they have now. Even if the power supply is not of high capacity, the locals are content that they no longer have to live in the 'darkness'. They have taken seriously the implicit hint of state officials to raise their own funds and finalize the work. When I revisited Kyzyl Zher in the winter of 2013, individual households were saving money to buy electricity pylons and cables, as well as ballast for paving streets. This is not to suggest that the people in Kyzyl Zher are politically passive in the sense that they do not demand their rights. After all, the numerous protests prove the opposite. However, they "have been unable to sustain protests or political organization enough to constitute a serious threat to government" (Hossain 2011:9). And, being pragmatic, they accept what cannot be changed and make the best of the situation.

Having the socialist past with the state provision of necessary services, Kyrgyzstanis had to reorient and adjust themselves to the needs of a market economy in post-Soviet times. With a struggling economy, the state's constant there-is-no-money attitude forced people in Kyzyl Zher to take initiatives into their own hands. This way, on the one hand, the locals do not completely rely on the state provision of services. On the other, they aid the state by raising their own funds and thus, filling the gap in what the state ideally was supposed to provide. Their nostalgic memories about the Soviet past reveal how the 'pain' of the new times is strong. Nevertheless, they do not become disheartened; on the contrary, they hope for a better future. It was interesting to listen to a group of men in Kyzyl Zher, who imagine their future in the settlement:

Man 1: When we all get electricity, water and our roads will be paved, we will become urbanites (*shaardyk*).
Man 2: If not ourselves, then hopefully our children will be able to call themselves *shaardyk*.

Man 3: We will start paying taxes and become 'state's people' (*ökmöttün kishisi*).
Man 4: When do you think this will happen? In ten years?
Man 2: No, not in ten years. I hope it will happen this year. You see, it is not so much work.
Man 1: Eliza, you should save money and buy a land plot. We will help you to build a house. If you do not want to live here this year, come back next year. Next year this place will already be *the city*.

This excerpt of a conversation demonstrates that the locals of Kyzyl Zher still feel themselves disconnected and detached from *the city*. Becoming *shaardyk* and belonging to *the city* seems to be a journey, at the end of which Kyzyl Zher inhabitants want to see themselves as fully-recognized and included Bishkek residents. By accessing basic material infrastructure and participating in formal governance by paying taxes, they would like to deconstruct their marginalization and become legal in the society which views them as *myrkas*[16], i.e. uncultured villagers.

There are, however, also some residents of Kyzyl Zher who would be happy to leave the settlement given the choice and the means to do so. When I met Aida, a young educated woman, she was not happy about living in Kyzyl Zher because, as she said, it was a backward life there: electricity that breaks down, no hot water, muddy roads, no internet cafes, etc. She said if she had more money, she would have left the settlement for a comfortable apartment in the city center. When I revisited Kyzyl Zher in the winter of 2013, Aida was living, as she dreamed of, in the city center, renting an apartment together with her friend. Her family, however, have stayed in Kyzyl Zher. When I asked Aida why she moved out of Kyzyl Zher, she replied, "I moved out only temporarily, until the end of winter but I don't think I will come in the spring because in the spring time the roads are muddy in Kyzyl Zher. You see, I work in the city for a Turkish company and I feel ashamed to come to work with my muddy boots."

Conclusion

The members of the informal self-governance body in Kyzyl Zher predict the population will increase in the settlement in the coming years. People, who have previously lived elsewhere, started coming back to their land plots to start or continue the construction of their houses. This is because there is basic infrastructure now in the settlement and living conditions have improved. Struggling all these years for better living conditions with their numerous protests, Kyzyl Zher locals refute the way they are usually portrayed. "[…] Socially and politically disfranchised, they barely survive, lacking real power to make meaningful changes in their lives" (Sanghera & Satybal-

---

[16] For more on *myrka*, see also Ph. Schröder's PhD dissertation (2011)

dieva 2012:7). As the example of Kyzyl Zher residents demonstrates, social and political disfranchisement does not necessarily lead to political passivity. When there is a dire necessity, people turn into 'quiet encroachers'. Furthermore, grabbing a piece of land, building a small house and being willing to become a city resident is a meaningful change for many *novostroika* inhabitants in Bishkek. Indeed, as the case of Kyzyl Zher illustrates, urbanization has become a place of illegality but not necessarily of despair and poverty because after all, it is in rural areas that people see no hope, lack work places and decide to move to Bishkek.

As it was the case with the Brazilian settlements called *autoconstructions* and nicely depicted in James Holston's account (1991), *novostroika* as a site enables internal migrants in Bishkek to develop and practice a new sense of agency, driven by economic necessity. In so doing, they construct a new of group of citizens who claim their rights even if they are not allowed to because of official laws.

This paper does not suggest that starting as squatters is a realistic way to become a part of a city and thus the trend of land squatting should continue. It simply shows how Bishkek is growing in real life, and how resourceful and resilient people are and can be if they are forced to.

References

Abazov, R. 1999: Economic migration in post-Soviet Central Asia: the case of Kyrgyzstan. *Post-Communist Economies* 11(2):237–252.
Alexander, C. et al. 2007: *Urban life in post-Soviet Asia*. London: UCL Press.
Alymbaeva, A. 2008: K voprosu ob urbanizacii (To the question of urbanization). *The Academic Review: The Journal of the History Institute of the Kyrgyz Academy Sciences* 1:65–77.
Anderson, J. 1999: *Kyrgyzstan: Central Asia's Island of Democracy?* New York: Routledge.
Bayat, A. 2000: From 'Dangerous Classes' to 'Quiet Rebels': Politics of the Urban Subaltern in the Global South. *International Sociology* Vol. 15(3):533–557.
Bichsel, C. et al. 2005: *'Should I buy a cow or a TV?': reflections on the conceptual framework of the NCCR North-South based on a comparative study of international labor migration in Mexico, India and Kyrgyzstan*. Berne: NCCR North South dialogue, NCCR North-South.
Heathershaw, J. 2012: *Protests in Kyrgyzstan: disorder or democratization?* Available at: http://cesmi.info/wp/?p=142.
Hirt, S.; Stanilov, K. 2009: Twenty years of transition: The evolution of urban planning in Eastern Europe and the Former Soviet Union, 1989–2009. UN Habitat. *Human Settlements Global Dialogue Series* No 5.
Holston, J. 1991: Autoconstruction in working-class Brazil. *Cultural Anthropology* Vol. 6. No. 4 (Nov.):447–465.
Hossain, Sh. 2011: Urban poverty, informality and marginality in the global south. *The Annual meeting of the Australian Sociological Association*.
Isabaeva, E. 2011: Leaving to enable others to remain: remittances and new moral economies of migration in southern Kyrgyzstan. *Central Asian Survey* 30,3–4:541–554.
Ivashenko, E. 2012: *OBON, ili baby osobogo naznacheniya v Kyrgyzstane: gde, zachem i pochem* (OBON, or the female troop for a special operation task in Kyrgyzstan: where, why and how much). Available at: http://www.fergananews.com/articles/7546.

Marat, E. 2008: March and after: what has changed? What has stayed the same? *Central Asian Survey* Vol. 27, No. 3–4:229–240.

Mavloni, D. 2010: *Znakom'tes: OBON – otryad bab spetsial'nogo naznacheniya* (Meet: OBON – female troop for a special operational task). Available at: http://rus.azattyq.org/content/obon_woman_kyrgyzstan_uzbekistan/2154268.html.

Oruzbaeva, B. 1984: Frunze. Entsiklopdia (Frunze. Encyclopedia). Frunze.

Reeves, M. 2012: Black work, green money: remittances, ritual and domestic economies in southern Kyrgyzstan. *Slavic Review* Vol. 71, No. 1 (spring):108–134.

Röhner, I. 2007: *National and International Labour Migration: A Case Study in the Province of Batken, Kyrgyzstan.* Unpublished MSc Thesis Work. University of Zurich, Switzerland.

Sanghera, B. 2010: Why are Kyrgyzstan's slum dwellers so angry? Available at: http://www.opendemocracy.net/od-russia/balihar-sanghera/why-are-kyrgyzstan%E2%80%99s-slum-dwellers-so-angry.

Sanghera, B. 2011: Illegal Settlements and city registration in Kyrgyzstan and Kazakhstan: Implications for Legal Empowerment, Politics and Ethnic Tensions. *OSI Occasional Paper.*

Sanghera, B.; Satybaldieva, E. 2012: Ethics of property, illegal settlements and the right to subsistence. *International Journal of Sociology and Social Policy* Vol. 32, Iss. $^1/_2$:96–114.

Sanghera, B. 2012: *The legal empowerment of the poor and the residential registration system in Kyrgzstan and Kazakhstan.* Available at: http://cesmi.info/wp/?p=197.

Schmidt, M.; Sagynbekova, L. 2008: Migration past and present: Changing pattern in Kyrgyzstan. *Central Asian Survey* Vol. 27, Issue 2.

Schröder, P. 2011: *From Shangai to Iug-2: Integration and Identification among and beyond the Male Youth of a Bishkek Neighbourhood.* Unpublished PhD Dissertation. Martin-Luther-Universität Halle-Wittenberg.

Thieme, S. 2008: Where to return to? Rural-urban interlinkages in times of internal and international labor migration. Social research center. In: Couper, J. (ed.), *Kyrgyzstan today. policy briefs on civil society, migration, Islam and corruption.* Bishkek: American University – Central Asia, pp. 108–113.

Han Migration to Xinjiang Uyghur Autonomous Region: Between State Schemes and Migrants' Strategies[1]

Agnieszka Joniak-Lüthi
Institute of Social Anthropology, University of Bern, Länggassstrasse 49a, CH-3012 Bern

Abstract. Post-1949 Han migration to the Xinjiang Uyghur Autonomous Region in northwest China is a hotly debated issue among Xinjiang scholars as well as among the population of the region itself. While it is often discussed as a large-scale historical process using statistical data, in this article I argue for a more differentiated view of Han migrants. I demonstrate that in the popular discourse, migrants are distinguished into numerous categories like Bingtuaners[2], Profit-Driven Migrants, Border Supporters, Qualified Personnel, Educated Youth and others. Accordingly, I argue that Han migrants to Xinjiang should not be understood as a homogeneous category of participants in a singular state project intended to establish state control over the region. High return rates demonstrate that state attempts to make Han migrants settle in Xinjiang are only partly successful and that migrants follow their own strategies when the situation permits, rather than fulfill the government's plans. Individuals who have migrated since the 1980s are especially careful in their assessment of the economic incentives of settlement and many decide to remain mobile.
[Xinjiang, Han immigration, Han-Uyghur interactions, migrants' strategies]

When analyzing the literature on Xinjiang Uyghur Autonomous Region as I prepared for my research, it occurred to me that although nearly every Xinjiang-related publication mentions Han migration, very few explore it *per se*. When it is discussed, Han migration tends to be viewed from a distant vintage point, through statistical data and as a large-scale historical process, far away from the qualitative perspective characteristic of social anthropology. Han migration is predominantly framed as a state strategy intended to "do something to Xinjiang" (spur development, placate ethnic unrest, integrate the region with other Chinese provinces, and so forth), as a historical process

---

[1] This paper is based on data collected during a ten-month period of fieldwork in 2011–2012 that focused geographically on the district of Aqsu, in southern Xinjiang. My fieldwork was generously supported by the Swiss National Science Foundation (Project no. 100013_132387/1) and UniBern Research Foundation (Project no. 4/2011).
[2] Xinjiang Shengchan Jianshe Bingtuan (Xinjiang Production and Construction Corps) is an almost exclusively Han organization. It was established in Xinjiang in 1954 to coordinate demobilized soldiers and early Han migrants. Since then, its population has grown to about 2.5 million (XWZCZ 2005). Bingtuan is directly under the jurisdiction of the central government and has its own universities, schools, research institutes, judicial system and police. On Bingtuan, see Hamann 2007; Becquelin 2004; Seymour 2000.

of colonization, as a collective "other" of the Uyghur,[3] as a threat to "Uyghur culture," as an agent of the central government in ethnic borderlands, and as a threat to Xinjiang's ecological environment (e.g. Rudelson 1997; Smith 2000 and 2002; Bovingdon 2004; Bachman 2004; Becquelin 2000 and 2004; Dautcher 2009; Erkin 2009; Hopper and Webber 2009; Caprioni 2011). While these interpretations are realized in some form or another, the homogenizing bird-eye perspective and sociometric representations of Han migrants do not reflect complex and fragmented social practices. They also do not reflect the differentiated ways in which Uyghur individuals perceive, react to, and interact with different Han. Although the dominant discourse among the Uyghur is indeed that of Han migrants encroaching onto their space, a careful observation reveals that Uyghur individuals distinguish between various categories of Han and interact with these categories accordingly.

In the present paper, I thus argue for a more differentiated view of Han migrants and Han migration. Halskov Hansen (2005:243) pertinently posits that when colonialist, modernist and civilizing projects are viewed through the representations of participants in these projects, "a fractured picture characterized by contradiction, fissures and plurality emerges." Likewise, Vasantkumar's (2012) study of Han in Qinghai Province makes clear that Han migrants and settlers in China's multi-ethnic borderlands are a fragmented category characterized by great internal differentiation and flexible identities. Elsewhere, I draw attention to the processes of othering, exclusion and discrimination that divide "the Han" into many competing identity categories (Joniak-Lüthi 2013). These processes must be considered when Han migration to Xinjiang and Han settlement are discussed. To counter the process in which the discourse of "Han migration" slowly acquires the characteristics of a Foucauldian "truth," I propose to pause and complicate the picture by focusing on the diversity of Han in Xinjiang and their life stories. Such an approach highlights the self-perception of those migrants who distinguish themselves along multiple coordinates. Among these, native place, length of residency in the region, income, education, and employment are most significant.[4] Furthermore, I argue that Han migrants should not be understood as a homogeneous category of participants in a grand state project to establish control over the borderlands. After all, high return rates demonstrate that state attempts to make Han settle in Xinjiang have been only partially successful, and that migrants follow their own strategies when situation permits, rather than fulfill government plans. Even if Han migration is a strategy to sinicize the region and draw it closer to the Chinese political orbit, as Becquelin (2004) and Rudelson and Jankowiak (2004:301) argue, migrants' life stories cannot be contained in these straight lines of political imperatives.

---

[3] The Uyghur constitute officially 45 % of Xinjiang's population (Toops 2013) and are the largest of its Muslim, Turkic-speaking peoples. On the Uyghur see Gladney 1990; Rudelson 1997; Smith 2002; Starr 2004; Bellér-Hann et al. 2007; Dautcher 2009; Bovingdon 2010.
[4] For other examples of intra-Han differentiations, see Halskov Hansen 2005.

It is necessary to recognize how migrants' heterogeneity is differently manifest in individuals' identification with Xinjiang, attachment felt (or not) to the region, sense of responsibility for it, integration with the non-Han population, language competencies, and structure of social networks which all significantly impact the ethnic relations in the region.

This paper focuses on Han migration to Xinjiang after 1949, the founding year of the People's Republic of China.[5] In 1949, Xinjiang's Han population constituted slightly more than six per cent (291,000) of the total 4,333,400.[6] The Turkic-speaking farmers and oasis-dwellers referred to today as Uyghur then made up about seventy-five per cent (3,291,100) of Xinjiang's population. The remainder was comprised of Kazakhs, Dungan/Hui, Kyrgyz, Mongols, Russians and others (XWZCZ 2005:205). Since then, Han immigration dramatically changed the demographic structure of the region, likely turning the Uyghur into a minority in the late 2000s.[7] In the first three decades of the Communist rule, many Han migrants to Xinjiang were motivated by political ideals and developmental discourses, and by the obligation to "volunteer" for state-organized campaigns. Some were given no choice but to migrate. For numerous others, migration was a means to escape persecution, violence, a repressive situation at home, or starvation. Economic profit was not the focus of this early migration. The late 1980s marked a significant break with the past: at this time, migration as a profit-driven endeavor began to dominate but it was also practiced as a strategy to evade the one-child policy or escape family feuds.

Because Han migration to Xinjiang is rooted in a mix of individual and state-generated motivations, choices and obligations, political and economic forces, and temporality and permanence, separating Han migrants into analytically helpful categories proves difficult. As a result, I ultimately decided to here follow the logic of public discourse on Han in Xinjiang. This discourse clearly distinguishes between Bingtuaners and non-Bingtuan Han, between post-1980s Profit-Driven Migrants and early Border Supporters and Qualified Personnel, between the politicized Educated Youth

---

[5] For information on Han migration prior to 1949, see Lattimore 1962; Perdue 2005; Millward 2007; Yuan, Yuan and Zhu 2009; and Li 2010.

[6] Until 1949, the Han population was concentrated in eastern Xinjiang, between Qumul/Hami and Urumchi/Dihua. After 1949, northern Xinjiang received most Han migrants: Becquelin (2000:68) reports that in 1997, 78 % of Xinjiang's Han population lived in the north. Until recently, the south remained predominantly Uyghur, with the exceptions of Korla, with a prominent oil industry, and Aqsu District, with a large Bingtuan population.

[7] According to the 2010 Census, of Xinjiang's population of 21.8 million, the Uyghur number 10 million and the Han 8.8 million (Toops 2013:21). However, both my Han and Uyghur informants argued that if the Census results were to be published truthfully, the number of Han would be significantly higher. Because many Han migrants do not transfer their *hukou* (permanent household registration) to Xinjiang and do not register with local authorities when they arrive for temporary stay, the actual number of the Han in Xinjiang is difficult for everyone, including the regional government, to assess.

and anyone else, and between the Floating Population and settled Xinjiang Han. Some of these signifiers, such as the Bingtuaners (*Bingtuan, Bingtuande, Bingtuanren*), Border Supporters (*Zhibian, Zhibiande, Yuanjiangde*) and Profit-Driven Migrants (lit. those "who come only for the money") were used by both my Han and Uyghur interviewees. Others, like Qualified Personnel (*Rencai*), Floating Population (*Liudong renkou*), Xinjiang Han, Second Generation (*Di'er dai*), Educated Youth (*Zhiqing*), and "Migrants who came during three years of natural disasters" were rarely used by Uyghur individuals but were regularly employed by the Han. The signifiers used by the Han are thus more numerous and more specific. Those used by the Uyghur, on the other hand, are less nuanced and manifest the rough distinction between those Han who live distant from the Uyghur (Bingtuaners), the early migrants of the 1950s, 1960s and 1970s (Border Supporters), and those who arrived since the late 1980s (Profit-Driven Migrants). In the following analysis, I adopt this Uyghur differentiation scheme but then separate the three categories further by using the signifiers I collected in conversations with Han. Because some of the identifiers overlap and are not mutually exclusive – e. g. a person can be a Bingtuaner and a Profit-Driven Migrant simultaneously – the analysis is not meant to be read as a neat characterization. Instead, it is a picture of entangled and not clearly-distinguishable migration and identity processes.

Bingtuaners

Demobilized soldiers and early migrants

> My father is from Gansu and my mother from Hubei. He came here as a soldier in August 1949 with the People's Liberation Army. He didn't know he would remain in Xinjiang. The soldiers thought they would conquer this area and then go back home. But this was not the case; they could not go back (*tamen hui bu qu le*). They were made to settle down and work [...]. My uncle was sent with his garrison to Nanjing and now he lives in Nanjing. My father was sent to Xinjiang, and so we are in Xinjiang. My mother was brought here by her older brother, a soldier too. He said to her: "Come to Xinjiang, have a look, it is good here. Afterwards, you can go back home." And she came, she made the whole journey, it took her more than two weeks. Later on, it became impossible to go back, transportation was too bad. It wasn't possible for her brother to bring her back home, not that year and not the year after. Their parents were very upset and cursed the brother. After the death of her parents, she didn't go back any more. She was introduced to my father and remained in Xinjiang. (Han official in Aqsu, between 50–60 years old)

The Xinjiang Production and Construction Corps (Xinjiang shengchan jianshe bingtuan, hereafter Bingtuan) was formed in 1954 to administer more than 20,000 demobilized soldiers of the People's Liberation Army and about 80,000 soldiers from the Nationalist (Guomindang) garrison who resided in the region prior to 1949. The demobilized soldiers were made to work in agriculture and animal husbandry, and to build irrigation channels, construct roads, and develop industry.[8] In 1955, another 20,000 soldiers were demobilized in China and resettled to Xinjiang (Zhang 2010: 271) to establish the foundations on which new state institutions and the Han population could further grow. However, it proved difficult to keep these soldiers in the region. The massive imbalance of sexes in the 1950s – the sex ratio in the 24–29 age group was 296.8 males to 100 females (Qiang & Yuan 2003:95–96) – was the foremost reason for high desertion rates. To stabilize the situation, the central government reacted swiftly by launching a campaign to recruit female soldiers for service in Xinjiang. Hunan Province, the homeland of Mao Zedong, was one of the first to recruit female soldiers (the so called "Eight Thousand Hunan Girls;" *Ba qian xiang nü*). Tianjin, Shanghai and Shandong Province sent substantial contingents as well.[9] Although officially recruited for border defense, these women quickly confronted their actual role in the state scheme, namely marrying male soldiers, settling down and giving birth to the next generation of Han settlers (Dai 2010:3). Though none of them expected to stay in Xinjiang for a lifetime, cases of resistance were rare. This was likely due to the desolate situation of the Chinese countryside in general, and also to government propaganda that celebrated the settlers as "masters" (*zhuren*) of Xinjiang. Further, as Kardos (2010:148–153) rightly points out, because some women were pressured into this endeavor by local authorities, and many other volunteered in order to escape repressive situations at home and/or utmost poverty and hunger, return was a viable option for only a few. Together with demobilized soldiers, the female soldiers were incorporated into Bingtuan.

Due to the recruitment of settlers in inner China and an influx of other migrants, by 1966 Bingtuan already boasted a population of 1.48 million. By 2004, the population had grown to 2.56 million (XWZCZ 2005:601). Owing to rather crude living conditions and limited opportunities for employment outside of agriculture, there is currently some outflow from the Bingtuan farms to nearby towns, and also to eastern China (Hamann 2007). The latter is particularly the case for younger generations who out-migrate for study and work. Yet at the same time, there is an influx of new migrants from eastern China into farms and Bingtuan's non-agricultural enterprises. This appears to keep the Bingtuan population stable.

---

[8] ZZWY (2010:91) places the number of demobilized soldiers at 90,000, Millward (2007:251) at 103,000; Seymour (2000:173) at 104,000, and Li (2009:44) at 110,000.
[9] Zhang (2010:271) reports that authorities introduced 8,000 females from Shandong and 3,000 from Hunan to senior veterans and army leaders for marriage.

Great Leap Famine Refugees

> I am from here, but my origins are in Sichuan. My parents came to Xinjiang in the 1960s, during the "three bitter years." In Sichuan there was no food to eat. Here it was better. They were migrants. They are still here, they do not want to go back. They went to Sichuan once for a visit and quickly returned; they were not used to it anymore after decades in Aqsu. The state provides for them here; they receive pension, medical care. Why should they go back? They worked for Bingtuan, they are Bingtuaners (*Bingtuande*). (Han taxi driver in Aqsu, 40 years old)

The frenzy of collectivization in the 1950s, accompanied by increasingly extravagant falsifications of harvest achievements to satisfy Party leaders and the disastrous Great Leap Forward campaign (1958–62) initiated by Mao overextended the new state's fragile economy in the first decade of recovery. While Chinese historiography commonly explains the famine of this period as a consequence of natural disasters, it was rather collectivization and the Great Leap Forward that were responsible for the starvation and death of as many as twenty to thirty million people. As illustrated in the above quote, many who faced starvation in their home provinces tried to flee. Between 1959 and 1961, Xinjiang population statistics registered 704,200 hunger refugees. However, the actual number is officially estimated at three times higher between 2–2.5 million (XWZDBW 2008:114). The famine refugees constitute the largest and most condensed wave of migration into Xinjiang in the first three decades of the Communist rule. Owing to the slower pace of land reform and collectivization, Xinjiang did *relatively* well compared to other provinces in the aftermath of the Leap. Nonetheless, food became scarce when refugees flowed into the area. The majority were received by Bingtuan farms and enterprises; there, refugees often relied on relatives and friends for introduction. As the situation improved, many refugees left Bingtuan farms and searched for employment elsewhere. Nevertheless, the return rates among hunger refugees and their children were among the lowest of all the Han settlers until today (XWZDBW 2008:114).

In my conversations with Han whose parents came to Xinjiang to escape the famine, a narrative of gratitude was always present. An ex-Bingtuaner in Aqsu said, "My parents would have died, had they not come here. They were lucky. Why would they ever want to return?" While these Han and their descendants who remain in Bingtuan farms are very similar to other Bingtuaners in their segregated way of living, there is a significant difference in their imageries of Xinjiang. In these imageries, Xinjiang is not a barren frontier and a place of exile. Likewise, it is not a border that needs to be "constructed" and "supported." Instead, it is depicted as a haven that received these Han in desperate times. Their relationship with the region is thus accordingly distinct from that maintained by other Bingtuan Han, such as the aforementioned demobilized soldiers or the Educated Youth I discuss in the next section.

Educated Youth (Zhishi qingnian)

Educated Youth (*Zhishi qingnian*, briefly *Zhiqing*), or Shanghai Educated Youth (Shanghai *zhiqing*) as they are sometimes referred to, is a broad category that nominally includes all high school and university graduates who arrived in Xinjiang in the early decades of Communist rule. However, in popular Han discourse, the signifier "Educated Youth" is typically used to denote one particular group of educated youth, namely the rusticated urban youth of the Cultural Revolution (1966–76). Unlike other educated migrants, rusticated urban youth comprised a highly politicized and sensitive population, one purged from eastern Chinese cities as fights between various fractions of Mao's Red Guards began to get out of hand. To calm the situation, Mao called upon militant youth to *shangshan xiaxiang*, to "go up to the mountains and down to villages" and learn from the peasants in a new proletarian and non-capitalist spirit. As the rusticated urban youth underwent a proletarian re-education among peasants, it was presumed that their presence would simultaneously enforce proletariat rule and inhibit the resurrection of capitalism on the countryside (Tian 2003:149–150). Millions of urban youth were rusticated in this massive resettlement action. Xinjiang, and Bingtuan farms in particular, received more than 400,000 of them from Shanghai, Wuhan, Tianjin and Hangzhou.

Concluding from my interviews with other Han settlers, rusticated youth did not warm to life in Xinjiang. Having realized that their urban household registration – an extremely precious item in Communist China[10] – was transferred to rural Xinjiang, thereby blocking any option of a legal return home, many rusticated youth felt betrayed. Numerous cases of sexual abuse and forced marriage among the female portion of the population further compounded the situation. In the wake of the Cultural Revolution, many of these forced migrants fled back east. Others publicly protested, demanding redress and the right to legal return, which they were eventually granted by Deng Xiaoping in 1981. Zhang and He (1999:31) report that until 1985, the return rate among the Educated Youth was as high as sixty-seven per cent.[11] Of course, after a decade on Bingtuan farms, reintegration to urban life and urban economies in eastern China proved difficult. Following return, youths' status was unregulated and thus negatively affected their employment, accommodation and health

---

[10] In the 1960s, '70s, and '80s, the type of *hukou* (agricultural and non-agricultural) and the place of *hukou* registration had a powerful impact on the life of an individual. These two things determined whether and where a person was entitled to employment, housing, education, grain ratios, medical care and other social welfare benefits. Only non-agricultural *hukou* gave access to these benefits; agricultural *hukou* did not, as life in the countryside was expected to be self-sufficient. See Chan and Buckingham 2008.

[11] Similarly high return rates were noted in Sipsong Panna/Xishuang Banna, where state farms that employed rusticated youth faced a drop of more than 47% in their labor force after youth were allowed to return home (Halskov Hansen 2005:60).

care. Moreover, the decade-long Cultural Revolution had deprived these individuals of the opportunity to complete vocational or tertiary education. According to my Han informants in Aqsu, a small number of rusticated youth returned to Xinjiang after unsuccessful attempts to reintegrate to urban life in the east. After all, and not insignificantly, in Xinjiang they enjoyed guaranteed employment with Bingtuan along with pension and health services. Although some eventually did settle down in Xinjiang, my interviewees emphasized that rusticated youth formed the only category of government-generated Han migrants officially released from the obligation to remain in Xinjiang.

Bingtuaners and their relationship with Xinjiang

Becquelin (2004:367) rightly points out that Bingtuan has been a "powerful colonizing force, reclaiming land to settle new immigrants from interior parts of China; securing the territory with a string of cities, farm complexes and industries; attracting demobilized soldiers to settle in Xinjiang; and consolidating territorial control." Han employed in Bingtuan farms and enterprises live spatially-segregated from other ethnicities, and from other Han.[12] They rarely speak local languages like Uyghur or Kazakh, have little knowledge of non-Han cultural and religious practices, and their social networks rarely include persons of other *minzu*.[13] Accordingly, on numerous occasions Uyghur informants highlighted the distance and separation they feel toward Bingtuan Han. Uyghur interviewees insisted that especially Bingtuan Han from the Han-dominated northern Xinjiang avoid mixed-ethnic settings. This was also reflected in conversations I had with Bingtuan Han. The words of one entrepreneur from a farm in Kuytun are particularly representative of this sentiment: "I have never traveled in southern Xinjiang. I think it would be inconvenient (*bu fangbian*). Imagine, I get on the bus and I am the only Han. This would feel very inconvenient."[14] In conversations, Bingtuaners frequently praised Uyghur foods such as *zhuafan* rice (*polo* in Uyghur), *banmian* noodles (*lengmen* in Uyghur), and Xinjiang mutton. However, even these Uyghur foods they would rather enjoy in Han-run restaurants than in Uyghur neighborhoods. That large Bingtuan farms not uncommonly come into conflict with

---

[12] This fact is also observed by Halskov Hansen (2005:51–58, 84), who studies military state farms in Sipsong Panna. In many respects, the history of Bingtuan Han in Xinjiang resembles that of Han on military farms in Yunnan. In a similar vein, Ma (2003:122) argues that large-scale state enterprises like Bingtuan have a negative influence on inter-ethnic group exchange in Xinjiang.

[13] *Minzu* are officially designated population categories. *Minzu* is translated either as "nation" or "nationality" (in Stalin's definition) or recently, and increasingly, as "ethnic group."

[14] However, it must be added that many Uyghur from the north or from Urumchi have never been in the south, albeit for different reasons. They imagine southern Xinjiang as very traditional, religious, and poor.

Uyghur farmers over water and land use further enhances the tensions that exist between the Uyghur and this portion of Han population.

Although Bingtuaners have formed a parallel society very poorly-integrated to the rest of Xinjiang's population, the Bingtuan Han I interviewed nevertheless feel strongly attached to Xinjiang. According to what felt like an ever-present metaphor, they believe they have transformed it "from a wasteland into a blooming garden" (*ba huangdi bianchang le ge huayuan*). While the Uyghur strongly oppose the notion of their homeland as a "wasteland," very few doubt that the work of early Bingtuaners was hard and physically oppressive. With limited tools and almost no machines, this first generation built irrigation channels, roads and bridges, factories, mines and towns. Having spent their lives "constructing" (*jianshe*) *their* Xinjiang, they understandably feel strongly attached to it. Among the second generation of Bingtuaners, self-denominations such as *bendide* ("local," "native") and *tusheng tuzhangde* ("born here and grown up here") are popularly used. Still, the Xinjiang they are attached to has little in common with the Uyghur, Kazakh or Mongol Xinjiang. The imagery of an empty frontier awaiting the determined Han migrant to settle and transform it into a "proper place" constitutes the core of the relationship between Bingtuaners and Xinjiang. Unavoidably, this further complicates their relationship with other ethnic groups.

Hamann (2007:97) reports that on farms north of Urumchi in Changji and Miquan, many Bingtuan employees reported feeling displaced and cherished the idea of returning home to eastern China. While this may be true of recently-recruited individuals, among the long-term Bingtuan Han I interviewed in Aqsu, no one expressed a similar wish, even if they did maintain an attachment to their idealized native places (*laojia, jiaxiang*) in China "proper" and even visited them once transportation became more convenient. Although Bingtuaners in Aqsu argued that "Xinjiang is terribly backward" (*luohou de hen*), they simultaneously praised Xinjiang's fruits, local specialties, landscape, weather and, let's not forget, central heating. The feeling of contentedness and pride that many long-term Bingtuaners display is significantly enhanced by guaranteed pension schemes, health insurance and accommodations provided by the state. Moreover, only in Xinjiang do these individuals and their descendants receive such a notable recognition for their contribution to the "stabilization of borderlands" (*gonggu bianjiang*). This awards an additional historical dimension to their lives and further binds them to the region.

Border Supporters and Qualified Personnel

> I am from here. I am the second generation of those who came to open up wastelands and protect the borders. My father came to Xinjiang in 1959. He was not among those who came to fight and plough, but among University graduates [...]; he was an intellectual. When he graduated, in every city Mao's call was publicized, which mobilized the youth to go to Xinjiang to support its development.

> Their heads were full of Chairman Mao's thought, so they followed it. People were like this earlier. And they came here, on a one-way ticket. Young graduates from all over the country were packed onto trains and sent to Xinjiang. (Han taxi driver in Shihezi, 40 years old)
>
> My parents came to Xinjiang in the 1950s following the call of Mao Zedong for young people from the east to develop the west. They were very enthusiastic and believed in their mission. They wanted to make a contribution. They were both workers; they worked in a cotton mill [...]. They lived among the local Uyghur [...]. Everybody was poor [...]. At the beginning, in the 1950s and 1960s, all the Han learnt Uyghur. Only later migrants stopped learning it and began to regard themselves as something better than the locals. (Han teacher in Kashgar, 30 years old)

Records show that the first group of 6,531 Border Supporting Youth (*Zhibian qingnian*[15]) arrived in Xinjiang from Shandong Province as early as 1954. It was followed in 1956 by another 55,000 so-called volunteers from Henan (Zhang 2010:272). Soon after, in 1958, Mao issued a nation-wide call mobilizing Han youth to go to borderlands and ethnic minority areas. The call had a dual purpose, namely to develop the frontier economically and populate it. 5.7 million "volunteers" were originally scheduled to be sent to border areas between 1958 and 1963 (ZZWY 2010:202–203). While the majority was to be recruited from among farmers, workers, artisans, economists, educators, doctors and other Qualified Personnel (*Rencai*)[16] were also to be mobilized to join the pool. Ultimately, Xinjiang was to receive about two million Border Supporters. Although the plan was only partially realized, between 1957 and 1960 more than 800,000 immigrants arrived in Xinjiang, where they were dispatched between Bingtuan farms and various government institutions, hospitals, educational institutions, enterprises and factories (Li 2009:46). Although Mao succeeded in mobilizing substantial numbers of Supporters, the return rates among this population, especially among the Qualified Personnel in this pool, were very high. Officially, government interventions kept return rates below twenty-five per cent (XWZDBW 2008:114) but the share of qualified workers in the total migrant population decreased significantly from 14.9% in 1957 to 8.7% in 1966, and then to 3.6% in 1976 (Li 2009:46). This suggests that many workers escaped from their assignments and that replacements were difficult to recruit.

Within the category of Frontier Supporters who followed the call of Mao was a not insignificant number of Han who opted to migrate to Xinjiang to escape the shame of a "wrong" family background. Those stigmatized as petty bourgeoisie, landlords and capitalists and discriminated in their home provinces by restricted access to education

---

[15] *Zhibian* is an abbreviation of *zhiyuan bianjiang*, lit. "to support the frontier."
[16] "Qualified personnel" is a broad category that includes vocational schools and university graduates. They constitute part of "border supporters" and are also referred to with this signifier.

and work, migrated to escape persecution and to improve their families' Marxist "karma." In Xinjiang, as informants from these families assured me, no one inquired about family background. All Han were equally welcome to settle and contribute to the "construction of the socialist borderland." My fieldwork data suggest that among this group of Border Supporters, return rates were rather low, not lastly because few of them had family or possessions to which to return.

From among the Frontier Supporters, some were dispatched to Bingtuan farms where, together with other Bingtuaners, they formed a parallel society that rarely interacted with others. Another significant segment was dispatched to Uyghur areas to populate government institutions and work in industry and agriculture. My data suggest that many of these migrants learned to speak local languages and established friendly and close relationships with their Uyghur neighbors and workmates. During my fieldwork, I became acquainted with a number of these settlers and observed Uyghur willingly and warmly socialize with them. On a train to Kashgar, for instance, I met a retired Han woman who arrived in Kashgar as a twenty year-old girl. She had worked there ever since as a teacher and learned to speak Uyghur fluently. Whenever she passed by, three Uyghur men who were traveling in the same hard-sleeper train car engaged her in a conversation. She herself also repeatedly visited their seats to socialize with them. The Uyghur men praised her in front of me and discussed her devotion to Xinjiang long after she returned to her spot. As Smith (2002) observes, some of these settlers and second-generation Han who maintain cross-ethnic relations will minimize consumption of pork or give it up entirely. One informant who arrived in Xinjiang in the 1950s with his parents, qualified factory workers, stated, "Uyghurs can smell pork after you have eaten it. That is why I gave it up. I cannot sit with them knowing that [they smell it]; it's been twenty years now."

While the mobilization of skilled personnel was actively pursued for "border support" in the Maoist period,[17] after which the majority left, smaller-scale assignments continued following Mao's death in 1976. Li (2009:45) reports that in the early 1980s, about 2,500 Chinese university graduates were assigned work in Xinjiang annually. After 1984, the government continued this practice but its scale rapidly decreased. In the late 1990s, the work assignment system in inner China was dismantled entirely. With the abolishment of this system, new policies were launched to attract Han professionals and university graduates to Xinjiang's government and educational system, and to state-owned enterprises. The centrally-coordinated campaign of "Partnership Assistance for Xinjiang" (*Duikou yuan Jiang* or *Duikou zhiyuan*), first launched around 1996 and again in 2010, is a principal structure through which graduates and professionals from outside Xinjiang are recruited for state sector jobs in Xinjiang today. Professionals also migrate individually. Struggling to launch their professional careers in

---

[17] Between 1957 and 1966, almost 30,000 university graduates were assigned work in Xinjiang (Li 2009:45).

overpopulated eastern China, young Han University graduates search for work in Xinjiang to gain professional experience and working contracts. Still clad in the state rhetoric of "border support," this employment experience in Xinjiang is particularly popular among junior cadres and young graduates, as it often serves to improve their chances on the job market after they return to eastern China. Yet both Uyghur and Han informants voiced that this "border support" – with cadres and professionals rotating at a maximum of three-year intervals – does not benefit the region as much as it does the young Han professionals who accumulate substantial financial resources during their tenure.[18] While junior professionals dominate numerically, a few hundred senior Han cadres and professionals from state-owned enterprises in eastern China are mobilized to contribute to "frontier support" through shorter-term assignments and projects each year. In financial terms, these mandatory assignments tend to be significantly less lucrative for senior cadres and professionals than assignments in eastern China.

According to a Uyghur government official in Urumchi, Xinjiang authorities hope to attract tens of thousands university graduates from eastern China to settle in southern Xinjiang cities for minimum three-year terms of employment. While the official argued that this would create a favorable economic climate and spur development, other Han and Uyghur informants instead highlighted the strategy as an attempt to alter the demography of the Uyghur-dominated Aqsu-Kashgar-Hotan region. In Kashgar, complaints about university graduates from eastern China (Shandong Province, in particular) assigned work there – in a situation where Kashgari University graduates themselves have difficulties finding local employment – were common. Although skepticism about this form of contemporary "border support" abounds, Han and many of my Uyghur informants actually agreed that Xinjiang does need ongoing "infusions" of skilled personnel to successfully launch necessary social and economic transformations. Still, the identification of ethnic bias in employment practices, resentment towards preferential conditions offered to contemporary Border Supporters as opposed to Xinjiang-born professionals, and an additional dose of state territorialization in these practices makes the issue controversial and contested.

Post-1980s Profit-Driven Migrants and Floating Population

> I came to Korla from Jiangsu one and a half years ago. I'm here with my husband. Our daughter is home in Changzhou with my parents and my older brother. We came here only because of money. We always return home during the Spring Festival. [...] I didn't transfer my household registration to Korla, it is in Changzhou. We plan to go back after some years. Our daughter goes to this famous school in

---

[18] In addition to a regular salary, these individuals are granted a "frontier allowance." Their accommodation is additionally provided by receiving working units.

Changzhou, we need to earn money to pay for it. [Han shop assistant, 40 years old]

There are many opportunities for investors in Xinjiang; the state policy is very good. I met many friends here. They all tell me: "It is good that people like you from inner China are coming to invest here, from you we learn how to make big money." I came here to make a contribution to Xinjiang. Our company is paying taxes, and in this way we make a great contribution to Xinjiang. If we don't come, the resources will remain untapped and the government of Xinjiang will receive no taxes [...]. There are many investment possibilities here [...]. We are operating an iron mine. I have been here for a year now. Xinjiang is really not bad. I got used to it, no problem. The climate is better than back home, [and] in winter you have central heating. The food is *qingzhen* (*halal*) but I have no problem with that. [Han investor from Sichuan, 50 years old]

The death of Mao Zedong, the subsequent transfer of power to Deng Xiaoping, and the introduction of economic and social reforms in the late 1970s had significant impact on the Han in Xinjiang. A number of "volunteers" from the 1950s and 1960s returned home, thereby reducing the Han share in Xinjiang's population. Between 1982 and 1990, this share diminished from 40.41 per cent to 37.58 per cent[19] (XWZDBW 2008:271). Yet in the 1990s, the central government's policies and the rising market economy succeeded in reversing the outflow. These political and economic factors eventually resulted in a massive influx of new migrants, one that has been increasing ever since. Anecdotal evidence suggests that periods of diminished influx and increased outflows of Han migrants occur only in the aftermath of major violent unrest, like that which took place in 1997 in Ghulja and in 2009 in Urumchi. While larger chunks of the Han population are still resettled to Xinjiang by the government,[20] economic, profit-driven migration has dominated the region since the late 1980s. As Zhang (2010:270) points out, the migration of peasant laborers to Xinjiang in the reform era parallels concurrent migration to urban areas and coastal regions. During the 1990s, the net migration to Xinjiang increased from 0.4 per cent to 2.4 per cent, making Xinjiang one of the top destinations for labor migrants following Beijing, Shanghai and southern Guangdong Province (Qiang and Yuan 2003:97). With its developing industrial base and large construction projects, Xinjiang offered employment to the Han migrant workers who first populated the industrial belt north

---

[19] The actual Han population grew slightly from 5.28 million in 1982 to 5.69 in 1990 (XWZDBW 2008:269), but the parallel increase in the non-Han population was larger, thereby effecting a decrease in the Han share of the total population.

[20] My informants posited that about 20,000 people were resettled from the earthquake area of Wenchuan in Sichuan Province to the Kashgar area to work in newly-established factories. Others asserted that Han displaced by the grand south-north water-transfer project (*Nanshui beidiao*) are being resettled in Xinjiang. However, these pieces of information are very difficult to verify.

of Tengri Tagh/Tianshan Mountains and who in the last decade began flowing in large numbers into southern Xinjiang. The main migrant workers' destinations in the south are the oil fields of the Taklamakan Desert and other extraction sites in the Tarim Basin, the cotton fields of Aqsu and Kashgar, road and railway construction sites, and various construction projects in urban areas. Most of these ventures are run by eastern Chinese companies. Favorable tax policies and low land prices attract state-owned and private enterprises from eastern China to set up factories and open new extraction sites in Xinjiang. Collected between 2011 and 2012, my observations in northern and southern Xinjiang prove that the workers employed in these factories and construction sites are overwhelmingly Han.[21] Workers arrive in the region in organized groups recruited from their home provinces, or they migrate individually, having gathered information about available jobs through native place networks. It appears that contemporary workers and entrepreneurs are encouraged to migrate either by the friends and family members who came before them, or by media reports in their home provinces. These reports represent Xinjiang as the land of opportunity where, as the popular saying has it, "money can be easily earned" (*zai Xinjiang qian haozheng*).

Most of the post-1980s migration to Xinjiang, including the skilled personnel I discussed above, appears driven by the search of economic profit. It also seems to be predominantly organized by individuals, and mostly voluntary. At the same time, however, this does not mean it is not political, centrally-planned and centrally- and locally-encouraged. The central and local governments have successfully created the favorable conditions necessary to attract Chinese companies to establish factories in Xinjiang. This, in turn, attracts workers to those regions where factories are constructed. Settlement in agricultural areas is also encouraged by favorable responsibility contracts (Becquelin 2000:76). However, the outcomes of these strategies are far from coherent, and migrants make use of state schemes in ways that do not always correspond with the government's expectations. For instance, although the government encourages immigration that should presumably result in long-term settlement, as well as the immigration of skilled personnel, most contemporary migrants are in fact peasant workers and entrepreneurs who come to Xinjiang temporarily or seasonally. As a result, while Han migration to Xinjiang has increased dramatically over the past decade, the actual number of Han settlers, that is, Han who transferred their *hukou* to Xinjiang, has decreased percentage-wise from 40.57 % to 40.48 % between 2000 and 2010 (Toops 2013).

Seen in this light, current state strategies produce relatively few Han settlers but many short- and long-term migrants. Even migrants who have lived in Xinjiang for as

---

[21] Bellér-Hann (2002:65) reports that Uyghur who lived in southern Xinjiang in 1995 resented the fact that even unskilled jobs in the profitable oil sector were offered to migrant Han. Hopper and Webber (2009) similarly demonstrate that the Han nearly monopolized the most profitable construction sector (with the help of native-place networks). This has significantly contributed to the current income inequality between the Han and Uyghur.

many as ten to fifteen years are reluctant to settle down in Xinjiang, i. e. relocate their *hukou*, since this would most likely close the cherished possibility of an eventual return home. As a number of my Han interviewees asserted, "Xinjiang is not a place where you want to live after retirement." Moreover, *hukou* transfer would deprive rural migrants of the farmland bound to rural *hukou* status which many still have in their communities of origin. During their absence, this land is leased; it often provides an additional source of income for the family. For Xinjiang authorities, non-*hukou* migrants are an ambiguous category. Even though these migrants are generally regarded as beneficial to the local economy, temporary and seasonal migrants are at the same time feared as potential sources of social disorder. They are difficult to control, as in the instance of birth-control policies. The official press blames this Floating Population (*Liudong renkou*) for threatening social stability, law and order, for breaching the one-child policy, and for living "unhygienic lifestyles" (Zhang 2010:279). The Floating Population – and even the Han Floating Population in Xinjiang – is similar to other non-sedentary populations in that it is treated suspiciously by the Chinese state and viewed as particularly difficult to discipline with the means of territorial states. When viewed in this way, a sizeable portion of the Han who have migrated to Xinjiang since the early 1990s does not actually fulfill the state's plan to increase Han settlement in this border region. Rather, most contemporary migrants are instable, individually-driven and prone to fluctuate between those places that offer the most lucrative employment opportunities.

In addition to the seasonal and temporary migrants who seek out employment in Xinjiang's mines, construction sites and cotton fields, petty Han entrepreneurs who establish their own businesses in Xinjiang constitute another significant group in the discursive category of Profit-Driven Migrants. Since some of them migrate with their entire families, they are different from the temporary and seasonal migrants. Those who have children also tend to transfer their *hukou* registration to Xinjiang in order to secure their children's access to local education and health care. In our conversations, many of these migrants reported that they felt displaced and had few friends, and that the friends they had were their *laoxiang* ("native place fellows"). As in the cities in eastern China, *laoxiang guanxi* ("native place bonds") constitute the basis of migrants' social networks in Xinjiang. As one of my Sichuan acquaintances said, "Those from elsewhere don't even understand my dialect. When I hang out, I do it with other Sichuanese who'll understand me." Just as seasonal migrants quite understandably do not learn to speak local non-Han languages during their employment in Xinjiang, so also is the case with petty entrepreneurs. Instead, the majority of them pursue a strategy of spatial detachment. These migrants maintain close links with their families back home; in their shopping, they focus on products they know from their home provinces;[22] they cook their own foods or eat out in restaurants offering dishes

---

[22] Frequenting one vegetable shop in Aqsu, I realized that there is a category of "Han vegetables" (*Hanzu cai*). This signifier was used by a Han shop keeper from Gansu Province; with it, she referred

they know from back home; and they deliberately spend time with "fellow natives." Similar to the Floating Population, their motivations to come to Xinjiang are principally to earn money for the education of their children or to support elderly parents. Some also intend to save money to start small businesses back home or to finance agricultural machinery for their farmland. Because individual entrepreneurs work independently and transportation connections are plentiful, they are able to wrap up their businesses one day and move to another place the next. Knowing this, these Han migrants rarely try to integrate or learn about the local society. Most work seven days a week, twelve hours a day, and live in the back of their shops, restaurants or garages to guard their property. Still, because they are savvy businesspeople, at least some of the well-established entrepreneurs maintain friendly, albeit limited, contact with their regular Uyghur customers and business friends.

Among my Uyghur informants, opinions about this recent segment of Han migrants were overwhelmingly negative. These migrants' singular economic motivation and corresponding disinterest in Xinjiang as a concrete place with a certain history and multi-ethnic population were frequently and extensively criticized. My observations reveal that the Uyghur avoid social interactions with seasonal migrant workers in particular, migrants the Uyghur look down upon as uneducated, poor and desperate to accept any kind of work. Interestingly, some long-term Han settlers and non-Bingtuan second-generation Han shared this opinion, emphasizing the detachment of migrants, their lack of responsibility for the region, their profit-orientation and the ecological costs of their immigration.

Concluding remarks

With the relaxation of the household registration regime in the 1980s, migration became much less definite. While Mao-era Han migrants remained in Xinjiang for decades, often without even returning home for a parent's funeral, the Han migration of the past twenty years is characterized by increasing flexibility, mobility and indefiniteness. Also, owing to a practically ever-present mobile phone signal, migrants are in daily contact with families back home. Along with the celebration of native place attachments in social networks, these intensively-maintained links result in migrants who live a largely de-territorialized life, one with little experience of Xinjiang as a concrete place. The frequent rotation and influx of immigrants greatly influence migrants' identification with Xinjiang, their relationships with the Uyghur and other ethnic groups, and their perceived need and readiness to integrate into the local society. The

---

to vegetables that are used by Han in their favorite dishes but are never purchased by Uyghur. One is the *doufucai* ("tofu vegetable"). Migrants from Sichuan, where this vegetable originates, love it stir-fried with tofu, she explained.

sheer numbers of incoming Han result in an ever-expanding transfer of Han spaces to Xinjiang. Because the number of temporary, seasonal, and permanently-settled Han in the region is greater than ever before, incoming Han are followed by yet other Han migrants and middlemen who offer their services to make the immigrants feel "at home." As a result, a huge immigrant-catering economy has developed: vegetables that Han migrants like are imported to Xinjiang, shops and markets open to sell products imported from their home provinces, Han butchers establish market stalls where they sell pork and other meat specialties appreciated by Han customers. Also restaurants and shops that cook Chinese regional dishes sprout out, massage salons open, and Chinese-medicine clinics are launched. Even bamboo chairs known from Chinese teahouses are now available in larger Xinjiang towns. Every year, tons of moon-cakes for the Han Mid-Autumn Festival and sticky-rice dumplings (*zongzi*) for the Dragon Boat Festival are shipped to Xinjiang from eastern China. These products are transported around Xinjiang through a network of Han intermediaries and Han truck-drivers. While Uyghur market stalls primarily display locally-grown carrots, onions, chili, celery, potatoes, melons and grapes,[23] Han market stalls offer a wide range of vegetables and fruit imported from other Chinese provinces. Further, all service people, like shoe-cleaners, house painters, plumbers, locksmiths, bricklayers, and mechanics, can now be organized within Han social networks. These networks produce and expand complex Han spaces. It is today possible for the Han to live in Xinjiang and have virtually no occasion to interact with Uyghur and other non-Han. Perhaps the only exception is when Han buy *nan* bread – a specialty that still, though maybe not for long, remains exclusively Uyghur-produced. Owing to their increasing numbers, and also to missing mechanisms that might otherwise control this phenomenon, the Han migrants of the past two decades have been able to recreate in Xinjiang their "spaces of familiarity" to an unprecedented extent. It is thus unsurprising that this wave of migrants has raised resistance, especially among local Uyghur. That most of the post-1980s migrants have arrived in the "gold rush," driven by money and opportunity, makes it even more difficult for the Uyghur, and also for local Han and earlier Han immigrants and their descendants, to establish a positive relationship with these newer arrivals.

A common "Han" denominator should not conceal the stark differentiation, fragmentation and even certain antagonisms among members of the Han *minzu* in Xinjiang. Similarly differentiated in social practice, if rarely in discourse, is the Uyghur perception of the Han. The Han who praise Uyghur cuisine and local produce, who speak the Xinjiang dialect with Uyghur-intonation and Uyghur loan words and, in the case of Han women, who wear earrings (an absolute rarity among Han women) are perceived differently from those who grew up in the closed compounds of Bingtuan

---

[23] Uyghur shops also display a rich variety of products from Turkey, Saudi Arabia, Malaysia, Indonesia, Russia, Poland, Ukraine, Germany and France; this provides an accurate reflection of Uyghur transnational trade networks.

towns. The Uyghur interact differently with Han settlers who publicly and in the presence of Uyghur workmates and neighbors refer to themselves as *Xinjiangren* ("natives of Xinjiang") or *Lao* Xinjiang ("old Xinjiang native") than they do with seasonal migrants who arrive to work the cotton fields. Furthermore, I observed that some of the local Han, non-Bingtuan early Han migrants, and the second generation Han feel closer to Uyghur on the basis of a shared regional identity than they do to recent Han immigrants whom they regard as strangers intruding upon an established *status quo*. A number of my Uyghur informants in Urumchi mentioned that they feel hopeful to see local Han and Han settlers become their partners in the struggle for more Xinjiang autonomy with regard to the management of resources and ecological sustainability. Lastly, among the Han are those who "disappear" (Morawska 1984 in Brubaker 2003:48) and become "Uyghurized," or identify as both Han and Uyghur. However rare, these encounters most powerfully deny the ubiquitous confrontational discourse of "us" against "them" and prove that social practice is much more diversified and "in between."

References

Bachman, David 2004: Making Xinjiang Safe for the Han? Contradictions and Ironies of Chinese Governance in China's Northwest. In: M. Rossabi (ed.), *Governing China's Multiethnic Frontiers*. Seattle and London: University of Washington Press, pp. 155–185.
Becquelin, Nicolas 2000: Xinjiang in the Nineties. *The China Journal* 44:65–90.
Becquelin, Nicolas 2004: Staged Development in Xinjiang. *The China Quarterly* 178:358–378.
Bellér-Hann, Ildikó 2002: Temperamental Neighbours: Uighur-Han Relations in Xinjiang, Northwest China. In: G. Schlee (ed.), *Imagined Differences: Hatred and the Construction of Identity*. Münster, Hamburg, London: LIT Verlag, pp. 57–81.
Bellér-Hann, Ildikó; Cesàro, M. Cristina; Harris, Rachel et al. (eds.) 2007: *Situating the Uyghurs Between China and Central Asia*. Aldershot and Burlington: Ashgate.
Bovingdon, Gardner 2004: Heteronomy and Its Discontents: "Minzu Regional Autonomy" in Xinjiang. In: M. Rossabi, *Governing China's Multiethnic Frontiers*. Seattle and London: University of Washington Press, pp. 117–154.
Bovingdon, Gardner 2010: *The Uyghurs: Strangers in Their Own Land*. New York: Columbia University Press.
Brubaker, Rogers 2003: The Return of Assimilation? Changing Perspectives on Immigration and its Sequels in France, Germany, and the United States. In: C. Joppke and E. Morawska (eds.), *Toward Assimilation and Citizenship: Immigrants in Liberal Nation-States*. Basingstoke and New York: Palgrave Macmillan, pp. 39–58.
Caprioni, Elena 2011: Daily Encounters Between Hans and Uyghurs in Xinjiang: Sinicization, Integration or Segregation. *Pacific Affairs* 84(2):267–287.
Chan, Kam Wing and Will Buckingham 2008: Is China Abolishing the *Hukou* System? *The China Quarterly* 196:582–606.
Dautcher, Jay 2009: *Down a Narrow Road: Identity and Masculinity in a Uyghur Community in Xinjiang China*. Cambridge and London: Harvard University Asia Center.
Erkin, Adila 2009: Locally modern, globally Uyghur: geography, identity and consumer culture in contemporary Xinjiang. *Central Asian Survey* 28(4):417–428.

Gladney, Dru C. 1990: The Ethnogenesis of the Uighur. *Central Asian Survey* 9(1):1–28.
Halskov Hansen, Mette 2005: *Frontier People: Han Settlers in Minority Areas of China*. London: Hurst and Company.
Hamann, Bettina 2007: *Der Südrand des Dsungarischen Beckens. Ökologie und Sozioökonomie des chinesischen Transformationsprozesses*. Saarbrücken: VDM Verlag Dr. Müller.
Hopper, Ben; Webber, Micheal 2009: Migration, Modernisation and Ethnic Estrangement: Uyghur migration to Urumqi, Xinjiang Uyghur Autonomous Region, PRC. *Inner Asia* 11:173–203.
Joniak-Lüthi, Agnieszka 2013: The Han *minzu*, local identities and ethnicity. *The Journal of Asian Studies* 72(4):849–871.
Kardos, Amy 2010: A Rock and a Hard Place: Chinese Soldiers in Xinjiang Caught between Center and Periphery after 1949. In: S. Cochran and P. G. Pickowicz (eds.), *China on the Margins*. Ithaca: Cornell East Asia Program, pp. 135–157.
Lattimore, Owen 1962: *Studies in Frontier History: Collected Papers 1928–1958*. Paris and La Haye: Mouton and Co.
Li Jie 2010: *Xinjiang Nanjiang diqu Hanzu yimin ji minzu guanxi yanjiu – Yi Akesu diqu Baicheng xian nongcun Hanzu yimin ji minzu guanxi wei li*. [A study of Han migration to southern Xinjiang and inter-ethnic relations: On the example of rural Han immigrants and inter-ethnic relations in Bai county in Aqsu district.]. Beijing: Minzu Chubanshe.
Ma Rong 2003: Population Distribution and Relations Among Ethnic Groups in the Kashgar Region, Xinjiang Uyghur Autonomous Region. In: N. Bilik, R. Iredale and F. Guo, *China's Minorities on the Move: Selected Case Studies*. Armonk and London: M. E. Sharpe, pp. 106–122.
Millward, James A. 2007: *Eurasian Crossroads: A History of Xinjiang*. New York: Columbia University Press.
Perdue, Peter C. 2005: *China Marches West: The Qing Conquest of Central Eurasia*. Cambridge and London: The Belknap Press of Harvard University Press.
Qiang Ren; Yuan Xin 2003: Impacts of Migration to Xinjiang Since the 1950s. In: R. Iredale, N. Bilik and F. Guo, *China's Minorities on the Move. Selected Case Studies*. Armonk and London: M. E. Sharpe, pp. 89–105.
Rudelson, Justin 1997: *Oasis Identities: Uyghur Nationalism along China's Silk Road*. New York: Columbia University Press.
Rudelson, Justin; Jankowiak, William 2004: Acculturation and Resistance: Xinjiang Identities in Flux. In: S. F. Starr, *Xinjiang: China's Muslim Borderland*. Armonk and London: M. E. Sharpe, pp. 299–319.
Seymour, James D. 2000: Xinjiang's Production and Construction Corps, and the Sinification of Eastern Turkestan. *Inner Asia* 2:171–193.
Smith, Joanne N. 2000: Four Generations of Uyghurs: The Shift towards Ethno-Political Ideologies among Xinjiang's Youth. *Inner Asia* 2(2):195–224.
Smith, Joanne N. 2002: 'Making Culture Matter': Symbolic, Spatial and Social Boundaries between Uyghurs and Han Chinese. *Asian Ethnicity* 3(2):153–174.
Starr, S. Frederick (ed.) 2004: *Xinjiang: China's Muslim Borderland*. Armonk and London: M. E. Sharpe.
Tian Weijiang 2003: *Xinjiang Bainian 1900–1999 [Xinjiang: One hundred years 1900–1999]*. Wulumuqi: Xinjiang Qingshaonian Chubanshe.
Toops, Stanley 2013: Spatial Results of the 2010 Census of Xinjiang. *The Annual Meeting of the Association of Asian Studies*. San Diego.
Vasantkumar, Chris 2012: Han at *Minzu*'s Edges: What Critical Han Studies Can Learn from China's "Little Tibet". In: T. S. Mullaney et al., *Critical Han Studies: The History, Representation, and Identity of China's Majority*. Berkeley, Los Angeles, London: Global, Area, and International Archive and University of California Press, pp. 234–255.

XWZCZ, Xinjiang Weiwu'er Zizhiqu Chengli 50 Zhounian Chouweihui Bangongshi and Xinjiang Weiwu'er Zizhiqu Tongjiju 2005: *Xinjiang Wushinian 1955–2005* [Xinjiang: Fifty years 1955–2005]. Beijing: Zhongguo Tongji Chubanshe.

XWZDBW, Xinjiang Weiwu'er Zizhiqu Difangzhi Bianzuan Weiyuanhui and Renkouzhi Bianzuan Weiyuanhui Xinjiang Tongzhi 2008: *Xinjiang tongzhi. Renkouzhi. Di shisan juan* [Xinjiang annals, Population annals, vol. 13]. Wulumuqi: Xinjiang Renmin Chubanshe.

Yuan Zuliang, Yuan Yansheng and Zhu Heping 2009: *Sichou zhi lu renkou yanjiu* [Exploration into demography of the Silk Road region]. Wulumuqi: Xinjiang Renmin Chubanshe.

Zhang Feng 2010: One Mouth, Different Tunes: Newspaper Representations of Migrants to Xinjiang 1949–2004. In: Peng De and Du Fachun (eds.), *Xibu kaifa ji qi shehui jingji bianqian: Zhong-Jia bijiao yanjiu//Western Development and Socio-Economic Change: China-Canada Comparative Studies*. Beijing: Zhishi Chanquan Chubanshe, pp. 266–284.

Zhang Yi and He Bingyu 1999: Xinjiang bingtuan renkou qianyi yu Xinjiang shehui fazhan [Migration of Xinjiang's bingtuan population and Xinjiang's social development]. *Journal of Xinjiang University (Social Sciences)* 27(4):30–34.

ZZWY, Zhonggong Zhongyang Wenxian Yanjiushi and Zhonggong Xinjiang Weiwu'er zizhiqu weiyuanhui 2010: *Xinjiang Gongzuo Wenxian Xuanbian 1949–2010* [Selection of working papers on Xinjiang 1949–2010]. Beijing: Zhongyang Wenxian Chubanshe.

Historical Homelands and Transnational Ties: the Case of the Mongolian Kazaks

Peter Finke
Ethnologisches Seminar, Universität Zürich, Andreasstrasse 15, CH-8050 Zürich

Abstract. Since the early 1990s, roughly half of the Kazak minority in Mongolia has left the country in several waves to re-settle in the newly independent Republic of Kazakstan, following an invitation to 'join the native homeland'. These successive migration movements have primarily reflected the changing economic situations in both countries but have had a number of unforeseen consequences. One is that integration in Kazakstan has proven to be much more difficult than expected. As a response, people have developed strong transnational ties manifested in frequent mutual visits with kin left behind and a strong nostalgia for their place of origin. It will be argued that this can be explained as a strategy to deal with a low degree of social integration, longing for what will be called 'institutional cosiness', i. e. for a geographical and social environment with which one is familiar, knows the rules of the game, and feels at home. Simultaneously, the migration has had deep impacts on those still in Mongolia where the expected outcome of decision-making is greatly dependent on those of others, creating a complex situation of incentives for leaving or staying.
[*Kazak(h)s, Mongolia, migration, transnational ties*]

Introduction

> During the day we live in Kazakstan, at night we are in Mongolia.
> Aygül, 72-year old Kazak woman from Khovd
> who resettled to Kazakstan in 2003

This paper deals with a group of people, members of the Kazak minority in western Mongolia, who the author has had the luck to have known for more than twenty years. I first met them in 1991 when most of them made a living as pastoral nomads struggling with the aftermath of the collapse of the socialist regime and a deteriorating economy. As of today, more than half of them have moved to Kazakstan, which, after gaining independence in that very same year, officially invited all its diasporas "to return home" (Diener 2005; Kuscu 2012). The reason for this invitation lay in the specific demographic (im-)balance with Kazaks making up only some 40 percent of the population of the new state (Svanberg 1996; Dave 2007). At the same time, four million Kazaks lived abroad with the largest numbers in China, Uzbekistan and Russia. If repatriated, so the idea, they could not only increase the number of ethnic Kazaks in the country but also serve as agents for a revitalization of traditional culture and language believed to be better preserved among the diasporas. While the latter aim has met with mixed results, at least the demographic hopes have proven justified. By now, roughly one million have followed this call helping to raise the proportion of Kazaks to more than 60 percent within just twenty years (Kuscu 2012; Mendikulova 2012).

The Kazaks from Mongolia occupy a particular place in this picture. During the early 1990s, they formed the overwhelming majority of the repatriants, or *oralman* as they are called in Kazak, and by now more than half have since moved to Kazakstan.[1] As such, they have been a paradigmatic case both for the public in that country as well as for international scholarship (Finke 1999, 2004; Diener 2005, 2009; Barcus & Werner 2007, 2010; Werner & Barcus 2009). What I will look at specifically in this paper are the impacts this migration has had on people in both sites and upon the interrelations between the two. In the case of Mongolia, the fact that half of one's people have left and the omnipresent option for the rest to follow suit are of utmost relevance in everyday life and conversation. These circumstances have had a profound impact on economic opportunities as well as social relationships. In Kazakstan, on the other hand, the integration of the migrants was to prove far more difficult than expected due to a lack of economic opportunities and social acceptance by the local population. Apparently, the imagination of a shared ethnicity and culture prevented people from anticipating that they would move to a foreign land where the institutional framework is not the one they were used to. The situation is thus quite similar, somewhat ironically, with the fate of those Germans who migrated from Russia and Kazakstan to Germany during the same period (Sanders this volume).

What this situation provoked was the emergence of a new transnational field uniting those who left and those who stayed behind. Apart from the fact that people attempt to maintain kin relations, which by now always cross borders, this has other reasons as well. In Mongolia, it is, of course, based on the recognized probability that one will follow one's kin in the not too far future and may then be dependent on their support. At the same time, mutual visits are also an important source for seeking up-to-date information that would help one's decision-making. For those in Kazakstan, this may be explained as a counter strategy against feelings of being excluded at their new homes. As a consequence, people largely refrain from encounters with the local population, irrespective of their ethnicity, while Mongolia and one's relatives there – even more so than in the opposite direction – remain key points of reference in much of daily life.

---

[1] In more recent years, most of the migrants stem from Uzbekistan and China, with the former today accounting for two thirds of the total number of *oralman* (Kuscu 2012; Mendikulova 2012; Finke & Buri forthcoming).

In theoretical terms, this paper will apply an institutional approach looking at the changing motives of migrants and non-migrants, their integration into local society and the transnational ties that evolve. As 'rules of the game' (North 1990), institutions form the background to human incentives and strategic planning as they define costs and benefits related with specific prescriptions for social interaction. They provide people with guidelines of what to expect as consequences of their acting in a particular situation in light of the likely strategies of others. At the same time, institutions are also the very product of these patterns, and as such are reproduced, manipulated and changed in the course of people interacting with each other (North 1990; Knight 1992; Ensminger 1992; Finke 2004). They are agreed upon on the basis of repeated interaction and are challenged by individuals who believe to be disadvantaged by the existing institutional framework or imagine to do better with a different one (Knight 1992). On the other hand, institutions need a certain degree of stability to be able to create the expectations for other actors' strategies that allow a reasonable calculation of one's own, although due to the lack of information and the potentially opportunistic behaviour of individual actors, the rationality of strategic planning is always bounded (Simon 1957; Tversky & Kahneman 1990).

This is not to challenge anthropological engagement with migration but to link with different strands of theorizing. In spite of the extensive critique (neo-)classic push and pull explanations have received, a calculation of the relative attractiveness of places of origin and destination is inherent in any migratory decision (Mitchell 1969; Massey et al. 1993). It is simultaneously clear, however, that these take place under circumstances of limited information and are of a very complex nature involving a multitude of individuals socially connected to each other (Chibnik 2011). This is also an issue in the literature on chain migration, which looks at the role of social networks rather than 'objective' economic criteria in determining destinations or dates of move (Sassen 1988; Castles & Miller 1993; Brettell 2000; Faist 2000). Arguing from a new institutional perspective, institutions thus guide the social logic of migration, of who is supposed to accompany or follow whom. I will further argue that familiarity with one's social environment as well as with the rules and regulations this entails has great impact on the decision as such. As these differ for every individual, this can shed light on the question why some, even within one kin network, migrate while others do not. Apart from individual skills, available resources and future perspectives, ones position within a social network and one's material and emotional dependence on institutional safety are important variables in this respect (Chibnik 2011).

The main concern in this paper is, however, not the motives for migration but the reasons to stay and the continuing meaning the place of origin has for those who left. This links it to the huge body of literature on transnational ties between place of origin and destination that has evolved in recent years (Massey et al. 1993; Basch et al. 1994; Portes & Guarnizo 1999; Levitt & Glick Schiller 2007; Vertovec 2007). The case of the *oralman* from Mongolia is a very peculiar one in this regard as it keeps people connected to an alleged diasporic place where they were previously a minority (though a local majority) after they moved to another state considered to be their native country. I will argue that besides the obvious importance of the role kinship ties play in this, it is a longing for what I would like to call 'institutional cosiness', to a place or social environment with which one is familiar, knows the rules of the game, and feels at home. As most institutions that deal with one's everyday life consist not only of rules and sanctions but also of ideas about appropriateness, they also include a strong ideological and emotional component (Ensminger 1992; Finke in press). This longing does indeed include geographical features and, to a certain degree, loyalty towards a state where one was born and educated (and apparently did not experience any discrimination). More crucial, however, is the respective memories, which these create in terms of a previous well-being connected primarily to one's social embeddedness and knowledge of institutional regimes.

Migration out of Mongolia

I will first turn to the place where the story began, namely the steppes of Western Mongolia, a region affected by succeeding migrations and ethnic reconfigurations over the course of time. In this setting, the Kazaks were relative newcomers who started to immigrate from neighbouring Xinjiang during the second half of the 19th century. This continued well into the middle of the 20th century until the borders with China were effectively closed. Due to immigration and higher birth rates, the Kazaks soon became a local majority and as early as 1940 the westernmost province of Mongolia, Bayan-Ölgiy, was created as a semi-official autonomous unit (Finke 1999, 2004). In political terms, it is held that Kazaks had equal rights and were, indeed, privileged in comparison to other minorities. Theirs was the only language used for school instruction or in public media. There were Kazak theatres and music ensembles, and in politics and business many were to be found in superior positions (including a number of ministers and high-ranking diplomats).

Outside of Bayan-Ölgiy, one district in the neighbouring province of Khovd is also predominantly Kazak. This district, the Khovd-*sum*, is the original home of the group of Kazaks whose fate I will follow in this paper. In ecological terms, the district is fairly typical for Western Mongolia. Located in-between high mountain pastures and desert steppes, characterized by a continental and harsh climate, the economy is dominated by livestock rearing. At the same time, the district harbours some of the more important agricultural areas in the region, which are mainly used for growing potatoes, some vegetables and fruits (in particular melons). Other jobs exist primarily in the local administration, schools and medical service. With the beginning of de-collectivization in the early 1990s, the number of state employees was drastically reduced and animal husbandry became a prime occupation for those now jobless. Due to the lack of marketing structures and high transaction costs, this period saw a retreat to subsistence and risk-minimizing strategy, including a rapid increase in herd sizes (Finke 2004).

As a consequence of the deterioration of living standards, Kazaks started to move to the republic bearing their name in the immediate years after 1991.[2] Within three years, some 40 percent (or 60'000 out of 130'000) left Mongolia and a similar figure is true for the Khovd-*sum* in particular. There was a rush that seemed unstoppable and affected everyone in a fever-like way, as it would later be stated. People sold off their livestock and other immovable property for next to nothing and abandoned their winter and spring quarters. Some of this would be bought by Mongols returning to the countryside or migrating from neighbouring districts, although their number remained low in comparison to other regions (Finke 1995, 2004). The motives of the early migrants were overwhelmingly economic. While in conversations the idea of a Kazak nation state was usually mentioned, the main arguments were about the perceived superiority of Kazakstan as a prosperous and modern state. Given the deep economic downturn in Mongolia during those days, people could simply not imagine a recovery that would promise a decent living in the future.

The situation would, however, change again soon. In 1994, out-migration stopped and within the following two years an estimated 10'000 individuals returned to Mongolia. The same development was true for the Khovd-*sum* (see table 1). When stating a reason, people mentioned three obstacles in Kazakstan: ecology, the economic crisis and the decay of social order. Mongolia may not be the most-favoured place in the world when it comes to climatic conditions, but with metres of snow and extreme altitudes between winter and summer, Kazakstan seemed even less admirable. Even more important was the degree of environmental destruction people referred to. One can hardly breathe there, so a frequent complaint, due to all the industrial pollution and the land being spoiled by pesticides (Finke 2004). The economic downturn was obviously another major concern but more often returnees would talk about Kazakstan in those days as a society in a state of disorder where no one helps each other and nobody can be trusted.

The following years saw things calm down. For some time there was little movement in either direction. Migration to Kazakstan started to set off again after the turn of the millennium when the economic boom began to be felt also by those not working in the oil business. Jobs again became available in the industrial towns, in trade or as small-scale entrepreneurs, but also schoolteachers or agricultural producers benefited from rising salaries and food prices. At the same time, rural Mongolia experienced a severe crisis with heavy livestock losses due to severe winters and summer droughts in the early 2000s and again in 2009 and 2010. For potential migrants this signalled that it might be a good moment to make a move, and again every year hundreds of families sold their belongings to migrate to Kazakstan. Thus, today about half of the original population – and their descendants – live on each side of the border. For the Khovd-*sum*, the figure of migrants is even higher and an estimated 700 families has by now

---

[2] In fact, some families had moved there even before as labour migrants (Finke 2004; Diener 2009).

Table I   Population of the Khovd-sum 1991–2010

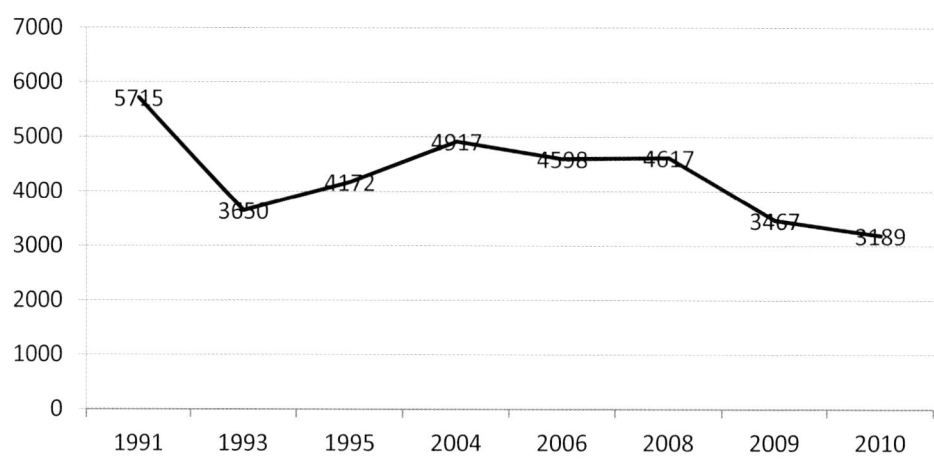

resettled in Kazakstan, while the number left in Mongolia is around 500 families (cf. table 1).[3]

In the early years, it had primarily been the urban or sedentary part of the population, including many of the specialized agriculturalists, that voted to leave, but in later days they were to be joined by pastoralists in growing numbers. No clear pattern can be discerned regarding the relative economic background of migrants who include representatives of all social classes, to use a somewhat exaggerated word for the local configuration. The same is true concerning arguments to stay. Many of the very poor have stayed as they have little to offer on the job market in Kazakstan, and are thus better off with their modest livestock holdings in Mongolia, while wealthy households have in recent years been able to build up a strong economic basis.

Arrival at the historical homeland

The organization of this migration in Kazakstan has been guided by a quota system that sets numbers of families per state of origin on an annual basis. These numbers have varied over the years from a peak during the early 1990s to an all-low of 500 families before gradually increasing again to the current number of 10'000 (Kuscu 2012). Not all states were included in the quota system though Mongolia was.

---

[3] Out-migration also included some of the local Uygurs and Dungans, both heavily kazakiced linguistically as well as culturally. For acceptance in Kazakstan, they had to re-register their official ethnicity beforehand.

Furthermore, people could also migrate outside the quota system but receive less state support in that case. In fact, in most years the numbers of actually migrating families exceeded the number foreseen by the quota. The early arrivals were usually allocated houses and, in some cases, jobs. In later years they would receive financial benefits, in the range of several thousand dollars, which was more or less sufficient to buy a house in a village in the not-so advantaged parts of the country. Rumours had it for several years that the quota system was to be suspended and, indeed, in 2012 the government in Astana stopped any financial support for migrant families for the time being.

Upon their arrival, the first migrants from Mongolia usually had no one to relate to as, mostly originating from China, none had any kinship ties in Kazakstan. The government in Almaty had its own plans anyway and attempted to settle them in the Northern provinces where Kazaks formed a minority, sometimes no more than 20 percent of the local population. This, on the one hand, would countervail claims by Russian nationalists who demanded these regions to be transferred to the Russian Federation and, on the other hand, was meant to strengthen the cultural and linguistic element among those local Kazaks particularly affected by "Russification". A third, more pragmatic issue was probably the fact that these regions also harboured the greatest amount of empty housing as hundreds of thousands of local Russians and Germans had just left the country. Many of the early migrants enthusiastically described the clean and beautiful houses they had been able to take over from Germans, highly acclaimed all over Central Asia for their hard working and orderly attitudes.

What happened in the years to come was a consolidation of migrant resettlement within Kazakstan. While initially people had been spread all over the northern provinces depending on the availability of housing, by the early 2000s a dominant trend was for kin and people originating from the same district to concentrate in specific places. Thus, for the migrants from Khovd, two major points of settlement have emerged. One is the southern part of Pavlodar province. Here, the village of Alpis Zhildik alone harbours over 200 families from Khovd-*sum*. Dozens more live in villages nearby. While not as striking, several smaller clusters exist in and around the industrial town of Temirtau, near Karagandy, hosting the other half of the 700 families originating from Khovd-*sum*.

Alpis Zhildik is a typical Russian-style village where few Kazaks (as well as some Germans and Chechens) lived until the arrival of the *oralman*. Today, the latter form the majority of the population. It is surrounded by lowland and small-hill steppe territories that often extend for dozens of kilometres without a single settlement in-between. Little can be grown here beside potatoes, grain and some vegetables. An even larger problem, however, is property relations. Land has as yet not been privatized but was allocated by the state in the form of long-term lease contracts. This happened before the bulk of the migrants arrived. Additional land would in fact be available, yet, due to the collapse of parts of the irrigation system, it is not of any use. As in other places, in Alpis Zhildik a few of the original families – mainly Russians – have been able to concentrate agricultural land in their hands and have others work for

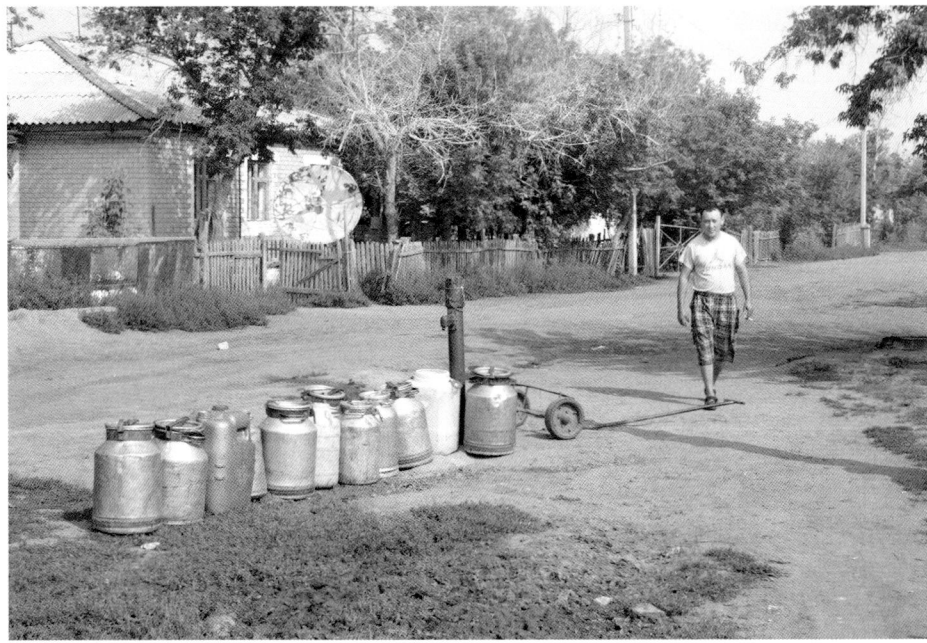

Figure 1   Village scene in northern Kazakstan, Pavlodar province (Photo: Peter Finke, 2011)

them. To make things worse for the migrants, the new landlords prefer Russian-speaking labourers (rather irrespective of their ethnicity). Only during harvest time, when labour is in particular demand, do the *oralman* have a chance to work for a couple of weeks.

In contrast to other parts of the country, the rural areas of Pavlodar (and other northern provinces) have thus not benefited as much from the ongoing boom in Kazakstan. When the first migrants arrived, jobs outside of school and administration hardly existed and market structures were largely dysfunctional. In the first years, many reported to have been employed as shepherds, although, as previously mentioned, few had the necessary skills, as they had been specialized agriculturalists or state servants back in Mongolia. Some of the migrants tried their luck as petty traders (which in those days did not make them more likeable in the eyes of the local population) or got jobs as teachers or medical personnel. The elders received pensions but these were rather low, as they had never worked in Kazakstan or the Soviet Union respectively.

This gradually started to change over the years, particularly since the beginning of the economic boom in the early 2000s. More jobs became available, the salaries of state employees increased and for everyone else the macro economic conditions for agriculture and trading business were greatly enhanced. The average income of a state-employee is now in the range of 300–400 USD and industrial workers, e.g. in the large metallurgical factory in Temirtau, where many migrants from Mongolia have found a job, receive up to twice as much. On the other hand, these jobs are less secure than being a civil servant.

In the villages, however, there continues to be hardly any work outside of schools and public administration, which are usually occupied by locals.[4] What most of the migrants do is keep some animals, usually in the range of 10–20 small stock and a few milking cows. If a household owns more than that, it is considered well off, but has to, due to the difficult ecological conditions, invest much of its labour force and additional food or hay for the animals in making things work. In spite of rising prices for meat in the cities, however, livestock rearing does little more than secure the survival of the household. What remains to be done for the young *oralman* in the village are odd jobs like collecting scrap metal. This was an attractive business for some years after the fall of the socialist regime, when remnants of the old technology and, sometimes, military equipment could be found scattered all over the steppes. Nowadays it is less profitable and more labour intensive. Every then and now groups of young men get together and search the surroundings with detectors for what is left beneath the ground. Other places to go are the industrial towns or the construction sites of the new capital of Astana to gather leftovers but here they may run into conflict with other groups striving for the same limited resource.

Thus, there is little one can do without a proper qualification, so a common understanding. That refers in particular to the many former pastoralists who have moved to Kazakstan within the last few years but have little to offer on the local job market. Some of them, indeed, consider going back to Mongolia but expect the future in Kazakstan to become better; if not for themselves than for their kids. Nowadays opportunities look brighter here (which was not the case ten years ago) and all one needs are some skills or capital to invest. Supporting ones children in higher education is therefore a key issue and particularly for daughters a university degree is highly sought-after, also among the *oralman*. If, however, they are not successful in getting a state grant, which is based on one's final school exams, this implies several thousand dollars per year for tuition, accommodation and subsistence as well as for occasional bribes to teachers.

Patterns of integration

The difficult economic situation during most of the 1990s also did nothing to help the *oralman* integrate into the local community. As indicated above, the early migrants had a particularly hard time. They felt themselves to be strangers and were perceived and treated as such. All reported that the first three to five years were extremely difficult

---

[4] Poor families receive state support. In 2012 this was reported to be around 100 dollars for a midsize household.

and unpleasant. Local Russians as well as Kazaks had no desire to share meagre resources in a time of crisis nor had they much sympathy for the idea of a revitalization of traditional culture. Rather, the migrants were excluded from much of everyday interaction, not least because they did not speak the locally relevant language properly, namely Russian. Any hint to the fact that they may, by contrast, be the only ones in the region reasonably comfortable with the official national language was more or less meaningless to everyone else around by that time.

In spite of the early hardships, today the situation of the first migrants in Alpis Zhildik is superior to the latecomers as they had easier access to houses and land. And while they are still not exactly well integrated into the village community, they have arranged themselves and, very important in that part of the country, learnt Russian to a reasonable degree. By contrast, the later arrivals are even less integrated and, as they encounter sufficient numbers of other *oralman*, have not bothered much to change this. This is partly transmitted to the next generation. In school, children have to take Russian classes but this is hardly ever used in everyday life perpetuating a structural disadvantage as for all better jobs fluency in Russian is still a precondition, even though the official state language is Kazak and the latter is increasingly implemented in public administration.

Social interaction with the local population is equally limited. Especially the later arrivals have hardly any contact with Russians and, indeed, rather little with local Kazaks. Many of those I met and visited did not know the name of the Russian neighbours down the street they had been living with for years, and have never spoken a single word or exchanged a greeting with them. Some of the earlier migrants mentioned do have individual Russians as friends but, as Erik for example admitted, do not invite even their immediate neighbour to a party for the birth of one's child. If advice is needed, one may ask a local Kazak but here as well familiarity is very low. When I asked about the lineage affiliation among local Kazaks in the village, migrants seemed to have little knowledge even about major kinship divisions.[5] Marriages are equally rare to non-existent but rather take place with other migrants. It is, however, rare to search for a spouse back in Mongolia.

Thus, the impact of the *oralman* on society in Kazakstan was initially rather limited. Instead of revitalizing traditional culture, the immigration movement has in fact provoked cause for conflict and contestation about proper Kazakness (Finke & Sancak 2005; Sancak 2007; Diener 2009). This concerned issues of language, Islam and, more broadly speaking, traditional culture. It did not, however, challenge the idea of a common identity. Based primarily on assumed blood ties rather than on cultural expres-

---

[5] Kazak kin organization is based on the idea of patrilineally defined exogamous descent groups, with three major units (the Greater, Middle and Smaller Horde) at their top, each sub-divided in multiple layers of clans and lineages (Hudson 1938). Those from Mongolia belong to the Kerey and Nayman subdivisions of the Middle Horde (Finke 2004).

sions, there is no criterion according to which others might be excluded from the Kazak ethnic group (cf. also Finke 2014). At the same time, while there is little contact with the local population, derogatory comments are rare. Local culture is not diminished as being Russified but as either neutrally different or, to some degree, accepted as the more civilized one, in contrast to *oralman* from China (Finke & Sancak 2005; Sancak 2007). Distinction is thus less a case of despise but more of mutual indifference.

Identification with Kazakstan is equally ambivalent and the state is a frequent target of complaints, primarily regarding ecology, school education, and politics. Air and water pollution is one of the most mentioned issues and many claim to have headaches or other types of illnesses attributed to climate. It is also held that people in Kazakstan are very obedient and often express their surprise at the self-confidence with which *oralman* approach authorities. On the other hand, Kazakstan is considered one's homeland and the critiques heard were never as fundamental as among *oralman* from China. What is criticized is the lack of democratic development in the country. In the prelude to the elections in 2007, local teachers in Alpis Zhildik reportedly told pupils to advice their parents to vote for the party of Nursultan Nazarbayev. This caused some consternation among the *oralman*. They would have done anyway, they said, so why would they need to tell us? Why have 88 percent if 60 of the electorate would also be nice? Equally criticized was the fact that after casting their ballots, people were asked for whom they had voted. "Isn't it that why we put our ballots in an envelope and insert it anonymously?", so Zhaylawxan.

Other reasons for the discomfort people feel in Kazakstan have been mentioned above. They refer both to the perceived differences in the natural geography of Mongolia and in the social setting left behind. This is universally expressed as homesickness. "We miss it *(saginamiz)*", is by far the most often heard phrase when conversation turns to Mongolia. Turning to the anthropologist, Qoyshibay said:

> You know what a wonderful place Mongolia is; you have been there. The clean air, the healthy food and the freedom you have. But you cannot tell people that here. They don't understand that and they feel offended because you do not praise Kazakstan enough. (Qoyshibay, 38-year old Kazak man in Alpis Zhildik, 2007)

As indicated above, this longing concerns both the physical space one got used to as well as the institutional familiarity with a known social environment. It is well captured in the quote in the beginning of this paper where Mongolia is the space of people's dreams. And it transfers in a way of life in Kazakstan that tries to preserve the previous one. In fact, internal relations among the *oralman* may have become even stronger than they used to be and mutual visits within the village and with close kin in neighbouring ones happen on an almost daily basis. Wherever I went – although, my presence and our common experience may have accelerated this to some degree – most of the conversation during these meetings focused on Mongolia and the kin left behind. Videos of past events are a frequent source of entertainment as is the singing of Mongolian songs when getting together.

Some weeks ago there was a music ensemble from Mongolia [that is to say, ethnic Mongols] playing in Pavlodar city. How wonderful that was! To hear that music again. We loved to sing Mongolian songs back in our childhood and later on. All the Mongols who had come, those in the ensemble, did not have to stay in a hotel. We took them here to the village and they would stay with us. We would take turns hosting them. It was such a pleasure. (Nurgül, 42-year old Kazak woman in Alpis Zhildik, 2011)

Remaining in Mongolia: new strategies and ongoing debates

While the described melancholia for Mongolia has not abated in all those years, the return migration has. This is not to say that people do not play with the idea. But while in the earlier period, due to the numbers of returnees and the known difficulties in Kazakstan, this was socially acceptable, it would now represent something of which one would be ashamed. Not to find ones place in a crisis-shaken Kazakstan is one thing, yet not being able to make it in a period of economic boom is a rather different one. It would be embarrassing, as I was told repeatedly.

Meanwhile, the Khovd-*sum* has also changed fundamentally. This is partly caused by migration, partly by recent developments in Mongolia. For the livestock sector the mentioned natural disasters have proven highly detrimental and many have lost a substantial part of their herd. On the other hand, incomes for those who have jobs have been rising constantly and today fall in a range of 200 to 300 dollars, approaching those in Kazakstan (while living costs, especially for those who possess animals, are much lower). Pensions average somewhere between 100 and 200 dollars. At the same time, prices for livestock and agricultural products increased, with cashmere and potatoes being the most important respectively. In this respect, the out-migration obviously was of economic benefit for those who stayed as they have more agricultural and pastureland at their disposal. There are also a few people digging for gold in the *sum*, as has become popular all over Mongolia, but this is of little importance and conducted mainly by outsiders.

As described above, those who have left Mongolia did not with any particular negative feeling towards their place of birth. The same is true for those still there. Mongolia is almost universally praised for unspoiled nature and healthy food, freedom and (relatively) democratic politics as well as honest and peaceful people. Also, Mongolia offers plenty of opportunities to make a living for those willing to work hard, according to a common saying. Regarding their status as a minority, the picture is ambiguous. Kazaks are aware that there are some people in Mongolia who would welcome their disappearance, although this is rarely stated so explicitly. In fact, it is probably a minority position among local Mongols. Within the Khovd-*sum*, frictions are not uncommon and usually have to do with the disregard of pasture allocation rules but these do not lead to violent encounters and are not a specifically inter-ethnic issue (cf. Finke

2004). On the other hand, so a widespread opinion, the local Mongols would rather prefer those Kazaks still around to stay.

> They became used to us. Many of them know our language. If we leave, other people will come. Who knows who will come; of course, these are also Mongols, but from different districts. They don't know them. So, they prefer living together with us. (Dargerxan, 52-year old Kazak in Khovd-*sum*, 2011)

Still, the question of whether to migrate is a dominant topic of conversation within the district and everyone seems to be more or less well-informed about the state of other people's decision making process. It is a conversation both about others as well as a direct inquiry. "So, have you made up your mind? Are you going to leave this year?" used to be a standard question posed in 2011. Answers tended to be elusive as long as no final decision and date were fixed. By 2013, the enthusiasm for migrating had decreased significantly, not so much due to developments in Kazakstan but much more to the fact that the situation in Mongolia had seen significant recovery, particularly concerning the livestock sector.

All agreed that migration is a long and often painful decision-making process, which is usually conducted within families or larger kin networks. Except in the cases of some of the young men, people hardly ever move alone and even individual families are the exception. If so, they follow others who have gone before them. In many cases, the option for leaving is discussed over a number of years until a final decision is taken. Seeking information about the wellbeing of relatives already migrated is therefore of prime concern as it gives an idea of what to expect for oneself. Yet, although the flow of information is much better than for those who migrated during the early 1990s, it is still perceived to be a situation of uncertainty, which is reduced, as much as possible, by previous visits. Many of those interviewed before their departure were well aware of the pain and had to some degree internalized the dominant discourse of homesickness in a pre-emptive way.

> Of course we will miss it here. This is the place we grew up. This is the place where we spent our childhood. Do you see the mountains over there? They don't have that kind of nature in Kazakstan. There it is spoilt. And the people as well. The relations between people are not as they are here. Yes, we will miss that. But still we go. (Tinishbay, 34-year-old Kazak in Khovd-*sum*, 2004, the week before he left for Temirtau)

Other things being equal, it is the younger generation and the female parts of the household who tend to prefer to go, but, in most cases, have less bargaining power in decision-making than others. Less clear is the relevance of particular skills and qualifications. While it is held that Kazakstan is a difficult place for those without any experience outside of agriculture, in recent years it was increasingly this segment of society that migrated due to the fact that they tend to be unemployed in Mongolia as well. What became an ever more important variable is the relative number of kin on both sides. In the past few years, many have left for that very reason, namely, according to their statements, that the majority of their extended family is already in Kazakstan. On the other hand, if most of one's children still live in Mongolia, the temptation to go is comparatively low. As important for the question of when to migrate is retirement for those who have a job and the school graduation of one's children. It has been gathered from earlier migrants that a change of the educational system may seriously harm grades and prevent children from entering university in Kazakstan. On the other hand, to wait too long may also be risky, as prices for houses increase, jobs become even rarer and the quota system may be terminated.

The future development is difficult to predict. On the one hand, those who still live in Mongolia are often well integrated and reasonably prosperous. They tend to have jobs and/or a sizeable number of animals. In addition, they benefit from the fact that so many have left, leaving them with twice as much agricultural and pasture land per head as before. On the other hand, the danger of further natural disasters seems to be in everyone's mind and is often mentioned as a reason to leave, although the climate has been much more favourable since 2010 and complaints have almost vanished. Furthermore, there is an all too real fear that a further decrease in the Kazak population will lead to the dissolution of the district. This, in turn, would not only endanger the modest degree of cultural and political autonomy but would also do away with those jobs linked thereto, namely schoolteachers and administrative staff. It would probably also affect land holdings. So far, Mongols from other districts tend not to move to Khovd-*sum* in search of pastures, or do so only seasonally during the summer months, as they feel uncomfortable among a Kazak majority. This would probably change with further out-migration. Thus, again, ones decision to stay or go, or the relative advantages of either, depends to a large degree on the future strategies of others. Important is to find the supposedly right timing, that is to say not to be the last to leave, as this may be a handicap in Kazakstan in terms of finding proper housing and getting state support.

Transnational ties

By now, practically all families have some of their members on either side of the border. Very often this goes along a male-female line as brothers have stayed or left together, although there are also cases when one or the other decides to move by himself or, in fact, was sent as a pioneer to test the attractiveness of migrating. This was more the case in the early years and by now the trend is more to follow those who have already gone. If male members of one extended family end up on different sides of the border, this usually expresses previously existing tensions. In the Khovd-*sum*, relations between fathers and elder sons, who have broken off from the joint household, are often strained. This is even more true for brothers after the death of their father. Only in very few cases will they stay together in one camp and particularly eldest brothers were often to be found alone (Finke 2004). This pattern is replicated at the migration level and it is in fact not unusual that brothers became separated as well. Married daughters or sisters usually have to follow the families of their husbands and are thus more often the ones separated from their natal families. This does not imply that women have no saying in migration decisions but once these are taken, they demand compliance among all members of patrilineally related households that move. Suffering from this divide is thus, to some degree, gendered.

From the very beginning in the 1990s, the division of kin networks caused a constant flow of people moving back and forth. These mutual visits are a heavy burden not only for those travelling, who have to pay for transport and bring gifts, but also for their hosts. People are expected to stay at least one night with every reasonably close kin household where in turn they have to be entertained and feasted. Depending on the respective economic situation this usually implies slaughtering a sheep. In Mongolia, I would frequently hear complaints about this.

> If they would only come back altogether, that would be okay. Then we have to give them a few sheep at one point, and that's it. But now they come every other year and stay for a month. You have to feed them; you have to serve them vodka. And you have to provide them with a horse or drive them around, so they can visit all the other relatives. This is really difficult. (Qongirbay, 67-year old Kazak in Khovd-*sum*, 2004)

The picture on the other side of the border is rather similar, although here it is less common that an animal has to pay for these visits with its life due to their rather limited number. On the other hand, the fact that slaughtering is often not an option makes an appropriate entertainment of visitors even more difficult. In addition, transport costs are low as long as one stays within one district but most people have relatives in at least the two major areas of settlement, namely Temirtau and Pavlodar.

In particular elderly people take every opportunity to visit their relatives, if possible once a year. Some, in fact, move even more often than that, although this may evoke some gossip. The younger ones usually have to work and are not as free to move. In addition, if money is scarce (which it usually is), the elder generation has more influence in deciding how to spend it, as they are often also the only people with a regular financial income, namely pensions. For some, visiting kin may take on a form of more or less commuting. There are people who spend around half of the year at either site, usually the summer in Mongolia and the winter in Kazakstan, but sometimes the other way around as well. For them, going back and forth has become part of a lifestyle. This is particularly the case when sons happen to end up being split between the two sites.

Commuting between both states takes place by car in most cases. There are regular buses (at the time of my latest fieldwork, there were three per month leaving Pavlodar for the Russian-Mongolian border), but private vehicles are the preferred choice. On the market in Ölgiy, drivers offer their services of driving to every city in Kazakstan where significant numbers of *oralman* from Mongolia live. Some, in fact, have made this their profession. In recent years, travelling has become trickier since entering Russia requires a visa for Mongolian citizens. In 2011, the latter chose to go to Kazakstan via China, where they do not need one, while those with a Kazakstanian passport go through Russia, making travel arrangements ever more complicated.[6]

The frequent visits to Kazakstan, apart from the fact that people want to see their relatives, of course also provide the opportunity to gather information on the current situation. Therefore, people constantly attempt to keep track on who is currently visiting or plans to do so in the near future. The information flow is facilitated by modern communication technology and one important criterion for choosing a particular mobile phone company is its rate for calling the other. This way, news from either side of the border spreads rapidly. In the summer of 2011, I was visiting a pastoralist household in one of the lower mountain valleys in the Khovd-*sum* and was told that my 'brother-in-law' (meaning the husband of one of the daughters of my long-term host family) had drowned the day before in an irrigation channel near the village of Alpis Zhildik. The man was neither a relative nor a friend of the family in question. In the end, it turned out that it was not the husband of my 'sister' who died but his elder brother. But the news had spread within hours across the whole community back in Mongolia. It was even known to everyone the same day that yet another brother of the deceased had learned about the loss at the moment he arrived at the Russian-Mongolian border on his way to Khovd.

Thus, while people try to make the best of the separation and attempt to keep relations as close as possible, the fact that half of one's people are gone or left behind is universally bemoaned and disputes about the future are common. Obviously, these transnational ties have consequences beyond the financial ones imposed by commuting and mutual hospitality. It also has a potentially negative effect on the willingness and ability to integrate into Kazakstanian society. As long as Mongolia and one's relatives there remain the main point of reference, temptation is high to consider the new settlements in Kazakstan as temporary or as a continuation of one's previous life. This is not so much because re-migration to Mongolia is an option given serious thought, but because a lack of necessity prevents people from pursuing encounters with the local population.

Conclusion

The story of the large-scale migration of Kazaks from Mongolia to the newly independent state of Kazakstan is important not only because of the number of people involved but also for the political consequences it has both within the country as well

---

[6] There used to be flights from the provincial centre of Bayan-Ölgiy to Almaty (with a stop in Öskemen) but these stopped in 2012.

as beyond. It has fundamentally reshaped the demographic and cultural outline of Kazakstan and causes concern among the minorities that may influence the relationship with neighbouring states, in particularly Russia. It has also fundamentally changed the lives of people, both those who followed the invitation to return to their 'native homeland' and those who stayed in the 'diaspora', to which the former have developed a strong sense of transnational belonging.

As was attempted to show, detecting the individual rationality for moving or staying is not an easy undertaking as it is influenced by a multitude of factors. Economic motives are clearly of prime importance in this case and the overall changes closely resemble the booms and crises in both countries. But other variables, social and cultural, play a role as well. What more, each decision, and its chance of future success, is dependent on those of others, directly or indirectly. Thus, on the one hand, migration is usually undertaken by households and very often by, at least parts of, extended families. Therefore, many – especially females – may not have much of a choice in this respect. On the other hand, people may refrain from migration precisely because other close relatives decided to do so. This, in turn, can be either a cooperative solution, namely to keep as many options open as possible as a strategy of diversification, or a conflictive one, in the sense of distancing oneself as far as possible from unloved kin. In other cases the choice is more driven by chance and based on individual decisions that take into account one's expected opportunities at either place. Mutual dependency is true for yet another reason. The fact that so many have left the Khovd-*sum* provides advantages in terms of land holdings for those still around; but if out-migration continues these may vanish very quickly and "the devil takes the hindmost".

What this paper was also about was the transnational ties that have developed between those who departed and those who stayed (but may follow in the near future). In this regard, the situation, particularly among those in Kazakstan, is truly remarkable. It seems that their place of origin became ever more important since migration. Being largely marginalized at the new place they live, people turn away from a place considered to be their historical home to an alleged diasporic site. To a large degree this may be interpreted as a counter strategy against the feeling of being not welcomed while at the same time contributing to an ongoing resistance to integrate. The need for transnational relations are somewhat less obvious on the other side, in Mongolia, but here almost everyone still plays with the idea of migrating as well or, as indicated above, is forced to consider the possibility unwillingly because everyone else does.

What I furthermore argued in the beginning of this paper is that a main variable for migrating and non-migrating as well as for the development and strength of transnational ties is the 'institutional cosiness' that either decision promises. In contrast to some of the migration literature, which seems to suggest that humans are fundamentally non-sedentary and on the move, I would rather argue that, other things being equal, people prefer to stay at the place they are familiar with, with the people they know, and within a game of which they know the rules. Economic incentives and social constraints may overrule this but they do not do away with the longing for the safety that a familiar environment, socially as well as geographically, provides. The retreat to a living that imitates the previous one in Mongolia as well as the intensity of relationships with the people left behind give ample proof of that. Rather than a return home, the migration to Kazakstan has been a move into a foreign land where people behave differently and one is not especially accepted, not to mention appreciated as a motor for cultural revival. The concept of home is therefore still very much connected to Mongolia. As elucidated in the citation above, this is an understanding for which locals have very little sympathy.

References

Barcus, H.; Werner, C. 2007: Transnational Identities: Mongolian Kazakhs in the Twenty-first Century. *Geographische Rundschau International Edition* 3(3):4–10.
Barcus, H.; Werner, C. 2010: The Kazakhs of Western Mongolia: Transnational Migration from 1990–2008. *Asian Ethnicity* 2(11):209–228.
Basch, L.; Glick Schiller, N.; Szanton Blanc, C. 1994: *Nations Unbound. Transnational Projects, Postcolonial Predicaments, and Deterritorialized Nation-States*. Amsterdam: Gordon and Breach.
Brettell, C. B. 2000: Theorizing Migration in Anthropology. The Social Construction of Networks, Identities, Communities, and Globalscapes. In: C. B. Bretell and J. F. Hollifield (eds.), *Migration Theory. Talking across Disciplines*. New York: Routledge, pp. 97–136.
Castles, S.; Miller, M. J. 1993: *The age of migration: International population movements in the modern world*. New York: Guilford Press.
Chibnik, M. 2011: *Anthropology, economics, and choice*. Austin: University of Texas Press.
Dave, B. 2007: *Kazakhstan: Ethnicity, Language and Power*. New York: Routledge.
Diener, A. C. 2005: Kazakhstan's Kin State Diaspora: Settlement Planning and the *Oralman* Dilemma. *Europe-Asia-Studies* 57:327–348.
Diener, A. C. 2009: *One Homeland or Two? The Nationalization and Transnationalization of Mongolia's Kazakhs*. Stanford: Stanford University Press.
Ensminger, J. 1992: *Making a Market: The Institutional Transformation of an African Society*. Cambridge: Cambridge University Press.
Faist, T. 2000: *The volume and dynamics of international migration and transnational social spaces*. Oxford: Clarendon Press.
Finke, P. 1995: Kazak Pastoralists in Western Mongolia. Economic and Social Change in the Course of Privatization. *Nomadic Peoples* 36/37:195–216.
Finke, P. 1999: The Kazaks of Western Mongolia. In: I. Svanberg (ed.), *Contemporary Kazaks: Cultural and Social Perspectives*, London: Curzon, pp. 103–139.
Finke, P. 2004: *Nomaden im Transformationsprozess. Kasachen in der post-sozialistischen Mongolei*. Münster: Lit.
Finke, P. 2014: *Variations on Uzbek Identity: Strategic Choices, Cognitive Schemas and Political Constraints in Identification Processes*. Oxford, New York: Berghahn Books.
Finke, P.; Buri, T. forthcoming: New transnational movements and relationships: The Case of the Kazaks from Gansu. *Etnograficheskoe Obozrenie* (special issue edited by G. Schlee and P. Finke).
Finke, P.; Sancak, M. 2005: Migration and Risk Taking. A Case Study from Kazakhstan. In: L. Trager (ed.), *Migration and Economy: Global and Local Dynamics*. Walnut Creek: AltaMira Press, pp. 127–162.
Hudson, A. 1938: *Kazak Social Structure*. New Haven, London: Yale University Press.
Knight, J. 1992: *Institutions and Social Conflict*. Cambridge: Cambridge University Press.

Kuscu, I. 2008: *Kazakhstan's oralman project. A remedy for ambiguous identity?* Ann Arbor: UMI.

Kuscu, I. 2012: Constructing the homeland: Kazakhstan's discourse and policies surrounding its ethnic return-migration policy. *Central Asian Survey* 31(1):31–44.

Levitt, P.; Glick Schiller, N. 2007: Conceptualizing Simultaneity. A Transnational Social Field Perspective on Society. In: A. Portes and J. DeWind (eds.), *Rethinking Migration: New Theoretical and Empirical Perspectives*. New York: Berghahn, pp. 181–218.

Massey, D. S.; Arango, J.; Hugo, G.; Kouaouci, A.; Pellegrino, A.; and Tylor, J. E. 1993: Theories of International Migration. A Review and Appraisal. *Population and Development Review* 19(3): 413–466.

Mendikulova, G. 2012: Some notes on the repatriation politics in the republic of Kazakhstan. *History of the Homeland. Research Journal* 59(3):18–23.

Mitchell, J. C. 1969: Structural Plurality, Urbanization and Labour Circulation in Southern Rhodesia. In: J. A. Jackson (ed.), *Migration*. Cambridge: Cambridge University Press, pp. 156–180.

North, D. C. 1990: *Institutions, Institutional Change and Economic Performance*. Cambridge, Cambridge University Press.

Portes, A. and Guarnizo, L. 1999: Transnational communities. Special issue, *Ethnic and Racial Studies* 22(2).

Sancak, M. 2007: Contested Identity: Encounters with Kazak Diaspora Returning to Kazakhstan. *Anthropology of East Europe Review* 25(1):85–94.

Sassen, S. 1988: *The Mobility of Capital and Labor*. Cambridge: Cambridge University Press.

Simon, H. A. 1957: *Models of Man. Social and Rational. Mathematical Essays on Rational Human Behavior in a Social Setting*. New York, London: Garland Publishing.

Svanberg, I. 1996: Kazakhstan and the Kazakhs. In: G. Smith (ed.), *The Nationalities Question in the Post-Soviet States*. London: Longman, pp. 318–333.

Tversky, A.; Kahnemann, D. 1990: Rational Choice and the Framing of Decisions. In: K. S. Cook and M. Levi (eds.), *The Limits of Rationality*. Chicago: The University of Chicago Press, pp. 60–89.

Vertovec, S. 2007: Migrant Transnationalism and Modes of Transformation. In: A. Portes and J. DeWind (eds.), *Rethinking Migration: New Theoretical and Empirical Perspectives*. New York: Berghahn., pp. 149–180.

Werner, C.; Barcus, H. 2009: Mobility, Immobility and Return Migration: The Impact of Transnational Migration on the Kazakh Diaspora in Mongolia. *Migration Letters* 6(1):49–62.

Deutsche im ländlichen Kasachstan: Das Streben nach besseren Lebensumständen und die Rolle von Ethnizität

Rita Sanders
Emser Str. 19, D-12051 Berlin

Germans in Rural Kazakstan: The Quest for Better Living Conditions and the Role of Ethnicity

Abstract. This article investigates the interplay between internal and international migration using the example of Germans living in rural Kazakstan. Gorbachev's policies of Glasnost as well as Germany's ethnically defined immigration laws were prerequisite for a massive outflow of Kazakstani Germans up until the mid-1990s. As a consequence, only about 20 percent (or 200 000 Germans) have stayed in Kazakstan. Within the country, most Germans as well as other non-Kazaks have moved from villages to towns in order to improve their housing conditions and to live among other Russian-speaking citizens. Those who stayed in the countryside usually had the intention of migrating transnationally but were denied immediate immigration permission by the German state. They then often had to wait for several years for a further response. During this time of uncertainty they refrained from making any future plans and therefore often missed the chance to migrate to a town, due to prices for urban housing having significantly risen after the 1990s. Therefore, an envisioned but failed diasporic migration often impeded alternative migration projects. However, this article also refers to those Kazakstani Germans who have deliberately stayed in rural areas. They mostly relate to a memory of Kazakstani German history, which displays the life of a self-sustaining and hard-working peasant. Such a life style is assumed to have saved the lives of many Germans after deportation to Kazakstan in 1941 and is, for some, therefore highly emotionally loaded. The article uses several case studies and seeks to account for the complexity of people's motives for staying or leaving, as well as when and where to go, and for these projects' successes or failures.
[*Kazakstani Germans, transnational migration, internal migration, Diaspora*]

Ich lebte seit rund drei Monaten an meinem Feldforschungsort Taldykorgan, einer mittelgroßen Stadt mit rund 135.000 Einwohnern im Südosten Kasachstans, als ich von den Mitarbeiterinnen des sogenannten ‚Deutschen Hauses' zunehmend deutlich darauf hingewiesen wurde, dass es an der Zeit wäre, aufs Land zu fahren und die dort lebenden Deutschen kennen zu lernen. Deutsche Häuser gibt es in über einem Dutzend Städten in Kasachstan; sie werden von der Organisation ‚Wiedergeburt' verwaltet und sind außerdem Teil des Minderheitenassemblees, das vom kasachstanischen Präsidenten Nazerbajev geleitet wird. In erster Linie verstehen sie sich als Kulturbewahrer und -vermittler, und in dieser Mission wurde auch die Ethnologin aufgefordert, sich mit dem Schicksal der Deutschen, die in Dörfern leben, zu befassen. So wurde für mich ein Termin mit einer deutschen Familie vereinbart, die eine gute Bus-stunde von Taldykorgan entfernt lebt. Meine damalige Gastmutter Vera[1] bot mir an, mich zu begleiten, da die Fahrt aufs Land – zumal im Winter – als ein schwieriges Unterfangen gilt.

Am frühen Abend trafen Vera und ich bei Irina und ihrer Familie ein. Irina lebt in einem kleinen Haus zusammen mit einer jungen Frau, Aigul, die ihr ein wenig Miete zahlt und im Haushalt hilft. Aigul wurde uns recht unvermittelt als halb Kasachin und halb Tatarin vorgestellt. Außerdem war noch Irinas Tochter Katja, die mit ihrer Familie ein paar Straßen weiter lebt, gekommen. Von allen wurden wir überschwänglich empfangen und direkt zu einem reichhaltig gedeckten Tisch geführt, während im Hintergrund deutsche Volksmusik spielte. Im weiteren Verlauf des Abends erzählte Katja von ihrer Tätigkeit als Leiterin des lokalen Deutschen Hauses und zeigte Fotos ihrer letzten Veranstaltungen. Zu sehen war ein Informationsstand auf dem Dorfplatz, der Handarbeiten und deutsche Trachten ausstellt. Außerdem schien es ihr wichtig zu sein, mit Dokumenten belegen zu können, dass sie auch wirklich deutsch ist. Katja erzählte weiter von ihrem festen Willen, Deutsch zu lernen und wenigstens einmal Deutschland zu besuchen. Am liebsten möchte sie allerdings nach Deutschland ausreisen.

Nach dem Essen führte uns Katja einen als ‚orientalisch' angekündigten Tanz in einem entsprechenden Kostüm vor. Anschließend werden Vera und ich aufgefordert, uns die Berlinvideos von Irinas Neffen aus Deutschland anzuschauen. Zu sehen sind verschiedene Supermärkte in Berlin-Marzahn, wie Irina erläutert. Irina betont während des gesamten Videos immer wieder, wie sehr sie an Deutschland schätze, dass es dort so sauber und geordnet ist. Außerdem erwähnt sie, dass ihre Verwandten sie finanziell unterstützen; so konnte sie sich einen Fernseher, einen Videorecorder und ein Telefon kaufen. Als wir das Video schauten, schlief Vera recht bald ein.

Einleitung

„Deutsche in Kasachstan?" wurde ich während meiner Forschung immer wieder mal erstaunt gefragt, die gibt es doch gar nicht mehr, die leben doch jetzt alle in Deutschland. In der Tat haben Kasachstandeutsche[2] in den letzten zwei Jahrzehnten vor allem durch ihren drastischen Schrumpfungsprozess auf sich aufmerksam gemacht: Ihre Zahl verringerte sich nach offiziellen Angaben zwischen 1989 und 2007 von ca. einer Million auf knapp über 200.000 Personen. Die massenhafte Auswanderung der Kasachstandeutschen (wie auch Kasachstanrussen) wird in zahlreichen wissenschaftlichen Betrachtungen und lokalen Analysen thematisiert (Diener 2004, 2006; Flynn 2007;

---

[1] Alle Namen sind anonymisiert. Ebenfalls sind die Namen der kleinen Ortschaften um Taldykorgan geändert.
[2] In Kasachstan wird für dort lebende Deutsche zumeist schlicht die Bezeichnung Deutsche [russisch: nemtsy, kasachisch: nemister] verwandt.

Peyrouse 2007; Yessenova 1996). Dass darüber hinaus auch noch tausende Deutsche wie Russen innerhalb Kasachstans vom Land in die Stadt zogen, scheint nebensächlich.

In diesem Artikel geht es um einen Migrationsprozess, der bezogen auf die interne Migration zumeist als Streben nach besseren Lebensbedingungen und bezogen auf die internationale Migration häufig als ethnisch-nationaler Prozess dargestellt wird. Anhand von Fallbeispielen[3] werde ich zeigen, wie sich in beiden Migrationsprozessen die Motive vermengen und wie ganz grundsätzlich beide Phänomene zusammenhängen. Interne und internationale Migration haben sich im Fall der Migrantinnen und Migranten[4] aus Kasachstan wechselseitig beflügelt, ohne direkt zusammenzuhängen, da ein Umzug in die Stadt selten eine Auswanderung nach Deutschland vorbereitet. Das heißt, die meisten Migranten entscheiden sich noch auf dem Land, ob sie entweder nach Deutschland, Russland oder in eine Stadt in Kasachstan ziehen möchten, wobei einige weiterhin im Dorf leben und gar nicht zu migrieren vorhaben. Ethnizität bzw. die Bedeutung, die ihr beigemessen wird, kann diese unterschiedlichen Migrationsprojekte nur unzureichend erklären. Alle Protagonisten streben nach einem guten und sicheren Auskommen für sich und ihre Kinder. Dabei haben sie jedoch unterschiedliche Vorstellungen von einem guten Leben und verschiedene zeitliche Planungshorizonte.

Meine Betrachtung setzt auf dem Land an und untersucht von dort aus den Migrationsprozess in Richtung Stadt und Deutschland. So werden andere Studien ergänzt, die fast ausschließlich aus Deutschland und aus der Stadt auf den Migrationsprozess blicken (z. B. Römhild 1998; Stoll 2007). Nach einer kurzen theoretischen Einführung werde ich im Folgenden auf Migrationsprozesse in Kasachstan seit Gründung des Staates 1991 eingehen und dabei besonders die Bedeutung von Ethnizität betrachten. Vor diesem Hintergrund werde ich schließlich die Fallbeispiele analysieren.

Das geringe Interesse an Land-Stadt-Ortswechseln in Kasachstan spiegelt einen allgemeinen Trend in der jüngeren Migrationsforschung wieder. So ist das vielbeschworene Zeitalter der Migration (Castles & Miller 1993) ein Zeitalter internationaler Ströme, auch wenn vielfach Ausmaß und Effekte interner Mobilität größer sind. (King & Skeldon 2010; White 2007:888) Bis in die 1960er Jahre war mit Migration jedoch vornehmlich der Wegzug vom Land in die Stadt gemeint. Forschungsarbeiten thematisierten die Auswirkungen von Industrialisierung und Urbanisierung im Zeichen von Modernisierungsprozessen. Vor diesem Hintergrund bildeten Ravensteins Migrations-

---

[3] Die Daten beruhen auf einer zwölfmonatigen Feldforschung in der Stadt Taldykorgan und den Dörfern und Kleinstädten der näheren Umgebung, die ich 2006 und 2007 durchführte. Ich danke dem Max-Planck-Institut für ethnologische Forschung in Halle/Saale für die Unterstützung des Projekts. Die hier verwendeten Fallbeispiele beziehen sich neben Feldforschungsberichten insbesondere auf Lebensgeschichten zur Bedeutung von ethnischen Identitäten und zu Migrationserfahrungen und -plänen (Linde 1993; Miller 2000).
[4] Aus Gründen der Lesbarkeit werden im Folgenden nicht immer weibliche und männliche Form gleichzeitig verwendet.

gesetze von 1876 die Grundlage für push-pull Konzepte, die das Anreizschema für potenzielle Migranten abzubilden und ihre Entscheidungen zu erklären versuchen (Dorigo & Tobler 1983). Mobilität ist damit das Resultat eines rationalen Anliegens nach sozialem und wirtschaftlichem Aufstieg. Dabei wird angenommen, dass Migranten besser dastehen als solche die bleiben; sie gelten als diejenigen mit dem größten Wunsch nach Erfolg, als Mutige, die bereit sind, die Kosten einer Migration auf sich zu nehmen (Coté 1997). Bis heute bestimmen theoretische Klüfte und ein Mangel an Austausch das Migrationsfeld, das sich in Studien zu interner und internationaler Mobilität teilt (King & Skeldon 2010; eine Ausnahme bildet Trager 2005).

Internationale Migration wird seit den frühen 90er Jahren zumeist als transnationale Migration verstanden (Basch u. a. 1997; Pries 2008). Implizit oder explizit werden Migrationen dabei in der Regel als nicht dauerhaft und als das Resultat von vorläufigen Entscheidungen interpretiert. Einige Ansätze gehen soweit, in der angenommenen Zunahme des Migrationsphänomens ein Verwaschen und Verschwinden jeglicher Grenzen bestätigt zu sehen, was neue Spielräume mit sich bringt und Kreativität freisetzt (Chambers 1994). Der Begriff Transnationalismus bleibt jedoch letztlich bei den alten Grenzziehungen. Argumentiert wird in erster Linie gegen die Annahme einer zwangsweisen Assimilierung und Eingliederung von Migranten in die USA; stattdessen wird die (dauerhafte) Inkorporation von Migrantinnen in zwei oder mehrere Nationen beschrieben. Um globale Vernetzungen und hybride Zugehörigkeiten formulieren zu können, erlangte neben dem Transnationalismus das Konzept Diaspora in den letzten Dekaden Popularität (Cohen 1997; Hall 1990; Safran 1991). Die Vorannahme, dass eine Art Ursprungsgemeinschaft für Menschen Bedeutung hat sowie die Ausweitung des Diaspora-Ansatzes auf eine Vielfalt von Phänomenen, wurden oft kritisiert (Anthias 1998; Brubaker 2005). Letztlich argumentieren beide Konzepte mit ethnisch-nationalen Identitäten und lassen andere Faktoren wie etwa regionale Identitäten oder staatliche Rahmenbedingungen oft unberücksichtigt.

Entscheidungen von Politikern, ein legislativer Rahmen und dessen de facto Durchsetzung sind jedoch für den vorliegenden Artikel bedeutsam, da die immensen Migrationsströme in Zentralasien mit dem Zerfall eines Staates und den Neugründungen vieler Nachfolgestaaten auf vielfältige Art und Weise zusammenhängen. Ein Staat ist allerdings kein Monolith, sondern eher als ein von unterschiedlichen Interessen geleiteter und ausgehandelter Prozess zu verstehen (Jones Luong 2004; Mitchell 1991), der Menschen z. B. in Phasen des Umbruchs verunsichern kann oder ihnen umgekehrt Anreize bietet und verspricht, mit einem Wohnortwechsel ihre Situation verbessern zu können. So beeinflussen politische Entscheidungen bzw. deren Effekte und Interpretationen auch die Abwägung, lieber in die nächstgrößere Stadt zu ziehen oder gleich das Land zu verlassen und sich Tausende Kilometer entfernt ein neues Zuhause einzurichten.

Der Artikel orientiert sich außerdem am Konzept der „mobile livelihoods". Dieses versteht Mobilität als individuelle Handlung, die sozial eingebettet und unter einer ökonomischen Rationalität zu betrachten ist (Fog Olwig & Sorenson 2002). Somit steht das Streben nach einem Auskommen, nach einer individuell unterschiedlichen Vorstellung von einem guten, sicheren und wirtschaftlich zufriedenstellenden Leben im Zentrum menschlichen Tuns. Die Kenntnis verschiedener sozialer Welten, die eventuell mit ethnischen und/oder nationalen Gruppen einhergehen, ist dabei die Voraussetzung dafür, ein Auskommen bestreiten zu können. Für die hier dokumentierten Fälle ist jedoch Mobilität nicht immer eine Option, so dass auch nicht-mobile Strategien und Projekte, sein Leben zu gestalten und sein Auskommen zu bestreiten, berücksichtigt werden.

Land der Migrantinnen und Migranten

Der Zusammenbruch der UdSSR bedeutete nicht nur das Ende eines politischen Regimes, sondern auch den Kollaps eines Wirtschaftssystems. Die Übergangsphase führte in den neuen Staaten zu einem Niedergang der Industrie, zu hoher Arbeitslosigkeit und unsicheren Rahmenbedingungen für die Neugründung von Unternehmen (Werner 1997). Hinzu kam eine drastische Verschlechterung der Infrastruktur. All diese Effekte zeigten sich in Kasachstan besonders deutlich auf dem Land (Finke 2001), so dass ein Umzug in die Stadt fast immer zu einer Verbesserung der Lebensumstände führte und führt. Urbanisierung wird somit in der Literatur zu Kasachstan – ebenso wie allgemein in der Literatur zu interner Migration – in erster Linie als Streben von Individuen und Haushalten nach einem besseren Lebensstandard betrachtet (Yessenova 2005; vgl. Stuart & Gregory 1977, die auch für die UdSSR zu einem ähnlichen Ergebnis kommen).

Anders verhält es sich mit Analysen zu internationaler Migration; hier werden neben wirtschaftlichen Beweggründen gleich- oder vorrangig ethnisch-nationale angenommen (Abazov 2009; Dave 2007; Diener 2004; Peyrouse 2007; zur Bedeutung wirtschaftlicher Migrationsmotive siehe Davis & Sabol 1998; Yessenova 1996). Dies mag naheliegen, da in der Tat die meisten Kasachstanrussen nach Russland und die meisten Kasachstandeutschen nach Deutschland migrierten. Eingewandert sind überdies viele ethnische Kasachen aus der Mongolei, aus China und aus Usbekistan (Diener 2009; Finke & Sancak 2005). Mit diesem Artikel möchte ich jedoch am Beispiel kasachstandeutscher Migranten und Nicht-Migranten aufzeigen, dass die Zuordnung von wirtschaftlichen und ethnisch-nationalen Motiven so eindeutig nicht ist.

Deutschsprachige Einwanderer wurden gegen Ende des 18. Jahrhunderts ganz überwiegend für die Besiedlung ländlicher Regionen im Wolgagebiet und an der Schwarzmeerküste angeworben. Dort lebten sie über viele Generationen hinweg zumeist als Bauern (Ingenhorst 1997). Die Deportation aller Russlanddeutschen nach Sibirien und Kasachstan 1941 ist als traumatischer Verlust der Heimat in das kulturelle Gedächtnis eingegangen (Brake 1998; Römhild 1998:124–126). Gorbatschows Glasnost-Politik ermöglichte Deutschen gegen Ende der 80er Jahre die Auswanderung aus der UdSSR. Die Zahl der Emigranten vervielfachte sich daraufhin von Jahr zu Jahr und wurde erst durch die Verschärfung der Einwanderungsgesetzgebung auf Seiten des deutschen Staates zu Beginn der 1990er Jahre gebremst.[5] Da dies in der Regel von den potenziellen Einwanderern nicht erwartet wurde, war nicht allen, die dies wünschten, die Einreise nach Deutschland möglich. Mangelnde Kenntnisse der deutschen Sprache sind dabei der entscheidende Faktor für einen Ablehnungsbescheid.

Die große Zahl der Auswanderer führte auch zu interner Migration, ein Zusammenhang, der bislang in der Literatur wenig dokumentiert ist (King & Skeldon 2010:1624–1626). Umgeben von leeren Häusern entschieden sich viele für einen Neuanfang in der Stadt. Dass darüber hinaus Wasser- und Stromversorgung häufig mangelhaft waren und Kindergärten und Buslinien eingestellt wurden, erleichterte sicherlich vielen den Abschied vom Land. Diejenigen, die noch im Dorf blieben, warteten und warten zum Teil immer noch auf ihre Ausreisebescheide nach Deutschland.[6] Erhielt man einen negativen Bescheid, entschied man sich ebenfalls oft für den Wegzug, entweder nach Russland oder in die nächstgrößere Stadt. Da die Immobilienpreise jedoch seit Ende der 1990er Jahre ansteigen, konnten nicht mehr alle einen Umzug in die Stadt finanzieren, so dass einige nun zum Bleiben auf dem Land gezwungen waren. Es sind also letztlich nur sehr wenige, die sich tatsächlich für ein Leben im dörflichen Kontext entschieden haben.

Zu berücksichtigen ist jedoch, dass nicht alle, wahrscheinlich nicht einmal die meisten der in Kasachstan gebliebenen Deutschen nach Deutschland auswandern möchten. Wenn ein Migrationsprojekt scheitert, kann es allerdings andere Migrationsvorhaben behindern. Sei es, weil man nun kein Geld mehr hat, sich das Preisniveau in den Städten verteuert oder weil man viel zu sehr an seinem alten Migrationsprojekt hängt. Migrationsentscheidungen sind somit oft schwer zu revidieren und können nicht immer flexibel an neue Rahmenbedingungen angepasst werden.

Der Prozess der Land-Stadt-Migration wie auch die Auswanderung nach Deutschland verlangsamen sich seit Ende der 1990er Jahre. Die Einwanderung nach Deutschland wird zunehmend schwieriger, die Preise in der Stadt steigen und die Infrastruktur auf dem Land verbessert sich ein wenig. Kasachstan wird dank eines Wirtschaftswachs-

---

[5] Unter Gorbatschow wurde 1987 ein neues Auswanderungsgesetz verabschiedet, das die Auswanderung auch ohne die Einladung eines Angehörigen aus Deutschland gestattete. Die Zahl der Emigranten stieg in Folge dessen sprunghaft an: von 753 nach Deutschland auswandernden Personen 1986 auf 14.488 Personen 1987 (und 47.572 Personen 1988, 98 134 Personen 1989, 147.950 Personen 1990, 147.320 Personen 1991 und 195.576 Personen 1992) (Eisfeld 1999:188). Um die Zahl der Immigranten zu reduzieren, wurden verschiedene gesetzliche Änderungen vorgenommen: Seit 1990 müssen Einwanderungsanträge vom Herkunftsland aus gestellt werden. Eine Quote von maximal 200.000 Immigranten jährlich wurde 1992 eingeführt. Zudem reduzierte die Einführung eines obligatorischen Sprachtests 1996 die Zahl der Einwanderer aus den Nachfolgestaaten der UdSSR. So konnte zwischen 1996 und 1998 nur ca. die Hälfte diesen erfolgreich abschließen (Info-Dienst Deutsche Aussiedler 2001: Heft Nr. 110; cf. Ingenhorst 1997:102–104; cf. Riek 2000:136–139).

[6] Insbesondere während der 1990er Jahre mussten Antragsteller nicht selten bis zu fünf Jahre auf ihren Bescheid warten (Stoll 2007:123).

tums von über zehn Prozent zwischen 2000 und 2006 zum Einwanderungsland für Arbeitsmigrantinnen und -migranten (Anderson & Hancilová 2011), und auch einige der Emigranten kehren aus Deutschland und Russland zurück, die, auch wenn sie vom Land kommen, doch selten dorthin zurück möchten. Sie bevorzugen das Leben in der Stadt, denn ein Problem verschärft sich aus Sicht von Deutschen und Russen in den Dörfern weiterhin: Ohne Kenntnisse der kasachischen Sprache ist das Leben dort kaum mehr möglich.

Das transnationale Feld zwischen Kasachstan und Deutschland, zwischen den Ausgewanderten und den Gebliebenen, ist vielfach spärlich und hat weniger Bedeutung als der Maßstab der Migrationsbewegung vermuten lässt und als dies für andere Migrationsprozesse dokumentiert wurde (Basch et al.1997). Ein Grund hierfür ist die Perspektive der Auswanderer, die häufig eine Rückkehr in ihre alte Heimat von vornherein ausschlossen, die alles verkauften und sich für immer verabschiedeten (Pfister-Heckmann 1998; Römhild 1998). Auch deshalb war man weniger bemüht, die Kontakte nach Kasachstan aufrecht zu erhalten als dies bei Arbeitsmigranten häufig zu beobachten ist. Hinzu kommt, dass in der Regel nicht einzelne Personen, sondern (Groß)familien migrierten (Dietz 1996:127; Ingenhorst 1997:172; vgl. dazu auch Römhild 1998:202). Und schließlich erschwerte nicht zuletzt die mangelhafte Infrastruktur das Schreiben von Briefen, das Senden von Geld und das Telefonieren, und noch heute ist z. B. das Senden von Paketen teuer und unsicher. In diesem nicht sonderlich engmaschigen transnationalen Netzwerk sind von daher jene, die auf dem Land leben, tendenziell weniger eingebunden als jene in der Stadt.

Stadt, Land und Ethnizität

In der Literatur werden interne Migrationsbewegungen zumeist weniger in Verbindung mit ethnischen Migrationsmotiven gebracht. In Kasachstan ist ethnische Zugehörigkeit jedoch nicht unerheblich für interne Mobilität. So migrieren die meisten Nicht-Kasachen vom Land in die Städte. Ebenfalls sind ethnische Kategorien omnipräsent, wenn es um öffentliche Debatten und Klischees über Land- und Stadtbewohner geht, denn die meisten ethnischen Gruppen gelten grundsätzlich als entweder rural oder urban. Stereotype sind dabei vor allem an der sowjetischen Version eines Modernisierungsprojektes orientiert; d. h. Landbewohner gelten als ungebildet und rückständig, wohingegen Stadtbewohner als kulturell in jeder Hinsicht fortgeschritten dargestellt werden (Hirsch 2005; Yessenova 2005). Die Zuordnung von örtlichen Attributen zu ethnischen Gruppen erinnert dabei an die Widersprüche um das Nationalitätenkonzept der UdSSR, das Nationalität sowohl territorial als auch an Personen gebunden fassen möchte (Brubaker 1999).

Urbanität hat nicht nur für die Sowjets den Traum von Modernisierung ausgemacht (vgl. Ferguson 1999), und bereits Marx und Engels konnten in ihrem ‚Kommunistischen Manifest' immerhin von der Bourgeoisie sagen, dass sie „einen bedeutenden Teil der Bevölkerung dem Idiotismus des Landlebens entrissen" hätte (2009[1848]):33; vgl. auch Alexander & Buchli 2007:8). In der UdSSR versinnbildlichten Städte Fortschritt und Zivilisation (vgl. ebd:2f), jedoch auch Europäisierung und ‚Russifizierung' aller Bürger (vgl. Slezkine 1994:443).

Ethnische Gruppen, deren nationalstaatliche Namensgeber in Europa liegen, werden heute in der Regel als urban betrachtet, wohingegen zentralasiatische als rural gelten. Die Tatsache, dass auch Zentralasiaten – und insbesondere Kasachen – in Städten leben, wird dabei häufig ethnisch angepasst, indem diese dann als ‚russifiziert' gelten. Umgekehrt werden allerdings ländlich lebende ‚Europäer' höchst selten als ‚kasachifiziert' betrachtet; der urbane Status kann quasi gar nicht verloren gehen, womit lediglich ein zivilisatorischer Aufstieg möglich erscheint.

Solche Betrachtungen zu ethnischen Gruppen und den ihnen zugeordneten räumlichen Kontexten sowie deren Bewertung anhand des Modernisierungsschemas werden unter Kasachstanern weitgehend geteilt. Die Stadt-Land-Kategorien sind somit relativ stabil. Allerdings hat sich die Einschätzung zur Urbanität von Städten (und auch von Dörfern, denen man aus der heutigen Perspektive zur Sowjetzeit auch ein gewisses Maß an Urbanität oder Zivilisiertheit zuspricht) gewandelt (Sanders 2009). Die Migrationsströme der letzten beiden Dekaden haben – so die Einschätzung vieler Bewohner Kasachstans – zu einer massiven Verdörflichung [Ruralizatsiya] von Städten geführt, was eine Furcht vor Rückschritt in vormoderne Zeiten ausdrückt (Alexander & Buchli 2007:29f). Drei verschiedene Wanderungsbewegungen unterstützen dieses Bild: der Wegzug vieler ‚Europäer', die Land-Stadt-Migration von Kasachen und der Zuzug von Exilkasachen aus der Mongolei, China und Usbekistan, von denen zumeist angenommen wird, dass sie noch ‚dörflicher' einzuschätzen sind als die hiesigen Kasachen, die ja nun zum Teil in die Städte abwandern. Bemerkenswert ist dabei, dass Land-Stadt Mobilität fast ausschließlich als kasachisches Phänomen behandelt wird.

Ein Ergebnis der Migrationsprozesse der letzten Jahre ist die sprachliche Segregation: Auf dem Land wird oft nur noch Kasachisch gesprochen und verstanden[7]; einige Städte hingegen avancieren zu kosmopolitischen Zentren, in denen neben Kasachisch und Russisch auch Englisch, Türkisch und Chinesisch gesprochen wird. Noch vor 30 Jahren waren eher dörfliche Räume multilingual, da hier Kasachisch, Russisch, Deutsch, Polnisch und viele weitere Sprachen der nach Kasachstan deportierten Gruppen gesprochen wurden. Städtische Räume hingegen unterlagen ganz dem sowjetischen Urbanitätsprojekt, was in dieser Zeit zu einem akzent- und fehlerfreien Russisch verpflichtete. Interne (wie auch internationale) Migrationsbewegungen der letzten zwei Jahrzehnte haben die ethnische Landschaft Kasachstans verändert, während zugleich ethnische Beweggründe interne Migration motivierten, denn der sprachliche und da-

---

[7] Damit ist jedoch in erster Linie gemeint, dass kaum noch Russisch gesprochen wird, denn es ist zu berücksichtigen, dass Kasachen, die aus China, Usbekistan oder der Mongolei nach Kasachstan migrierten, neben Kasachisch auch noch die jeweilige Landessprache sprechen.

mit auch zumeist ethnische Segregationsprozess auf dem Land ist ein sich selbst verstärkender, der jüngst oft die letzten Nicht-Kasachisch-Sprechenden in die Stadt ziehen lässt.

Im Folgenden werden Ursachen und Konsequenzen von Migrationsprozessen und ihren Bewertungen anhand von Fallbeispielen erläutert. Vera und Irina wurden zu Beginn bereits eingeführt. Ausgewählt wurden sie, da sie das Zusammenspiel von Ethnizität und Migration besonders gut veranschaulichen können. Ihre Migrationsprojekte stehen dabei für die vieler anderer Personen, deren Lebenswege und -pläne mit in die Analyse einfließen konnten.[8]

Die Migrationsprojekte von Vera und Irina

Irina wurde 1937 in der Ukraine geboren. Anfang September 1941 wurde sie zusammen mit ihrer Familie nach Kasachstan in die Nähe des Balchaschsees deportiert. Sie sprach ausschließlich Deutsch mit ihrem Vater, der laut Irina kaum Russisch konnte. Ihr Vater blieb jedoch nach der Deportation verschollen. Irinas Mutter musste nun den gesamten Tag über arbeiten und kam erst abends um zehn Uhr zurück, weshalb Irina in einer kasachischen Familie aufwuchs, Kasachisch lernte und ihre Muttersprache vergaß. Um zur Schule gehen zu können, musste sie erst Russisch lernen. Ihre Mutter schickte sie deshalb zu einem russischen Kindermädchen, mit dem sie ein Jahr lang Russisch lernte; 1947, mit zehn Jahren, wurde Irina schließlich eingeschult. Nach acht Schuljahren wollte sie arbeiten gehen, doch ihr Schuldirektor, der ebenfalls, wie Irina hervorhebt, Deutscher war, ermutigte sie, doch noch zwei weitere Jahre zur Schule zu gehen. Nach der Schulzeit konnte sie noch eine Zeit lang als Laborantin an der Schule arbeiten, aber dann wollte Irina nach Russland. Sie ging nach Barnaul, in die Nähe von Omsk, und besuchte dort drei Jahre lang eine Fachschule für Bibliothekswesen. Die Russen mochten die Zugereisten aus Kasachstan nicht besonders und so kam Irina 1961 zurück nach Kasachstan. In Akbulak fand sie eine Arbeit im Fleischkombinat, doch träumte sie davon, als Lehrerin zu arbeiten. Ihre Mutter las eines Tages in der Zeitung, dass es ein Stipendium für die Lehrerausbildung in einem nahe gelegenen Ort gibt, und so begann Irina eine Ausbildung als Mathematiklehrerin. Über 30 Jahre lang arbeitete sie fortan als Lehrerin.

Einen Russen geheiratet zu haben, bereut Irina heute sehr, und damit ebenfalls ihren Aufenthalt in Russland, wo sie ihren Mann und Vater ihrer Kinder kennen lernte. Hätte sie, wie ihre Geschwister, einen Deutschen geheiratet, so wären sie, ihre Tochter und die Enkel längst in Deutschland, mutmaßt Irina. Die verpasste Chance einer Ausreise nach Deutschland ist für sie besonders schmerzhaft. Viele Jahre haben sie und

---

[8] Für meine Dissertation konnte ich ca. 60 Lebensgeschichten zu Migrationsprojekten und zur Bedeutung von Ethnizität in Kasachstan auswerten.

ihre Tochter auf einen Aufnahmebescheid gewartet; auch deshalb blieben sie im kleinen Akbulak und zogen nicht in eine größere Stadt in Kasachstan, um dort ein neues Leben in der alten Heimat zu beginnen, wie es die meisten anderen Kasachstandeutschen taten. In Akbulak sind Katja und ihre erwachsenen Kinder arbeitslos und ohne anderes Einkommen, in Taldykorgan oder Almaty könnten sie sicherlich viel leichter eine Arbeit finden. Auch jetzt nach dem Erhalt eines endgültigen Ablehnungsbescheids halten Irina und Katja an ihrem Ausreisewunsch fest. Hinzu kommt allerdings, dass sich städtischer Wohnraum innerhalb der letzten zehn Jahre stark verteuerte, so dass auch deshalb ein Umzug nach Taldykorgan kaum mehr möglich ist.

Die Veränderungen in ihrem Dorf betrachten Irina und Katja mit viel Skepsis. Irina spricht im Gegensatz zu den meisten Nicht-Kasachen fließend Kasachisch. Außerdem pflegt sie eine intensive Freundschaft zu einer Kasachin, mit der sie kürzlich das 50-jährige Freundschaftsjubiläum feierte. Dennoch folgt Irina nicht einer weit verbreiteten Narration der Besonderheit deutsch-kasachischer Beziehungen, die in der Aufnahme während des Zweiten Weltkriegs deportierter Russlanddeutscher in kasachische Haushalte begründet liegt. In den Erzählungen der meisten Kasachstandeutschen wird dabei berichtet, dass sich Kasachen aufopfernd um sie kümmerten und mit ihnen das Brot teilten (Sanders 2009:108–113). Irina hingegen erzählt, dass die Kasachen, bei denen sie und ihre Mutter nach der Deportation lebten, sie schlecht behandelt hätten, ohne ihre Erzählung als Sonderfall der ansonsten sehr gastfreundlichen Kasachen zu kennzeichnen. Es ist davon auszugehen, dass Irina diese Narration vertraut ist, da sie auch durch Fernsehberichte verbreitet wird. Vermutlich sucht Irina also gar keine positiven Anknüpfungspunkte an ein Leben unter Kasachen, sondern ganz im Gegenteil möchte sie sich eher darin bestärken, dass nur die Ausreise aus Kasachstan positiv für ihren und den Lebensweg ihrer Nachfahren sein kann.

Vera wurde im selben Jahr wie Irina an der Wolga geboren. Auch sie wurde als Kind deportiert, heiratete einen Russen und lebte eine Zeit lang in Akbulak, wo sie bis zu ihrer Pensionierung als Ökonomistin arbeitete. Im Gegensatz zu Irina wollte Vera allerdings nie nach Deutschland auswandern, obschon dies für sie bedeutend einfacher wäre, da sie muttersprachlich Deutsch spricht. So plante sie in den 1990er Jahren ihre Zukunft in Kasachstan. Kurz nach ihrer Pensionierung 1991 zog Vera von Akbulak in die nächstgrößere Stadt Taldykorgan und kaufte sich dort eine Wohnung.[9] Angesichts der widrigen Bedingungen in den ländlichen Gebieten während der 1990er Jahre versprach eine Wohnung in der Stadt mehr Annehmlichkeiten. Mit der klaren Perspektive der Mutter, in Kasachstan zu bleiben, gründeten ihre Kinder kleine Unter-

---

[9] Die meisten Migranten strebten auch in der Russischen Föderation in die nächstgrößere Stadt und nicht etwa nach Moskau (White 2007:893). Die Infrastruktur war jedoch auch in Taldykorgan in den 1990er Jahren problematisch, da insbesondere die Stromversorgung oft nicht gewährleistet werden konnte. Dies änderte sich allerdings mit dem Umzug der Oblastverwaltung von Almaty nach Taldykorgan 2001.

nehmen in Taldykorgan und gehören mittlerweile zu den wohlhabenden Einwohnern der Stadt. Vera lebt heute allein in einer Dreizimmerwohnung mit Zentralheizung und fließendem Wasser.

Obwohl Vera im Gegensatz zu Irina nicht plant, Kasachstan zu verlassen, betrachtet sie die soziale und politische Entwicklung des Landes dennoch skeptisch. Insbesondere missfallen ihr die demografische Veränderung des Landes zugunsten der Kasachen und die steigende Bedeutung der kasachischen Sprache. Vera spricht kein Kasachisch, da sie als Kind nach Sibirien deportiert wurde, dort aufwuchs und erst mit Ende 20 aus beruflichen Gründen in die Kasachische SSR migrierte. Dennoch ist Vera alles in allem zufrieden mit ihrem Leben in Taldykorgan und sieht auch für ihre Enkel eine Zukunft in Kasachstan. So werden sie von ihr häufig aufgefordert, sehr gut Kasachisch zu lernen.

Obschon die Lebenswege von Vera und Irina sehr ähnlich verlaufen sind, ist ihre heutige Situation doch sehr verschieden, was sich in erster Linie aus ihren unterschiedlichen Migrationsvorhaben nach dem Zusammenbruch der UdSSR ergibt. Ausschlaggebend war dabei die unterschiedliche familiäre Situation. Irinas Geschwister trafen 1991 gemeinsam den Entschluss, nach Deutschland auszuwandern. Bloß stellte Irina ihren Antrag etwas später. Zwischenzeitlich änderte sich jedoch die Einwanderungsgesetzgebung in Deutschland, die nun auch einen Sprachtest forderte. Diesen konnte Irina nicht bestehen, da sie kein Deutsch spricht und dies auch muttersprachlich, wie von der Gesetzgebung gefordert, kaum lernen kann. Vera und ihre Geschwister, die in Russland lebten und zu denen sie wenig Kontakt pflegte, hatten hingegen nie die Absicht zu migrieren. Hinzu kommt, dass Veras Sohn und Schwiegersohn zu Beginn der 1990er als Autohändler häufig in Deutschland waren und nahezu ausschließlich Negatives über die Deutschen und ein Leben in Deutschland berichteten.

In Irinas Fall trägt also gerade der gescheiterte Versuch auszuwandern dazu bei, dass die Lebensumstände heute eine Auswanderung erst recht nahelegen. Denn auf der Hand liegt, dass Irinas Lebensumstände in einem schlecht isolierten kleinen Haus mit Außentoilette und Ofen schlicht widriger sind als Veras in der Dreizimmerwohnung mit Dusche, WC und Zentralheizung. Allerdings könnte auch Irina heute so leben wie Vera, wenn sie bereits in den 90er Jahren in die Stadt gezogen wäre. Diese paradoxe Situation betrifft nahezu alle Familien, die noch auf dem Land leben: Fast jede wünscht sich ein Leben in Deutschland, da die bereits investierten Kosten für dessen Vorbereitung ein Leben in Kasachstan erschweren. Die Chancen für eine Migration nach Deutschland stehen jedoch heute ungünstiger denn je, und auch ein Umzug in die Stadt ist deutlich kostspieliger geworden. Eine anvisierte transnationale Migration wird somit nicht durch eine Land-Stadt-Migration vorbereitet, wie dies in anderen Migrationsprozessen häufig zu beobachten ist (King & Skeldon 2010:1623 f.), sondern steht dieser eher im Wege

Hinzu kommt die unterschiedliche Situation der Kinder, deren Wohl und Ausbildung zumeist das Hauptmotiv für Migrationsentscheidungen liefert. Irinas Tochter Katja ist ausgebildete Kindergärtnerin. Da sie allerdings kein Kasachisch spricht sind ihre Aussichten, eine Anstellung in Akbulak zu finden, sehr gering. Auch Veras Kinder sprechen beide kein Kasachisch. In Taldykorgan können sie aber dennoch ihr Auskommen als selbständige Unternehmer bestreiten; sie betreiben beide eine Autoreparaturwerkstatt. Veras Kinder hatten genau wie sie selbst nie die Absicht, aus Kasachstan auszuwandern. Da sie deshalb ihre finanziellen wie sozialen Ressourcen ganz für die Gründung zweier Betriebe einsetzten, konnte ihnen dies gelingen. Eine jahrelange Unsicherheit hinsichtlich des zukünftigen Wohnortes, wie dies bei Katja und Irina der Fall war, hält jedoch davon ab, mittel- und langfristige Pläne für den Aufbau einer wirtschaftlichen Existenz zu entwickeln und umzusetzen.

Die Frage, inwieweit Irinas und Katjas Im-Dorf-Bleiben rational war, ist schwierig zu beantworten, denn politische Entscheidungen in Deutschland senden höchst widersprüchliche Impulse nach Kasachstan und erschweren damit die Abwägung. Auf die freimütige Einladung an alle Deutschen der UdSSR, nach Deutschland zu migrieren, und das Propagieren der deutschen Nation jenseits deutscher Grenzen, erfolgte die schrittweise legislative Rücknahme dieser Absichten und Ideen. Letztlich ist allerdings entscheidend, wie staatliche Politik und deren Entwicklung eingeschätzt werden. Aus dörflicher Perspektive in Kasachstan sind politische Entscheidungen aus Deutschland jedoch kaum einschätzbar. Die vergebliche Hoffnung, doch noch nach Deutschland auswandern zu können, ist von daher nicht unbedingt eine irrationale.

Eng verbunden mit der Rationalität von Migrationsentscheidungen ist die Frage ‚wer ist gegangen', und ob dies nur die Mutigen und Erfolgreichen sind. Nur aus heutiger Perspektive sind jedoch die Erfolglosen die, die geblieben sind, da das Landleben und seine Bewohner seit den 1990er Jahren insgesamt eine massive Statusabwertung erfahren haben und zudem auf dem Land lebende Nicht-Kasachen besonders marginalisiert sind.

Diaspora-Identität?

Internationale Migrationsprozesse werden im Hinblick auf Kasachstan häufig in Verbindung mit der Rückkehr einer Diasporagemeinschaft und ethnischer Diskriminierung als Nicht-Kasache gebracht (Dave 2007:139). Auch wenn man die Lebensgeschichten von Vera und Irina betrachtet, so ist bemerkenswert, welch große Bedeutung die Themen Deutsch-Sein und die deutsche Muttersprache in Irinas Leben spielen, wohingegen sie in Veras Erzählungen über ihr Leben kaum Raum einnehmen. Es ist naheliegend anzunehmen, dass auch die deutsche Identität Motor für Veras Migrationswunsch in eine historische Heimat war und ist. Die starke Verknüpfung dieses Themas mit dem Umstand, dass eben dieses Projekt gescheitert ist, lässt allerdings auch den Schluss zu, dass die ethnische Identität eher der Umgang ist, mit dem das Scheitern behandelt werden kann, als dass diese stets bedeutsam war.

Sowohl Irinas als auch deren Tochter Katjas Alltag prägt die Beschäftigung mit der deutschen Identität, die immer auch an das gescheiterte Lebensprojekt der Auswanderung erinnert, womit umgekehrt wieder das Gedächtnis an die deutschen Vorfahren wachgerufen wird. Katja besucht häufig die verbliebenen Deutschen in ihrem Dorf und versucht diese für gemeinsame Aktivitäten wie das Ausrichten von Festen zu gewinnen. Alle teilen Irinas und Katjas Schicksal in gewisser Weise, wenn auch ihr Engagement für die ‚deutsche Sache' geringer ausfällt.

Katja arbeitet – wie oben geschildert – für eine Filiale des Deutschen Hauses in Akbulak. Ihr war es ein besonders großes Anliegen, mich mit allen Deutschen im Ort bekannt zu machen. Dafür lud sie sogar jene, die mich nicht zu sich nach Hause einladen mochten, zu sich ein, damit ich dort ein Interview mit ihnen machen konnte. Nach Aussage von Katja war es ihnen schlicht zu unangenehm, mir ihren ärmlichen Lebensstil zu zeigen. Darunter war ein Ehepaar in den 50ern, die sich während des gesamten Nachmittags über den ihrer Ansicht nach ungerechten Sprachtest des Goethe-Instituts beklagten, bei dem sie schon mehrfach durchgefallen waren.

Ein anderes Paar im selben Alter wirkte ungewöhnlich reserviert und wenig begeistert von Katjas und meinem Spontanbesuch. Ihr vornehmliches Thema war die rasante negative Veränderung des nachbarschaftlichen Umfelds durch den Zuzug von Kasachen. Eine andere Familie zeigte uns Videos ihres Deutschlandbesuchs und lobte die deutschen Tugenden, die sich sogar bei ihrem deutschen Schäferhund zeigen würden. Eine ältere alleinstehende Frau betonte, wie gut es doch wäre zu wissen, dass sich Deutschland (in Form meiner Person) um die Kasachstandeutschen kümmern würde. Dabei lobte sie auch die Arbeit der GTZ[10].

Diese hier nur kurz angerissenen Lebensgeschichten und weitere andere sind höchst unterschiedlich hinsichtlich des Migrationswunsches, ihrem Deutschlandbild und der Wahrnehmung von Veränderungen in ihrem Umfeld. Alle Besuche wurden jedoch von Katja dahingehend kommentiert, dass sie doch zeigten, wie schwer ihr Schicksal hier ist und wie schlecht es den Leuten geht. Damit verband sie die Aufforderung an mich, dies auch so aufzuschreiben. Hier ist sicherlich von Bedeutung, dass Katja sich als Vertreterin der Deutschen und ihrer Anliegen betrachtet. Dabei möchte sie die Chance nutzen, die Nöte und Probleme der Kasachstandeutschen durch meine Person in Deutschland publik machen zu können. Durch ihre Tätigkeit für das Deutsche Haus weiß sie auch um die Finanzierung durch die GTZ, die die besondere Bedürftigkeit der deutschen Empfänger an Hilfslieferungen und finanzieller Unterstützung voraussetzen. Das eingangs erwähnte Bedürfnis einiger Deutscher in Taldykorgan, mich mit den Deutschen auf dem Land bekannt zu machen, ist ebenfalls in diesem Zusammenhang zu sehen: Es soll dokumentiert werden, dass Deutsche zum Teil unter sehr schwierigen Bedingungen leben und hilfsbedürftig sind.

Regelmäßig besucht Katja darüber hinaus alle Kulturveranstaltungen des *Akimats* (Kasachisch: Rathaus), bei dem sie sich als Repräsentantin der Deutschen versteht.

---

[10] Nach dem Zusammenschluss von GTZ, DED und Inwent 2011 wurde die GTZ (Gesellschaft für Technische Zusammenarbeit) in GIZ (Gesellschaft für Internationale Zusammenarbeit) umbenannt.

Auch wenn Katja durch ihr Engagement relativ gut im Ort vernetzt ist, so marginalisiert sie sich doch gleichzeitig. Ihr Projekt ‚deutsches Leben zu aktivieren' hat eigentlich keine Zukunft. Es leben kaum noch Deutsche in ihrem Ort, und alle Kulturveranstaltungen werden seit kurzem ausschließlich auf Kasachisch abgehalten, was Katja und die meisten anderen Vertreterinnen der Minderheiten nicht verstehen. Ich begleitete Katja zu einer dieser Veranstaltungen, die sie schließlich vorzeitig und frustriert verließ, weil sie sich ausgegrenzt fühlte. Es scheint fast, als wollten Katja und auch Irina ihrem gescheiterten Migrationswunsch mit Realitätsflucht begegnen. Sie ziehen sich auf eine deutsche Identität zurück und blenden damit andere Optionen aus. Die deutsche Muttersprache, deren Bedeutung für ihre Identität von beiden fortwährend herausgestellt wird, erscheint dabei als intrinsischer Motor für ihr Tun. Die Tatsache, dass beide gar kein Deutsch sprechen, veranschaulicht jedoch das Scheitern ihrer Lebensprojekte, was von ihnen nicht verwunden werden kann.

In Veras Lebensgeschichte fällt das Gegenteil ins Auge: Wegen ihrer ethnischen Zugehörigkeit wurden sie und ihre Familie nach Sibirien deportiert, sie wurde als Kind beschimpft und konnte (wie Irina) erst mit 10 Jahren die Schule besuchen. Dennoch beschreibt Vera ihr Leben nicht als maßgeblich bestimmt durch ihr Deutsch-Sein. Zudem ist die deutsche Muttersprache lediglich eine Randnotiz in ihrer Erzählung; stattdessen betont sie, dass sie die russische Sprache liebt und auch ihre Eltern sehr gut Russisch sprachen. Auch wenn Vera mit ihrem Leben in Kasachstan nicht in jeder Hinsicht zufrieden ist, hat sie sich dort in einer Stadt bestmöglich eingerichtet und verlegt ihre und die Lebenspläne ihrer Kinder und Enkel nicht in ein fernes Land.

Katjas und Irinas Suche nach einem besseren Leben ist in erster Linie der Wunsch nach einem wirtschaftlich besseren Leben, das sie allerdings nur dann gewährleistet sehen, wenn sie unter ihresgleichen in Deutschland leben. Ethnizität ist in ihrem Fall somit ein wichtiger Motor für Diaspora-Migration. Zu berücksichtigen ist jedoch, dass nur die Vorstellung, dort – in seinem ‚historischen Heimatland' – ein besseres Auskommen für sich und seine Kinder zu haben, Ethnizität bedeutsam werden lässt. Wenn diese Vorstellung – wie im Fall von Vera – nicht da ist, ist auch der Wunsch, dorthin auszuwandern, nicht vorhanden. Wichtiger ist jedoch, dass es nur auf den ersten Blick um die richtige Ethnizität im Zielland geht, es geht vielmehr um die falsche Ethnizität am Herkunftsort, die den Wunsch, gehen zu wollen, stärkt, da sie ein finanzielles Auskommen behindert (vgl. auch Radnitz 2006 zur Auswanderung aus Usbekistan). Dies trifft besonders in einem kasachischen Dorf und weniger in der Stadt zu. Ethnizität ist von daher bedeutsam für interne und internationale Migration in Kasachstan, aber es geht dabei in erster Linie um die als ungünstig empfundene ethnische Zugehörigkeit in Kasachstan und weniger um eine diasporische Identität.

Das Fallbeispiel von Irina und Katja zeigt darüber hinaus, dass das Scheitern eines Migrationsprojektes andere Migrationsvorhaben behindern kann. Dabei spielt es eine Rolle, dass äußere Rahmenbedingungen wie teurer städtischer Wohnraum, ein allgemeiner Preisanstieg und Arbeitslosigkeit heute ungünstiger sind. Darüber hinaus ist nicht unerheblich, dass Katja und Irina ihr Leben rund um das Migrationsprojekt eingerichtet haben. Indem an das alte Migrationsziel immer neu erinnert wird, werden andere verunmöglicht. Migrationsentscheidungen können somit nicht unter allen Umständen an sich verändernde Rahmenbedingungen flexibel angepasst und revidiert werden und sind damit häufig weniger vorläufig als im Zeitalter des Transnationalismus vielfach angenommen.

Im Folgenden wird das dritte Fallbeispiel, der Lebensentwurf von Adas Familie, vorgestellt. Dieser steht in starkem Kontrast zu Veras und Irinas Vorstellungen von einem guten Leben in einem städtischen ‚modernen' Kontext, denn für Ada und ihre Familie verkörpert gerade das Landleben Sicherheit und Wohlstand. Dabei stellen sie ihren Lebensentwurf auch in den Kontext einer russlanddeutschen Identität.

Der Lebensentwurf von Ada und ihrer Familie

Gulder galt bis Anfang der 1990er Jahre als ‚deutsches Dorf', etwa die Hälfte der ca. 1.000 Bewohner hatte einen Pass mit dem Eintrag ‚deutsch' in der Rubrik ‚Nationalität'[11], bei den meisten anderen stand dort ‚russisch'; Kasachen lebten dort nur wenige. Seitdem hat sich die demografische Situation genau umgekehrt: Heute leben in Gulder nur noch wenige deutsche Familien, die allesamt nicht die Absicht haben, nach Deutschland auszuwandern bzw. sogar aus Deutschland zurückgekehrt sind. Russische Familien gibt es ebenfalls kaum noch. Die Häuser standen allerdings nur für sehr kurze Zeit leer; sie wurden rasch von kasachischen Familien bezogen, zum Teil auch von solchen aus China. Heute leben in Gulder insgesamt mehr Menschen als gegen Ende der UdSSR; dafür wurden sogar zwischen den alten recht weit auseinanderliegenden Straßen neue errichtet. Das Dorf hat zahlreiche kleine Geschäfte und eine Schule, und auf der anderen Seite der großen Straße, die in nur 30 Autominuten nach Taldykorgan führt, steht seit Kurzem sogar ein Hotel.

Mein Besuch bei einer der deutschen Familien in Gulder wurde von einer Mitarbeiterin des deutschen Hauses in Taldykorgan organisiert, die ebenfalls früher dort lebte, in den 90er Jahren aber in die Stadt zog, während ihre gesamte Familie nach Deutschland auswanderte. Eine ihrer Freundinnen aus Kindertagen, die bislang nicht aus Gulder wegzog, war von ihr gebeten worden, mich an einer Bushaltestelle an der großen Straße abzuholen und zu einer der deutschen Familien zu bringen. Auf dem Weg dorthin erzählt sie, dass sie sehr zufrieden mit ihrem Leben in Gulder ist. Sie ist

---

[11] Seit 1932 war die Nationalität der Bürger im Pass notiert; seit 1938 musste sie für die Bewohner der sogenannten ‚Regimezonen', in der die meisten Sowjetdeutschen lebten, auch in Übereinstimmung mit der Elternnationalität sein (vgl. Hirsch 2005:268 f.). In Kasachstan ist heute der Eintrag der Nationalität nicht mehr obligatorisch, dennoch geben die meisten Bürger ihre Nationalität im Pass nach wie vor an.

Lehrerin an der Dorfschule, die ganz modern mit Computern ausgestattet ist, wie sie betont. Sie entschuldigt sich mehrfach für den Dreck auf der Straße. Im Sommer wäre es aber wunderschön, wenn alles blüht. Dann erzählt sie von ihrem Besuch bei ihrer Schwester, die vor zehn Jahren nach Deutschland ausgewandert ist. Dort hatte es ihr allerdings gar nicht gefallen. Ihre Schwester begann in Deutschland zu trinken, sie wurde dick, hat keine Arbeit und spricht kaum ein Wort Deutsch. So möchte sie nicht leben, und deshalb wäre sie lieber hier in Gulder geblieben. Sie verabschiedete sich am Gartentor und entschuldigte sich damit, dass sie so viel im Haus zu tun habe. Zuvor hatte sie mir noch mitgeteilt, dass die Familie, die ich heute besuchen werde, sehr religiös sei.

Ich wurde sehr herzlich von der Großmutter Ada und ihrer Tochter Rosa empfangen. Wie sich herausstellte, war ich gerade rechtzeitig zu ihrem Gottesdienst gekommen, den sie immer sonntags um zehn Uhr in ihrem Haus abhalten. Ada lebt gemeinsam mit ihrem Mann Viktor. Im Nachbarhaus leben ihre Tochter Rosa, deren Mann und ihre sieben Kinder; ein weiterer Sohn lebt mit seiner Familie ebenfalls in Gulder, die anderen drei Kinder von Ada und Viktor sind nach Deutschland ausgewandert. Zum Gottesdienst war neben Ada, Viktor, Rosa und ihren Kindern noch Igor[12] gekommen. Viktor übernahm die Leitung und predigte auf Russisch, gesungen und gebetet wurde überwiegend auf Deutsch.

Die meisten Deutschen, die früher in Gulder lebten, waren wie Ada und Viktor Lutheraner. Ihre Gottesdienste hielten sie immer in verschiedenen Häusern ab, bis zu Beginn der 90er Jahre eine kleine Kirche errichtet wurde. Zu dieser Zeit waren jedoch die meisten Deutschen bereits ausgewandert oder planten dies. In der Kirche werden heute noch Gottesdienste gefeiert, allerdings ausschließlich in russischer Sprache, so dass Ada und Viktor lieber selbst einen abhalten, so wie sie dies früher auch immer taten. Die beiden sprechen untereinander Deutsch, das ihre Tochter Rosa versteht und gebrochen auch selbst spricht. Deren Kinder kommunizieren jedoch ausschließlich auf Russisch und nur der jüngste Sohn, der 12-jährige Max, spricht neben Russisch auch Kasachisch, da er sonst mit fast niemandem mehr spielen könnte, wie seine Mutter erklärt.

Ada und Viktor hatten nie die Absicht, nach Deutschland auszuwandern, und überhaupt nie den Wunsch, ihr Dorf zu verlassen, in dem sie nun seit nahezu 50 Jahren leben. Mit Blick auf die russlanddeutsche Geschichte betont Viktor, dass das ‚Leben in der Natur' die Russlanddeutschen schon oft gerettet hätte, wie etwa in der schwierigen Zeit nach der Deportation. Nur weil sie sich stets mit Nahrungsmitteln selbst versorgen konnten, haben sie überlebt. Das Leben auf dem Land bedeutet für beide von daher, eine sichere Existenzgrundlage zu haben und gesund zu leben. Die Möglichkeit, sich auf dem Land selbst versorgen zu können, mögen beide nicht aufs

---

[12] Igor ist einer der Rückkehrer. Er lebte für mehrere Jahre in Deutschland und kehrte vor ca. zwei Jahren zurück. Er ist nicht mit der Familie verwandt.

Spiel setzen und gegen ein möglicherweise bequemeres, aber in ihren Augen unsicheres Leben eintauschen. Auch aus diesem Grund kommt so weder eine Migration in eine Stadt in Kasachstan noch eine Migration nach Deutschland in Frage.

Ihre Tochter Rosa teilt diese Einschätzung, die durch die Erfahrungen ihres Bruders, der seit ca. 15 Jahren in Deutschland lebt, bestärkt wird. Dieser hatte aufgrund von Rückenproblemen seinen Arbeitsplatz verloren. Nach dreijähriger Arbeitslosigkeit wurde ihm schließlich eine Umschulung zum Computertechniker finanziert, die er mit nun knapp 50 Jahren vor kurzem abschloss. Aufgrund seines Alters fand er jedoch erneut keine Arbeit. Rosa beschreibt allerdings im gleichen Atemzug die Schwierigkeiten, mit denen ihre Kinder in Kasachstan bei der Arbeitssuche konfrontiert sind. Ihre Töchter können als Näherinnen keine Anstellung finden und arbeiten so den Sommer über ‚in den Rüben' (in der dörflichen Kooperative) und in ihrem Garten. Außerdem halten sie drei Kühe und ihre Eltern zwei Schweine und mehrere Hühner. Ihr ältester Sohn wurde auf verschiedenen Baustellen mehrfach um seinen Lohn geprellt. Schließlich übernimmt er nun zumeist schwere körperliche Tätigkeiten in der dörflichen Kooperative. Rosa hilft dort ebenfalls manchmal aus. Ihre Arbeit wird mit Naturalien wie Mehl oder Zucker entlohnt.

Alles in allem scheint Rosa mit ihrem Leben in einem kasachischen Dorf zufrieden zu sein. Ein Problem sieht sie jedoch: Es gibt in Gulder keine deutschen Heiratspartner mehr für ihre Kinder. Ihr ältester Sohn hat seit Kurzem eine russische Freundin, was ihr eigentlich nicht passt, dennoch sagt sie, dass sie ein nettes und schönes Mädchen ist. Kasachen scheinen als Heiratspartner gar nicht zur Diskussion zu stehen; sie werden von Rosa als ‚Schwarze' [tschjernye] bezeichnet. Dennoch hält sie fest, dass sie zu ihren ‚schwarzen' Nachbarn ein gutes Verhältnis hat und dass ihr das nachbarschaftliche Leben hier in Kasachstan viel besser gefällt als jenes in Deutschland, von dem sie gehört hat, dass es sehr formell sei, da man für jedes Treffen zuvor einen Termin vereinbaren muss.

Viktor, Ada und Rosa sind mit ihrem Leben zufrieden und wissen, dass sie ihr Lebenskonzept wahrscheinlich an keinem anderen Ort besser verwirklichen können als in Gulder. Die Tatsache, dass sich die Lebenswirklichkeit im Ort in den letzten 20 Jahren drastisch verändert hat, wird von ihnen nicht als bedrohlich empfunden, da sie ihr Leben unbeeindruckt dessen fortführen können. Sie leben nahezu autark – nur den Mangel an deutsch-lutherischen Heiratspartnern können sie nicht durch eine bestimmte Lebensführung kompensieren. Dieser aber wird die ethnisch-religiöse Spezifik der Großfamilie dennoch über kurz oder lang verändern.

Identität, Migration und das Streben nach einem guten Leben

Die traumatische Erfahrung der Deportation aller Russlanddeutschen nach Sibirien und Kasachstan 1941 ist Teil des kulturellen Gedächtnisses. Gleichermaßen ist aber deren Überwindung grundlegend für ein russland- und kasachstandeutsches Selbstverständnis. Das Überleben unter höchst widrigen Bedingungen wird dabei auch mit den russlanddeutschen Eigenschaften Fleiß, Ordnungssinn und Zuverlässigkeit erklärt, von denen angenommen wird, dass sie sich durch viele Generationen von arbeitsamen Bauern herausgebildet haben (Sanders 2009:97–116). Die russlanddeutsche Geschichte wie auch das kulturelle Gedächtnis scheinen daher kaum zu der Position im Modernisierungsprojekt zu passen, die ihnen von den meisten Kasachstanern und im öffentlichen Diskurs zugedacht wird. Die ‚Vertreter' einer westlichen Kultur- und Industrienation gelten nämlich als gebildet, zivilisiert und kulturell weit entwickelt. Dazu kann aus sowjetischer und kasachstanischer Perspektive eigentlich nur ein urbaner Lebensstil passen.

Dieser Widerspruch ebnet sich erst in den letzten 20 Jahren durch massenhaftes Abwandern der Deutschen nach Deutschland oder in die Städte Kasachstans ein. Das kasachstandeutsche Selbstverständnis bleibt allerdings – wenigstens zum Teil – ein rurales. Die ausgeprägte Beziehung zur Natur und dem ‚einfachen' ländlichen Leben dient dabei auch als das Differenzkriterium gegenüber den Deutschen in Deutschland. Geschichten vom Jagen und Angeln in der Natur ohne Verbotsschilder und von Menschen, die nach ihrer Migration nach Deutschland durch ein Leben ohne Garten krank wurden, sind zumeist die Antwort auf die Frage nach den Motiven fürs Bleiben in Kasachstan (Sanders 2009:193–199).

Das deutsche Selbstverständnis vom fleißigen ländlichen Arbeiter hat jedoch durch die massenhafte Abwanderung der Deutschen in die Städte und nach Deutschland seine Entsprechung in der Alltagspraxis verloren. Dies hat allerdings nicht dazu geführt, dass ein solches Leben als leider verlorenes dargestellt wird, das eigentlich immer noch erstrebenswert ist. Ganz im Gegenteil gilt nun ein städtisches Leben als geeignet für die Deutschen und andere Europäer, wohingegen ein ländlicher Lebensstil den Kasachen zugeschrieben wird. Das heißt, dass das rurale Selbstverständnis zumeist nur durch ein zeitweiliges Sein in der Natur gelebt wird und Aktivitäten wie Jagen und Angeln dabei lediglich eine kurze Erholung vom urbanen Lebensstil darstellen. Somit hat sich die sowjetische Evolutionsidee – wenn auch erst nach Ende ihrer politischen Umsetzung – schließlich verwirklicht. Obschon der Lebensstil heute zumeist nicht mehr ländlich ist, ist doch die Vorstellung von den ‚typisch russlanddeutschen Charaktereigenschaften' geblieben und markiert neben der Idee einer gemeinsamen Abstammung kasachstandeutsche Identität.

Das Lebenskonzept von Viktor, Ada und Rosa stellt heute eine Ausnahme dar, es repräsentiert aber die Lebensphilosophie vieler Generationen von Deutschen zur Zeit der UdSSR und davor. Das hervortretende Element ihrer Lebenskonzeption ist dabei die Autarkie, so dass auch die Gründung eines neuen Staates von ihnen kaum wahrgenommen wird.

Die Vorstellungen von einem guten Leben sind unterschiedlich und somit auch die Migrationsabsichten. Ein Leben in vertrauten und als sicher empfundenen Bahnen zu führen, stellt die Hauptmotivation fürs Bleiben dar. Dabei können Lebensumstände sogar dann noch als vertraut empfunden werden, wenn sich fast alle äußeren Rahmenbedingungen ändern. Dies erklärt sich auch mit dem kulturellen Gedächtnis und der Vorstellung, dass Russlanddeutsche lange Zeit ein Leben mit wenig Anbindung an den Staat führten.

Der Wunsch nach einem sicheren Auskommen für sich und die Kinder ist in allen hier vorgestellten Fallbeispielen die treibende Kraft hinter der Entscheidung zu bleiben oder zu gehen. Trotz ähnlicher Absichten sind jedoch die Migrationsprojekte höchst unterschiedlich: Einige möchten nach Deutschland auswandern, andere sind vom Land in die Stadt gezogen und wieder andere möchten im Dorf bleiben. Dabei spielen zeitliche Aspekte und sich verändernde äußere Rahmenbedingungen sowie unterschiedliche Vorstellungen von einem guten und sicheren Leben eine Rolle.

Diasporische Identität steht hier nicht in direktem Zusammenhang mit Migrationsvorhaben und noch weniger mit deren Ergebnissen. So haben die Fallbeispiele gezeigt, dass sich russlanddeutsche Lebensentwürfe in einem ‚kasachischen Dorf' verwirklichen lassen, dass diejenigen, die Deutsch sprechen, in Kasachstan bleiben und die, die kein Deutsch sprechen, nach Deutschland auswandern möchten. Natürlich ist einzuwenden, dass eine deutsche Identität nicht anhand von Sprachkenntnissen bemessen werden kann, wie dies die deutsche Gesetzgebung vorsieht, denn gerade diejenigen ohne deutsche Sprachkenntnisse geben an, dass ihnen eine deutsche Identität besonders wichtig ist und sie deshalb ein Leben unter ihresgleichen bevorzugen. Vieles spricht jedoch dafür, dass die ethnische Identität erst im Verlauf des Wartens auf den Bescheid und während der Auseinandersetzung mit der Ablehnung an Bedeutung gewann. Der Ausreisewunsch wird so stark, weil man bei seiner Familie leben möchte. Hinzu kommt jedoch, dass Irina und Katja auch die einzigen sind, die so deutlich keine Perspektive für ein Leben in einem kasachischen Umfeld für sich sehen und auch das weit verbreitete Narrativ über die deutsch-kasachische Freundschaft nicht teilen. Ein gescheiterter transnationaler Migrationsversuch erscheint in ihrem Fall somit kaum revidierbar und zeigt, dass Entscheidungen nicht bloß vorläufig sind. Alle hier vorgestellten Familien treffen darüber hinaus Migrationsentscheidungen mit der Absicht, an dem neuen Ort dann für *immer* leben zu wollen bzw. zu müssen.

Die massenhafte Ausreise nach Deutschland und Russland führte zu interner Migration in die Städte. Da politische Entscheidungen des deutschen Staates jedoch oft falsch eingeschätzt wurden, war nicht allen, die dies wünschten, die Einreise nach Deutschland möglich. Ein Umzug in die Stadt, der für viele eine weitere Option darstellt, war jedoch Ende der 1990er Jahre ebenfalls schwierig, so dass einigen nur das Bleiben auf dem Land möglich war.

Die transnationalen Bezüge wirken sich höchst unterschiedlich aus: In zwei der drei Fälle verstärken sie den Wunsch zu bleiben, im dritten Fall bekräftigen sie den Wunsch auszuwandern. Dies ist nicht mit der Qualität der Beziehungen zu erklären. Transnational versendete Gelder und Güter erleichtern in einigen Fällen das Leben in Kasachstan; das führt allerdings in dem hier vorgestellten Fallbeispiel gerade nicht dazu, sich als Profiteur von Migrationsprojekten anderer zu fühlen, sondern bekräftigt vielmehr den Wunsch, selbst zu gehen. Unterstützungsleistungen können aber in Kasachstan gleichermaßen von wohlhabenderen Familienangehörigen aus der Stadt erfolgen, so dass eine internationale Migration nicht unbedingt notwendig ist, um seine Vision eines guten und sicheren Auskommens auf dem Land zu verwirklichen.

Literatur

Abazov, R. 2009: Current Trends in Migration in the Common Wealth of Independent States. *Human Development Research Paper* 36.
Alexander, C.; Buchli, V. 2007: Introduction. In: C. Alexander and v. Buchli (eds.), *Urban Life in Post-Soviet Asia*. London: University College London Press, pp. 1–39.
Anderson, B.; Hancilová, B. 2011: Migrant Labour in Kazakhstan: A Cause for Concern? *Journal of Ethnic and Migration Studies* 37:467–483.
Anthias, F. 1998: Evaluating 'Diaspora': Beyond Ethnicity? *Sociology* 32:557–580.
Basch, L.; Glick Schiller, N.;Szanton Blanc, C. 1997: *Nations Unbound. Transnational Projects, Postcolonial Predicaments, and Deterritorialized Nation-States*. Amsterdam: Gordon and Breach.
Brake, K. 1998: *Lebenserinnerungen rußlanddeutscher Einwanderer. Zeitgeschichte und Narrativik*. Berlin: Reimer.
Brubaker, R. 1999: *Nationalism Reframed. Nationhood and the National Question in the New Europe*. Cambridge: Cambridge University Press.
Brubaker, R. 2005: The 'Diaspora' Diaspora. *Ethnic and Racial Studies* 28:1–20.
Castles, S.; Miller, M. J. 1993: *The Age of Migration. International Population Movements in the Modern World*. Basingstoke: Palgrave Macmillan.
Chambers, I. 1994: *Migrancy, Culture, Identity*. London and New York: Routledge.
Cohen, R. 1997: *Global Diasporas. An Introduction*. Seattle: University of Washington Press.
Coté, G. 1997: Socio-Economic Attainment, Regional Disparities, and Internal Migration. *European Sociological Review* 13:55–77.
Dave, B. 2007: *Kazakhstan. Ethnicity, Language and Power*. London: Routledge.
Davis, S.; Sabol, S. 1998: The Importance of Being Ethnic: Minorities in Post-Soviet States – the Case of Russians in Kazakstan. *Nationalities Papers* 26:473–491.
Dietz, B. 1996: Rückwanderung in eine fremde Gesellschaft. Zur sozialen Integration rußlanddeutscher Aussiedler in der Bundesrepublik Deutschland. In: I. Graudenz und R. Römhild (Hrsg.), *Forschungsfeld Aussiedler. Ansichten aus Deutschland*. Frankfurt/M.: Peter Lang. S. 123–137.
Diener, A. C. 2004: *Homeland Conceptions and Ethnic Integration among Kazakhstan's Germans and Koreans*. Lewiston: E. Mellen Press.
Diener, A. C. 2006: Homeland as Social Construct: Territorialization among Kazakhstan's Germans and Koreans. *Nationalities Papers* 34:201–235.
Diener, A. C. 2009: *One Homeland or Two? The Nationalization and Transnationalization of Mongolia's Kazakhs*. Stanford: Stanford University Press.
Dorigo, G.; Tobler, W. 1983: Push-Pull Migration Laws. *Annals of the Association of American Geographers* 73:1–17.
Eisfeld, A. 1999: *Die Russlanddeutschen*. München: Langen München.
Ferguson, J. 1999: *Expectations of Modernity. Myths and Meanings of Urban Life on the Zambian Copperbelt*. Berkely u. a.: University of California Press.
Finke, P. 2001: Kasachstan und Kirgizstan im 20. Jahrhundert: Tradition und Wandel. In: P. Finke und M. Sancak (Hrsg.), *Zwischen Markt- und Mangelwirtschaft. Berichte eines Feldforschungsaufenthaltes im ländlichen Kasachstan und Kirgizstan im Jahre 1999*. Almaty: Friedrich-Ebert-Stiftung, S. 10–15.

Finke, P.; Sancak, M. 2005: Migration and Risk Taking. A Case Study from Kazakstan. In: L. Trager (ed.), *Migration and Economy: Global and Local Dynamics*. Walnut Creek: AltaMira Press, pp. 127–162.

Flynn, M. 2007: Reconstructing 'Home/lands' in the Russian Federation: Migrant-Centred Perspectives of Displacement and Resettlement. *Journal of Ethnic and Migration Studies* 33:461–481.

Fog Olwig, K. 2003: 'Transnational' Socio-Cultural Systems and Ethnographic Research. Views from an Extended Field Site. *International Migration Review* 37:787–811.

Fog Olwig, K.; Sorenson, N. N. 2002: Mobile Livelihoods: Making a Living in the World. In: idem (eds.), *Work and Migration: Life and Livelihoods in a Globalizing World*. London: Routledge, pp. 1–20.

Hall, S. 1990: Cultural Identity and Diaspora. In: J. Rutherford (ed.), *Identity: Community, Culture, Difference*. London: Lawrence & Wishart, pp. 222–237.

Hirsch, F. 2005: *Empire of Nations. Ethnographic Knowledge and the Making of the Soviet Union*. Ithaca: Cornell University Press.

Info-Dienst Deutsche Aussiedler. Zahlen, Daten, Fakten. 2001. Bundesministerium des Inneren, Vol. 110.

Ingenhorst, H. 1997: *Die Rußlanddeutschen zwischen Tradtition und Moderne*. Frankfurt/M.: Campus.

Jones Luong, P. 2004: Conclusion: Central Asia's Contribution to Theories of the State. In: P. Jones Luong (eds.), *The Transformation of Central Asia: States and Societies from Soviet Rule to Independence*. Ithaca: Cornell University Press, pp. 271–281.

Linde, C. 1993: *Life Stories. The Creation of Coherence*. New York: Oxford University Press.

King, R.; Skeldon, R. 2010: 'Mind the Gap' Integrating Approaches to Internal and International Migration. *Journal of Ethnic and Migration Studies* 36:1619–1646.

Marx, K.; Engels, F. 2009(1848): *Manifest der Kommunistischen Partei*. Zittau.

Miller, R. L. 2000: *Researching Life Stories and Family Histories*. London: Sage.

Mitchell, T. 1991: The Limits of the State: Beyond Statist Approaches and their Critics. *The American Political Science Review* 85:77–96.

Peyrouse, S. 2007: Nationhood and the Minority Question in Central Asia. The Russians in Kazakhstan. *Europe-Asia Studies* 59:481–501.

Pfister-Heckmann, H. 1998: *Sehnsucht Heimat? Die Rußlanddeutschen im niedersächsischen Landkreis Cloppenburg*. Münster: Waxmann.

Pries, L. 2008: Transnational Societal Spaces. Which Units of Analysis, Reference, and Measurement? In: L. Pries (ed.), *Rethinking Transnationalism: the Meso-Link of Organisations*. London: Routledge, pp. 1–20.

Radnitz, S. 2006: Weighing the Political and Economic Motivations for Migration in Post-Soviet Space: The Case of Uzbekistan. *Europe-Asia Studies* 58:653–677.

Riek, G.-A. 2000: *Die Migrationsmotive der Rußlanddeutschen: Eine Studie über die sozial-integrative, politische und ökonomische Lage in Rußland*. Stuttgart: Ibidem.

Römhild, R. 1998: *Die Macht des Ethnischen: Grenzfall Rußlanddeutsche. Perspektiven einer politischen Anthropologie*. Frankfurt/M.: Lang.

Sanders, R. 2009: *Why Did They Stay Behind? Identities, Memories, and Social Networks of Kazakhstani Germans in Taldykorgan/Kazakhstan*. Dissertation, Halle a. d. S.

Safran, W. 1991: Diasporas in Modern Societies. Myth of Homeland and Return. *Diaspora* 1:83–99.

Slezkine, Y. 1994: The USSR as a Communal Apartment, or How a Socialist State Promoted Ethnic Particularism. *Slavic Review* 53:414–452.

Stoll, F. 2007: *Kasachstandeutsche. Migrationsstrategien Kasachstandeutscher im Übergang von ethnischer zu transnationaler Migration – aus der Sicht von Kasachstan*. Kisslegg: STOLLVerlag.

Stuart, R. C.; Gregory, P. R. 1977: A Model of Soviet Rural-Urban Migration. *Economic Development and Cultural Change* 26:81–92.

Trager, L. (ed.) 2005: *Migration and Economy. Global and Local Dynamics*. Walnut Creek: AltaMira Press.
Yessenova, S. 1996: The Outflow of Minorities from the Post-Soviet State: The Case of Kazakhstan. *Nationalities Papers* 24:691–707.
Yessenova, S. 2005: "Routes and Roots" of Kazakh Identity: Urban Migration in Postsocialist Kazakhstan. *The Russian Review* 64:661–679.
Werner, C. A. 1997: *Household Networks, Ritual Exchange and Economic Change in Rural Kazakhstan*. Bloomington: Indiana University.
White, A. 2007: Internal Migration Trends in Soviet and Post-Soviet European Russia. *Europe-Asia Studies* 59:887–911.

Grounding Mobile Ideas: Kyrgyzstani NGO-leaders and the Notion of 'Knowledge Transfer' as a Source of Social Cohesion

Jeanne Féaux de la Croix
Asien-Orient Institut, Abteilung Ethnologie, Schloß Hohentübingen, Burgsteige 11,
D-72070 Tübingen

Abstract. Investigating activist responses to what is often thought of as 'instability' in Kyrgyzstan, this paper asks how notions such as democracy and knowledge transfer are propagated, transformed, localized, rejected or appropriated in Central Asia. Rather than seeing Kyrgyzstanis solely as the objects of donor policies, the article asks how influential actors in the NGO-sector actually negotiate categories of 'own' and 'foreign' ideas in order to construct what they consider the right 'mix' for peace and prosperity. Of particular concern here are the notion of spreading knowledge as ideology or inner wealth, and desirable relations between younger and older people. At one level, the sorting of ideas into binary categories looks something like a Latourian constitution. At another level however senior NGO activists routinely cancel out these divisions to create their vision of social change. I argue that such ongoing acts of structuring continuously posit donor organizations or international NGOs as extraneous to Kyrgyzstani society, while in fact such organizations should be viewed as an established and integral part of Kyrgyzstani society.
[development, knowledge transfer, activism, ideology, generations, Kyrgyzstan, NGOs]

Educated people now don't know their roots, they have a Western education. So they have two cultures in their bodies. They have been picked out from their own culture and trained elsewhere. Their body and mind fight with each other. But I'm whole in my body; there is no conflict in my mind. The problem is people fighting in their own mind. We have to force ourselves to overcome this. The West is not from Mars. . . . Kyrgyzstan will go its own separate way [K: jolu bölökchö]; it will be a combination of features. (Anarbek, Director of an agricultural NGO, 2008)[1]

Recent literature on mobility and identity in Central Asia has largely been built on the study of borders and migration, i. e. the complexities of people moving from one place to another (Finke and Sancak 2005, Reeves 2007 and 2011, Sahadeo 2012, Thorez 2005 amongst others). But Central Asia has also become a competitive place for supra-national agents who wish to participate in shaping the independent states and

---

[1] All names are pseudonyms, the identity of organizations has also been disguised. I here use the Library of Congress transliteration system, minus the diacritics. Kyrgyz terms are labelled (K), Russian terms as (R).

'new' societies that were supposed to emerge from the former Soviet republics. Just as influential as the current large-scale migrations of Central Asian citizens, are the modes and effects of 'foreign', 'imported' ideas and practices. Some of these are actively propagated by Kyrgyzstani NGOs, many of whom are supported by international donor organizations. These efforts are widely weighed up and discussed critically, no less so by actors such as Anarbek, whose livelihood in the NGO-sector depends on cooperating in such 'knowledge transfer' projects.

Studies of development efforts in the region have largely provided an institutional analysis that assumes mobile, global ideas being brought to Central Asian recipients (cf. Buxton 2011, Jones-Luong and Weinthal 2002, Roy 2002). While this to some extent mirrors the perception of all actors concerned of 'local' and 'global'/'international'/'Western' categories of people and ideas, this paper investigates how influential actors in the NGO-sector actually negotiate these categories in order to construct what they consider solid values and appropriate paths towards a more peaceful and prosperous Kyrgyzstan. I thereby show when these categories bear political force, in a positive or negative sense. What senior Kyrgyzstani development actors like Anarbek seek, is an appropriate, correct mixing of these categories. Rather than discussing Kyrgystanis as the *objects* of donor or state policies, or as reacting to them, I here engage with senior Kyrgyzstani NGO-workers as reflective actors and activists of a very particular kind.

Activists navigating a heaving sea of ideas and political 'instability'?

In order to understand the political force of the local/non-local categorizations, one needs to cast an eye over the heaving sea of competing influences, or what some have called a 'marketplace' of ideas and life-styles (Kirmse 2013:164).[2] Kirmse recognizes that the 'market' of possibilities is not a level playing field. I would go further in suggesting that to the actors discussed in this article, this is not a morally unambiguous space of 'consumer choices', but heavily inflected by the political and economic clout of the agents propagating certain ideas, as well as anguished reflections on what choices are positive for individuals and society in Kyrgyzstan. These more or less powerful actors include official and mediated influences by powerful states such as Russia, China and the United States, as well as the personal projects of Kyrgyzstani politicians and businessmen.

In the Kyrgyz context the 'travel' of new ideas and practices is further shaped by high levels of rural, urban and transnational mobility. Large donors include UN agencies, the Aga Khan Development Network and a wide range of bilateral donor agencies and faith-based organizations such as the Fethulla Gülen movement (Balci 2003,

---

[2] Such an idea of the process of globalization or cultural mixing has been put forward elsewhere, for example in conceiving of the nineteenth century urban Indian religious landscape (Green 2011).

Jailobaeva 2011). All these projects of influence come to bear among historically-rooted notions of national self and otherness/foreignness shaped by the Soviet experience. All these actors pursue their ends in a climate of – by Central Asian standards – permissive politics. Unless they are religious missions of various ilk, few international actors are actively discouraged from putting in their oar. Depending on the political moment, this can look like a canny political balancing act of the government in playing off the great powers against each other and reaping bilateral aid – or as bowing to greater powers, without being able to make a choice. Because of the high level of dependency on such donors and their consequent influence on legislation and economic decisions, Kyrgyzstan has been called a 'globalized protectorate' (Pétric 2005).

Kyrgystani citizens tend to worry about the literal survival of the country: will it be torn apart, one way or the other? Will it be 'sold off' by the rapacious political elite? People also worry about the number of competing missions, Muslim and otherwise, bringing the 'wrong kind of religion', radicalizing and dividing the country (McBrien and Pelkmans 2008:99). Rumours abound on China's supposed tactics in gaining a hold over Kyrgyzstan: perhaps the cheap Chinese-made toys in the bazaar are poisoned? Suspicion of Chinese products sometimes comes paired with the claim that China is actually afraid of the Kyrgyz (as an ethnicity rather than a state), because the Kyrgyz had a powerful empire long ago, and might become a threat again. Since the late 2000s, and especially since the 2010 violence between Kyrgyz and Uzbeks in the South of the country, a significant rise in ethno-nationalist sentiment, particularly on the part of the Kyrgyz titular nationality, signals this sense of beleaguerement.[3] Not incidentally, both the sense of beleaguerment and nationalist sentiment has grown alongside the volume of people seeking work and a future abroad. Who will be left in the country, people worry, if all the brightest and best, as well as ordinary householders leave the country? Those who gain a liveable wage elsewhere, might even chose to renounce their Kyrgyz citizenship in return for a Russian passport. Despite widespread discriminatory practices by e. g. the Russian police, Putin enjoys a good reputation as a legitimate leader who provides a sense of national pride, order and international clout. In other terms however, Russia is rarely evoked as a model for desirable social change.[4]

It is in this heaving, restless political context often characterized as 'instable', that people like Anarbek attempt to put forward models for changing society, to successfully navigate pulls in different directions.[5] Despite the clamour of initiatives, the per-

---

[3] Kalb and others have analysed this search for national or ethnic pride as a defensive move in the face of neoliberal shock therapies that have multiplied social inequalities (Kalb 2005).
[4] Even members of the dwindling ethnic Russian minority tend to have ambivalent relationship to their so-called 'homeland'.
[5] One should be careful in taking the idea of Kyrgyzstan as essentially 'unstable' and other countries as 'stable' at face value: notions of stability and instability are heavily politicized and manipulated for different interests in the region.

ceived insecurities feel to many like 'treading water' rather than any kind of opening. Senior NGO-activists like Anarbek see theirs as a heavy responsibility: not only for their own happiness and peace of mind, but as civic leaders. The metaphor of commercial offers and 'shopping' for ideas does not adequately convey the moral weight of such decisions, the sense of precariousness and urgency that actors like Anarbek feel. This article highlights some varieties of what this socially active intelligentsia strive for in Kyrgyzstan. The concrete case studies of how globalizing concepts 'travel' here are also intensely personal answers to a sense of social unease.

In discussing the 'transfer' of ideas, I focus on relatively successful and authoritative figures in the NGO-sphere, who have been able to shape their organization's program with a degree of independence.[6] These actors are also of particular interest because they consider themselves to be part of the educational elite, are of an age and standing to wield a degree of political force with their voice, if they so wish. But they are also interstitial actors, fluent and at home in the language of international development aims, the habitus of cosmopolitan civic activists, development bureaucrats and the techniques of reporting on projects. While these are authoritative people in one sense, yet they are in-between figures in another sense: the actors introduced below all came of age in the Soviet era, many already embarking on the beginnings of a career in the Soviet era. Yet that experience is rarely articulated as beneficial or valuable to their current work. Their negotiations of the crowded field of persuasion, and sometimes fleeting support, are nevertheless also conclusions drawn from this varied life-experience.

The paper asks how notions such as democracy and knowledge transfer are propagated, transformed, adapted, localized, rejected or appropriated in Central Asia. Elsewhere I have focused on the young 'trainers' employed by people like Anarbek to convey the ideas they support, and the *'treningi'* methods they use to persuade Kyrgyzstani audiences (Féaux de la Croix 2013). This article looks at the convictions and choices made by their managers, the Kyrgyzstani leaders and shapers of the NGO-landscape. Without exception, I encountered a group of people that actively reflected on their social role, the degree of their influence and who eloquently articulated the struggles and convictions they tried to work by. The NGO-leaders who shared their life-histories and goals with me were long-term urban residents in the capital Bishkek or the regional capital Jalalabad. They were all from a professional or academic background e. g. former economists, school teachers and university lecturers. Despite the instability of employment in the NGO-sector, they had all been successful in establishing themselves as professionals in the field, running country offices of international NGOs or establishing their own organization and funding streams. I conducted extensive (frequently several) semi-structured interviews with such actors in the context of a wider research project on age relations and knowledge transfer exercises in Kyrgyzstan. Be-

---

[6] I discuss degrees of NGO workers' agency, and in how far their financial dependence forces acquiescence to donor ideas in more detail below.

low, I draw on conversations between 2007 and 2012 with twenty-two such actors, out of a pool of 71 formal interviews and many more informal conversations and forms of participant-observation that included taking part in training sessions for NGO-workers and editing grant applications.[7]

Research encounters are also political encounters, a fact that became eminently obvious in the course of this study. The relationship of development work and scholarship is a complicated one: on the one hand we find many similarities in the background of employees, methodologies and vocabulary of these two fields, such as writing 'grant proposals' and 'reports'. Indeed, in the role of 'consultants' individuals frequently move between the two spheres. On the one hand, this usually makes initial access to and communication with development actors easy. On the other hand, communication may be more closely guarded, since scholarly commentary can be potentially damaging to individuals and organizations, as the development anthropologist Mosse found in a litigation case (Mosse 2006). There is a degree of mutual critique, even suspicion between the two 'camps': development actors sometimes regard scholars as the proverbially useless 'ivory tower' thinkers, whose funding could be more immediately used to alleviate suffering. Scholars meanwhile see their critical point of view as essential, and the development sphere as often implicated in morally dubious projects and frameworks (Yarrow 2008). The tensions between these positions often came to light obliquely, in the conversations elaborated below.

As I will demonstrate below, the NGO managers here *both* hold a politically and morally weighted model of their relationship with donors in mind, *as well as* holding much more differentiated views on the sources of moulding a positive future in Kyrgyzstan. As Ferguson (2006) notes, 'global' and 'local' here function as opposite ends of a scale, each valued in its own way. How do Kyrgyzstani development workers make sense of these, how do they manage their complexities in striving for what they often describe as a 'third' or own way towards a thriving future in Kyrgyzstan?

One influential thinker on the practice of upholding binaries such as nature and society, or people and things, is Bruno Latour. While much can be said of his 1993 polemic '*We have never been modern*', I adopt a Latourian perspective here for more limited aims than those he proposes. Latour argues that people believing themselves to be modern adhere to a 'constitution' that firmly purifies, divides the natural from the social, the human from the non-human, the traditional from the modern. However, they do so in order to then unconsciously maximize mixings of all kind: conceptual, technological, moral. Moderns only differ from premoderns not in what they do,

---

[7] This research was supported by the Carnegie Trust for the Universities of Scotland, the University of St. Andrews, as well as a research fellowship at Zentrum Moderner Orient funded by the German Bundesministerium für Bildung und Forschung (funding code 01UG0713). I would also like to thank the participants of the 2012 Zurich workshop on mobility in Central Asia for their helpful questions. The author is of course fully responsible for the content of this publication.

but what they *say* they do: they do not acknowledge mixings, even as they create more and more of them (Latour 1993:112). He argues further:

> *'the idea of an identical repetition of the past and that of a radical rupture with any past are two symmetrical results of a single conception of time. We cannot return to the past, to tradition, to repetition, because these great immobile domains are the inverted image of the earth that is no longer promised to us today: progress, permanent revolution, modernization, forward flight.'*

It is the act of sorting that creates the timing, not vice versa (Latour 1993:76). Similarly, the 'local' and the 'global' have no content except as each other's opposite. They do not admit any in-betweens, although in fact, almost everything is in-between (Latour 1993:123). This view of the work of creating and shifting categories is useful for examining the real-life mixings that result from such ideal binaries of identity and mobility as the ones that Anarbek feels are *'fighting in people's minds'* – even though, as he puts it, the West is not a totally different planet.

In the conversations below, we are able to trace how the actual practice of mixing goes together with efforts to create and keep apart clear categories of 'local' and 'foreign'. The structuring of the NGO-sector and work environment in development is itself thoroughly structured by such notions. One thing that such a structuring does is to continuously posit donor organizations or international NGOs as somehow extraneous to Kyrgyzstani society, as if they would somehow one day 'lift off' and leave some kind of pure 'inside' Kyrgyzstan behind. However, it makes much more sense to see NGOs as an established and integral part of Kyrgyzstani society, with or without the label 'international'.[8] In the following discussion, I focus on topics of particular concern among NGO-leaders that high-lighted choices in adopting, adapting, rejecting 'local' or 'foreign' ideas: the notion of spreading knowledge as a solution to societal ills such as injustice and poverty, and desirable relations between younger and older people.

Concepts and Practices of 'Knowledge Transfer'

Knowledge as a basis for economic growth in 'knowledge societies' emerged as an academic hypothesis from the 1960s, that then gradually found advocates in institutions such as the OECD. The digital and online revolution further spurred ideals of the freedom of information (now enshrined in a number of constitutions) and goals of

---

[8] I do not mean to thereby neglect the unequal power relations between these 'partners' and donors, but to emphasize that this 'state of exception' is unlikely to be 'left behind' by developed 'normality' in Kyrgyzstan, or indeed many other relatively impoverished countries. One could equally question the degree of national sovereignty of EU-states or states with multiple business and aid involvement abroad.

bridging the 'global digital divide'. A number of countries such as Singapore adopted this notion of knowledge (academic and creative industries, IT-software development etc.) as a motor of economic development. By 1999, the World Bank was advocating its program as 'Knowledge for Development' (Hornidge 2012:397). Transporting or giving access to knowledge came to be seen as a powerful form of social action. As philosophers and anthropologists have long pointed out, knowledge however only exists as a part of a power-inflected relationship, and 'quality' of a person (Foucault 1972, Boyer 2005, Harris 2007). Hobart (1993) has highlighted knowledge as a judgmental term that is only meaningful in relation to 'ignorance': the notion of knowledge transfer thus constructs groups and societies bathed in the light of knowledge as opposed to those who remain in the dark. Development efforts to 'transfer knowledge' acknowledge what some theories of globalization tend to obfuscate: precisely this channel-bound, person-bound character of having or not having knowledge, and the need for active outreach, rather than celebrating technology distributed through equalizing 'networks' as a facilitator in itself (Tsing 2000, Harvey 2007).

In practice, techniques for bridging 'gaps' in knowledge in order to overcome poverty and inequality have included a handful of measures in Kyrgyzstan, as elsewhere. Some select individuals, especially government actors or NGO-leaders may be invited to be schooled in 'best practices' abroad or visited by foreign experts. But the most widespread and rather standardized tool is the *trening* (Russified version of the English 'training'): pre-fabricated units of training modules exist for any imaginable subject: on communal water management, child nutrition, fund-raising skills. Such modules are usually developed elsewhere in the world and then 'adapted' to various extents, translated in the literal and also metaphoric sense by people like Anarbek. The *trening* format is a voluntary seminar held, often in rural locations, by NGO-employees over the course of a couple of hours or days. They employ quite different pedagogic tactics to those familiar from school, home or work-place: open discussion in mixed groups, brainstorming, role play or board games. Vocabulary that has apparently become familiar in areas with a strong NGO-presence, includes the *aisbreker* (ice-breaker) and the *kofibrek* (coffee-break: this actually involves a lot of tea). These small examples point to a process that looks like colonization, transplanting a term and associated practice wholesale from one context to another. Certainly in the case of knowledge transfer exercises such as the *trening* model described above, large amounts of money facilitate the 'travel' of ideas from 'elsewhere'. As imagined by donors, this process and relationship might be summed up as neat 'tutelage': instruction, coaching, sponsorship, guidance from a dominating position that leaves 'learners' little choice in determining content. However, as we will see, Kyrgyzstani NGO-leaders themselves are not at all uncritical of such tutelage, nor do they perceive themselves as unable to adjust the thrust of ideas. Indeed, for many Kyrgyzstani citizens, judging an idea like democracy as 'ours' or not, as culturally and historically alien or familiar, proven and valued is one important criteria for judging ideas on the direction Kyrgyz citizens should take.

Managing relationships between us and them

In conversations I often attempted to ascertain how NGO-workers felt about the influence of donor funding and policy. Could their priorities perhaps deflect what would be most useful for Kyrgyzstani society? Immersed in such dependencies themselves, respondents tended to reply very pragmatically on this sensitive point, commenting that *'Well, you always have to put the key words in applications, that's true'* (BKh, 14. 3. 2012) or noting that *'there is so much to be done, you could work on so many issues. So what the donors suggest is fine, there is always a need'* (SI, 15. 3. 2012) As we will see below, there can indeed be much lee-way in matching up 'foreign' and 'own' ideas and aims, without the disjunctures necessarily becoming apparent to either party. We find here examples of what Anna Tsing calls zones of 'sticky engagements'. Rather than being universal abstracts, notions like 'justice' work to bridge divides by positing that no gap in fact exists, thus bringing very different actors into alliance, for example in the environmental movement (Tsing 2005:6–7). The most common way of talking about bringing new ideas to Kyrgyzstan was as 'adaptation': re-interpreting to a greater or lesser degree, what e. g. democracy might best look like in Kyrgyzstan.

Saikal is in her mid-fourties and heads an organization with a dozen employees, concerned with fostering and recovering folk knowledge on the environment, for example on horse training and medicinal plants. This project is financially supported by a private American foundation and researches these topics, organizes training sessions and publications. Saikal previously worked for a number of NGOs and was then known as a particularly effective *trener*. She commented on the need to adapt training methods to the Kyrgyzstani context:

> '*I didn't want to introduce the training with everyone going 'my name is Ömürbek Ata and it starts with an Ö, like this and this vegetable'...'You can do these modules with fifteen-year olds or with NGO leaders, but for authoritative people* (chong adamdar) *you need to adapt them.'...'So I changed how I started the seminar, I talked about how* 'we all love the mountain pastures, go there after the 15th of May'... *The ideal of the seminar is to treat everyone the same, but in practice, this doesn't work. You have to show respect to elders, call them 'uncle' etc. The modules aren't adapted at all to Kyrgyz culture, it would be more appropriate for the most senior local person in the seminar group to introduce it*'. (KA, 4. 4. 2011)

While in some instances, Saikal communicated her discomfort to the funding organization, at other points she decided to work in ways she considered appropriate, without seeking the approval of her employers and simply keeping such details to herself: she felt fully justified in pursing training in a way that she felt realized the organizations goals.

But assessments of the usefulness of methods brought to Kyrgyzstan could also go in another direction. Aida, a former teacher and senior NGO-worker is engaged in projects to strengthen civil society in the south of Kyrgyzstan. I asked what she thought of Soviet forms of knowledge, since some in Kyrgyzstan argued it was no longer useful.

> *'After the 80s, the level of education fell. Society didn't develop much. ... Now teachers are using old methods, but children's biology and consciousness isn't adequate for these methods. I went to America in 2010, saw lots of different teaching methods, like choosing your courses according to your preferences. We have to reform the syllabus, adapt it to the children, otherwise they just get tired of school and are prepared really badly.'*
> (CJ, 13. 3. 2012)

She noted that Soviet teaching methods had been appropriate to its time, but was no longer fitting in children's current situation. I asked further what she thought of so many people complaining that young people no longer respect elders. She responded: '*I think it's a political problem. Because of the democracy thing: we don't fully understand it. People don't understand children's and parents' rights.*' She thought the democracy idea was interpreted as a free-for-all, and then returned to her concern for the drop in the quality of education. Perhaps surprisingly, younger people's attitude and behavior towards their elders in particular raises quite a lot of outraged social commentary and passion.[9] The judgments we find below on this situation are clearly associated with certain trends of capitalism and democracy, as introduced and practiced currently in Kyrgyzstan.

Relations between younger and older people as an index of social cohesion and morality

Cholpon has long headed the local branch of an international NGO that is particularly concerned with the fate of pensioners. Before taking on this work, she had been among the first generation of Kyrgyz language teachers for Peace Corps volunteers. Unsurprisingly, she has a lot to say about the way the position of older people in society has declined.

> '*Ten, fifteen years ago the saying 'we respect our elders' was true, whether they were Kyrgyz or not. Teachers in villages used to be very respected. Now the young just care about money.'...'we say we respect elders, but no one can say what that means, concretely. The most simple example: offering someone a seat in the bus or marshrutka* [young people don't always get up for older people anymore]'.
> (BE 28. 3. 11)

---

[9] It should be said that to some degree, complaints about the declining valour of youth are a staple in human history. It seems however a particularly painfully felt issue currently in Kyrgyzstan. The topic was also encouraged by the line of conversation I took, being particularly interested in age dynamics.

She partially blamed the state for not instilling respect in elders, for example by not demonstrating respect through the provision of adequate pensions. She added that it was not just about money, that there was *spiritual* respect that needed to be shown, a depth of feeling. Having volunteered in the Komsomol, and been sent to elderly people to help with the housework, she also considered this lack of respect and care a capitalist problem: people rushing about to earn a good living, not having time for each other, and yet not being taught the right kind of discipline.

Aida, working in the South of the country, also saw a real change in the moral, inner wealth of the soul (R: *dukhovnii bogatstvo*) among young people. She worried about young folk's attention being taken up by email and texting, rather than reading novels and going to the theatre, as she had done in her youth. She also blamed these preoccupations for a new lack of communication between parents and children. It became clear that Saikal had also thought much on this issue. When we discussed the difficulties young trainers face in communicating with a mixed, sometimes entirely older audience, she also noted relations changing for the worse. '*Previously, young people learnt about keeping livestock, about using healing herbs and so on from their elders: each needed the other.*' She added that in Soviet times, young people were taught to honor older generations for '*building collectivization for them, for defending them in the Great Patriotic War*', and so giving them a reason to respect them. '*But now youth are thinking: was collectivization good? Did we have to participate in the war? Should I respect elders for this?*'

Neither of these senior social activists rejects technologies such as email, or the arrival of a new kind of political economy after Communism wholesale. Indeed, they are all actively engaged in fostering particular aspects of social life that they found lacking in the late Soviet period, and have enrolled in projects funded from abroad, in order to pursue their ideas, as well as making a living. Yet they clearly differentiate the uses, and social costs of change – in the case of Cholpon, new social media and technologies. In all three examples, the narratives see a very definite break (á la Latour) of 'then' (Saikal's "previously", Aida's youth, Cholpon's Soviet era) and 'now'. But looking closer, these divisions are actually combinations of a time when life was 'traditional' and Kyrgyz, with times that were overwhelmingly marked by Soviet modernization efforts (Komsomol activism, students going to the theatre). Yet at the same time, these actors use thoroughly non-traditional means for pursuing goals of preserving, re-shaping, maintaining past practices (of different pasts) that they consider valuable. The actors profiled here were neither unaware of such combinations, nor did they think these particularly problematic, on the whole.[10] The most important loss reflected in the conversation excerpts above, is the loss of 'inner wealth', a wisdom of the heart and spiritual values. This was a theme that frequently recurred, particularly among this

---

[10] Compare however Saikal's critique of typical introduction's to trening sessions, which are insensitive to locally respectful forms of communication (page 7). Details such as these were certainly vigorously contested, rather than the overall principles.

generation of socially engaged intellectuals. And they drew very particular, different consequences from this concern. Saikal was particularly eloquent on this subject.

Knowledge transfer as a way to a unifying *ideologiya* and *inner wealth*?

According to Saikal, the Kyrgyz were polytheists and Tengrianists until the 8th century. She describes Islam first entering softly, then with bloodshed. She felt strongly that much had been lost:

> '*The Kyrgyz used to respect nature, then lost that connection. Young farmers say their wives don't want to come to the mountain pastures because they are afraid* ('What if I'm ill? …and my face will get all brown!'). *Knowing 'ecological philosophy', rituals and so on would help them feel better and encourage them to go to the pastures.'* …'*I'm worried that I can't transmit a proper Kyrgyz way of life to my children: it's all muddled with other things in my head. Every generation receives less percent of* [the knowledge that existed, people's wisdom] *before.*' (KA, 4. 4. 2011)

Saikal had lately been really embarrassed when her teenage son made a toast that sounded completely ridiculous, because of his awkward Kyrgyz. She tried to explain to her son that without understanding his Kyrgyz roots, '*you are a slave, … without knowing yourself, who are you? You are a hybrid* [of many influences]: *you don't have any strength, no core* (paraphrased KA 4. 4. 11). She then resolved to take him to the high pastures, to '*make his Kyrgyz blood respond*', as she put it and to help him orientate himself. Lately her son had met uneducated, patriotic Kyrgyz from the countryside at university: this had made him feel small, she said. But now he asserted '*I am a kochevnik* [R: nomad]'. Saikal commented that perhaps this was a '*primitive philosophy, but for now it is helping* [my] *son, giving him strength.*' When I asked after the dangers of nationalism, Saikal judged this as way to fill a vacuum, like in all other post-soviet societies.

To Saikal, knowledge of the Kyrgyz language, identifying oneself as a nomad *in the blood*, is a source of strength and a guiding principle. Elsewhere, Murzakulova and Schoeberlein have identified the need for a unifying *ideologiya* as one of the big themes of public discussion in contemporary Kyrgyzstan (2009: 1243).[11] The concern expressed here by NGO actors is similarly pursued by politician's and government efforts to devise a national ideology. They shared, and sometimes spear-headed, public de-

---

[11] There was a notable absence of talk of Islam as a potentially useful ideology among my respondents in NGOs, despite some of these practicing Islam quite intensively in their personal lives. Indeed, though quite popular as a means of solving some of the problems of lacking 'inner wealth' described by my respondents, Islam is viewed with a lot of suspicion in the educated elite, particularly by older generations. Indeed, some conceive of their activities as trying to establish a bulwark, an alternative to Islamic ideologies.

mands in the media for an *ideologiya* that unites people and directs their efforts, as well as those of the government.[12] One university lecturer, participating at a conference on Soviet legacies, spoke enthusiastically about the need for ideology. When I asked her in the *kofibrek* about the difference between ideology and identity, she reflected for a moment, and then decided there was none. Since the 1990s there have been a series of attempts to cultivate ideologies, such as former president Akaev's celebration of the epic hero Manas and his 'Seven Principles', which continue to be taught at schools. None of these efforts were however considered successful in acting as a focal point for moral education and national unity. The felt urgency of establishing such an ideology of consensus can be understood in relation to a regional context where more authoritarian neighbours such as Karimov's regime in Uzbekistan have proclaimed what authentic national identity is about, or celebrate 20-year national development plans, as in Kazakhstan. In other words, here is a goal of 'knowledge transfer', both from the 'West' and from the 'past', that is unlikely to meet with approval by Saikal's liberal American funders.

As we saw earlier, respondents also detected a lack of *duxhovnost'* (R: soulfulness, humane-ness, morality. This is sometimes translated into Kyrgyz as *ichki bailygy*). Like Anarbek, Saikal and her colleagues found themselves trying to sort out which bits of the past should be preserved, reconstructed or which offers or pressures from 'outside' should be heeded. They saw this as a means of building individual and collective 'inner wealth': NGOs were thought to play an important part as a forum for communicating and preserving morality for a 'lost generation'. Interestingly, despite common emphasis on many things being better in the Soviet era, none of the organizations I encountered attempt to foster knowledge of the Soviet past, or re-establish Soviet practices.[13] Saikal's organization was also exceptional in aiming to rediscover practical skills. When I suggested this pragmatic way of using the past to other NGO employees, this seemed a very novel idea, even though they might be enthusiastic about rediscovering Kyrgyz history – as identity and ideology. The need for this kind of *patriotizm* (this currently includes a spectrum of values ranging from a sense of civic duty and responsibility, national pride to the most strident ethnic nationalism) was also often related to working on developing people's 'consciousness' or 'awareness' (K: *ang sezim*), unity (K: *birimdik*) or solidarity. Sometimes my respondents also saw their job as changing the current '*mentalitet*' of 'eating money', for example. Rather amazingly to me, all these qualities were spoken of as things that could be achieved, or at least attempted, through the *trening* model.

More broadly, most development workers voiced a firm conviction that better education (R: *obrazovanie*) and upbringing (R: *vospitanie*) would lead to peace and prosper-

---

[12] One NGO was in fact instructed to teach ministry employees Kyrgyz traditions, in order to foster patriotism.
[13] A Kyrgyz Communist Party does exist, but does not command a large following.

ity. For example, the Uzbek leaders of a tiny NGO in Jalalabad, a city that had recently experienced the burning of dozens of Uzbek-owned restaurants and businesses, spoke to me of this. Their dogged, yet woefully under-funded organization advertises writing competitions and gives away books in an attempt to encourage school children to read. The emphasis on education to some extent reflects both the social background of NGO personnel, including many former teachers in the older generation. The conviction is also mirrored and supported by the current international policy of eradicating social ills through 'knowledge transfer' – thus fitting like a hand in a glove to Soviet-inspired reform efforts by a certain generation of Kyrgyzstani activists.[14] But the emphasis on education also reflects a wider social faith in education as a means of improvement: despite widespread corruption and the concurrently low market value of degrees, Kyrgyzstani universities take in up to 70 % of university-age citizens. At the same time, the emphasis on the need for knowledge is felt urgently in a context of catastrophically declining rates of school enrollment and literacy, with a growing, deskilled migrant labour force keeping the country afloat (DeYoung 2010).

In the paragraphs above, knowledge covers an enormous range of bases and purposes: as education, practical skills, source of morality and proper conduct towards elders, ideology and source of social cohesion or peace. This semantically wide field of 'knowledge' seems a good example of Tsing's 'universals': notions that look like everyone can agree on them, that function as bridge-builders, and yet disaggregate into quite different understandings, under closer inspection. Such bridge-building is clearly going on to mutual satisfaction between Saikal's conceptions and that of the American donor, while the small Uzbek organization fostering enjoyment of education in Jalalabad is being left out of such 'sticky engagements'. We can separate out some of the assumptions about propagating new, or reviving old ideas.

People's assumptions about the uses of knowledge to some extent follow some of the theories discussed above. Knowledge turns up firstly, as 'stuff', as valuable information that can be passed on, as in the knowledge transfer doctrine. Secondly, it operates in Saikal's conception as a form of dormant, tacit knowledge that can be woken through activities such as visiting the high pastures, to allow it to 'speak' to, stir people's Kyrgyz blood. Such knowledge however also needs to be made explicit, verbalized, preserved and handed on, for example by publishing books.[15] To some extent,

---

[14] Efforts to share knowledge are to some extent undermined by the language barriers and orientation of NGOs to satisfy donor demands, in the first instance. This is evident in the strong representation of information on such organizations on the internet in English, with a much weaker knowledge base provided in Russian or Kyrgyz. More generally, the development sector is strewn with acronyms, insider knowledge that is supposed to facilitate communication between like-minded organizations, but creates barriers to ordinary Kyrgyz citizens.

[15] We may have here a classic example of James Scott's distinction between *techne* (planning-type, codified knowledge) and *metis*, the improvisation and subtlety of human interaction necessary to achieve what e. g. project programme's demand (Scott 1998: 62).

the training model reflects an assumption that teaching is about 'lifting the lid and pouring knowledge in'. Such a version of learning and knowledge is evident in the more or less universal 'module' concept, whose content is slightly adapted to new contexts. However, the training model also puts forward the importance of face-to-face contact, of relationships as crucial channels of knowledge transfer. As mentioned above, a number of philosophers and anthropologists have pointed to this phenomenon. Indeed, the new profession of 'knowledge management' and talk of institutional memory has spawned a whole new industry based on this premise, it seems. Rather than knowledge 'parcels' being able to move independently, arriving like unmanned space-crafts, knowledge here appears as fundamentally linked to persons. Harvey has called this essentially socially characteristic of knowledge 'sticky': like oil, it does not move particularly easily around the 'channels' built for it (Harvey 2007).

As we can see in the case of the training model unintentionally introducing by-the-way notions such as the *kofibrek* and *aisbreker* to colloquial language, ideas rarely if ever travel in isolation, in a disembedded or disembodied manner. Thus the third way that knowledge is understood by respondents here, is as a form of power: hence the wide range of social goals that better knowledge, be it in the form of ideology or practical skills, is hoped to achieve. This fluidity in conception and practice sits alongside moves to separate out classes of knowledge under labels such as 'traditional' or 'foreign'. In this sense, this case study encounters a classic Latourian 'modern' constitution that allows for mixings that are rhetorically strenuously separated out

Conclusion

Anna Tsing has described movement as travel, but also reminds us that it can be a mental impulse of desire or aversion. Hence the expression 'to be moved'. She also connects this notion of mobility to mobilization, which she argues requires friction (Tsing 2005:213–14). It became evident in the conversations with senior development activists described here, that the notions of being moved, of mobilization and of seeking and examining fresh impulses for their society, was a strong current in their lives.

This article has taken a novel approach to the topic of mobility in Central Asia by addressing not the physical movement of people, but notions of 'external' and 'internal' ideas that Kyrgyzstanis come into contact with, accept, reject, modify or reproduce. The examination focused on how senior staff in non-governmental organizations negotiate what they consider to be most beneficial to their society. Anarbek, Cholpon, Saikal and Aida all actively reflected and negotiated influences interpreted as 'own' or 'foreign'. Although on one level, such analytical distinctions remind one of the modern 'constitution' invoked by Latour, and the predilection by 'moderns' to recognize pure forms while enabling lots of mixing, there are other levels these actors discussed, that do not fit this model. One can see the struggles Anarbek and his colleagues go through as a serious play (more or less successful) with sameness and difference. These modestly influential figures drew down from such absolute binaries as 'internally' and 'externally' generated ideas what they considered the right 'mix' to heal Kyrgyzstani society. In doing so, they weighed in the balance issues of sovereignty, of degrees of trust, accessibility and desirability. They clearly differentiated for example, 'good' and 'bad' traditions, as when Aida praises Soviet measures to assure respect for the elderly, while Cholpon does not consider Soviet pedagogy worth reviving. The Soviet past is an excellent example in demonstrating the way 'pure' forms of ours/not ours allow Soviet experiences to selectively be included or excluded from the idea of desirable traditions.

I further demonstrated that knowledge transfer as a method, mainly propagated through the *trening* model, was not fundamentally questioned by this constituency. Rather, it is the content and concurrent goals of knowledge transfer that were at issue. As I highlighted in the case of Saikal's felt need for *ideologiya,* such a notion of the role of knowledge as the basis of national solidarity and identity co-habited tacitly and easily with conceiving knowledge as a set of practical skills to eradicate poverty and inequality.

In this research, I listened to an influential, familiar and yet analytically largely invisible group. The Kyrgyzstani citizens working in the hundreds of active NGOs in the country, need to be recognized as one of the central nodes of processing, translating, or – as they would have it – 'adapting' notions such as democracy or valuable knowledge to their society. In this sense, they are intermediaries as well as potentially influential political agents. Since in their work they do not fit the binaries of 'foreign' and 'local', 'donors', 'government' and 'the people', their crucial role as mediators and their own initiative have often escaped notice. Such a 'go-between' role might be considered as a kind of mobility in its own right.[16] However, such a concept replicates the assumption of two discreet worlds, which as I have shown, is a popular, yet highly selective way of viewing interactions. Just as NGO-leaders like Saikal have to shift back and forth in performing 'local-ness', so they switch back and forth between structures of pedagogy that on the one hand aim to foster equal exchange, and on the other, are embedded in hierarchies of knowledge.

---

[16] Indeed, conversations with informants were conducted in in Kyrgyz, Russian, English and even German: neat divisions of points of view or notions of homogeneity are clearly out of place here. Caroline Humphrey's discussion of Soviet concepts and critique of *kosmopolitanizm* are bound to resonate with people like Anarbek, Cholpon and their generation, but this is a topic for a different article (Humphrey 2004).

References

Balci, B. 2003: *Missionnaires de l'Islam en Asie centrale: Les écoles turques de Fethullah Gülen.* Maisonneuve and Larose: Paris.
Boyer, D. 2005. Revisiting the anthropology of knowledge. *Ethnos* 70(2):141–148.
Buxton, C. 2011: *The Struggle for Civil Society in Central Asia: crisis and transformation.* Kumarian Press: Stirling, VA.
DeYoung, A. 2010: University Experiences among Youth in Contemporary Kyrgyzstan. *Central Asian Survey* 29(4):421–434.
Féaux de la Croix, J. 2013 forthcoming: How to build a better future? Kyrgyzstani development workers and the 'knowledge transfer' strategy. *Central Asian Survey* 32(4):448–461.
Ferguson, J. 2006: *Global Shadows:Africa in the Neoliberal World Order.* Durham: Duke University Press.
Finke, P.; Sancak, M. 2005: Migration and Risk-Taking. A Case Study from Kazakstan. In: Trager, L. (ed.), *Migration and Economy. Global and Local Dynamics.* Walnut Creek (CA): Altamira, pp. 127–161.
Foucault, M. 1972: *Archaeology of Knowledge.* Pantheon: New York.
Green, N. 2011: *Bombay Islam: The Religious Economy of the West Indian Ocean, 1840–1915.* New York: Cambridge University Press.
Harris, M. 2007: *Ways of Knowing: anthropological approaches to crafting experience and learning.* Oxford: Berghahn Books.
Harvey, P. 2007: Arresting Mobility or Locating Expertise: "Globalisation" and the "Knowledge Society". In: M. E. Lien and M. Melhuus (eds.), *Holding Worlds Together: ethnographies of knowing an belonging.* New York and Oxford: Berghahn, pp. 163–183.
Hobart, M. (ed.) 1993: *An Anthropological Critique of Development: the Growth of Ignorance.* London: Routledge.
Hornidge, K. 2013: ‚Knowledge', ‚Knowledge Society' & ‚Knowledge for Development'. Studying Discourses of Knowledge in an International Context. In: R. Keller and I. Truschkat (eds.), *Methodologie und Praxis der Wissenssoziologischen Diskursanalyse.* VS Verlag für Sozialwissenschaften: Wiesbaden, pp. 397–424.
Jailobaeva, K. 2010: *The Return of the State to Development: The State, Donors, and NGOs in Post-Soviet Kyrgyzstan.* Unpublished PhD diss., University of Edinburgh.
Kalb, D. 2005: From Flows to Violence : Politics and Knowledge in the debates on globalization and empire. A*nthropological Theory* 5(2):176–204.
Kirmse, S. 2013: *Youth and Globalization in Central Asia: Everyday Life between Religion, Media, and International Donors.* Frankfurt and New York: Campus.
Latour, B. 1993: *We Have Never Been Modern.*: Cambridge, Massachusetts: Harvard University Press.
McBrien, J.; Pelkmans, M. 2008: Turning Marx on his Head: missionaries, 'extremists' and archaic secularists in post-soviet Kyrgyzstan. *Critique of Anthropology* 28(1):87–109.
Mosse, D. 2006: Anti-social anthropology? Objectivity, objection, and the ethnography of public policy and professional communities. *Journal of the Royal Anthropological Institute* 12:935–956.
Murzakulova, A.; Schoeberlein, J. 2009: The Invention of Legitimacy: Struggles in Kyrgyzstan to Craft an Effective Nation-State Ideology. *Europe-Asia Studies* 61(7):1229–1248.
Paasiaro, M. 2009: Home-grown strategies for greater agency: reassessing the outcome of civilsociety strengthening in post-Soviet Kyrgyzstan. *Central Asian Survey* 28(1):59–77.
Pétric, B. 2005: Post-Soviet Kyrgyzstan or the Birth of a Globalised Protectorate. *Central Asian Survey* 24(3):319–332.
Reeves, M. 2011: Introduction: contested trajectories and a dynamic approach to place. *Central Asian Survey* 30(3–4):307–330.

Reeves, M. 2008: *Border Work: An Ethnography of the State at its Limits in the Ferghana Valley.* Unpublished PhD thesis: University of Cambridge.

Roy, O. 2002: Soviet legacies and Western aid imperatives in new Central Asia. In: A. Sajoo (ed.), *Civil Society in the Muslim World.* London: I. B. Tauris, pp. 123–148.

Sahadeo, J. 2012: Soviet Blacks and Place Making in Leningrad and Moscow. *Slavic Review* 71 (2):331–358.

Thorez, J. 2005: *Flux et dynamiques spatiales en Asie centrale: géographie de la transformations post-soviétique.* Unpublished PhD thesis: l'université de Paris X-Nanterre.

Tsing, A. L. 2005: *Friction: an ethnography of global connection.* Princeton and Oxford: Princeton University Press.

Tsing, A. L. 2000: The Global Situation. *Cultural Anthropology* 15(3):327–360.

Weinthal, E.; Jones Luong, P. 2002: Environmental NGOs in Kazakhstan: democratic goals and non-democratic outcomes. In: S. Mendelson and J. Glenn (eds.), *The Power and Limits of NGOs.* New York: Columbia University Press, pp. 152–176.

Yarrow, T. 2008: Paired Opposites: Dualism in Development and Anthropology. *Critique of Anthropology* 28:426–445.

Ainuras Amerikanische Karriere – Räumliche und Soziale Mobilität einer jungen Kirgisin

Philipp Schröder
Institut für Asien- und Afrikawissenschaften, Humboldt Universität zu Berlin, Invalidenstrasse 118, D-10115 Berlin

Ainura's American Career: The Spatial and Social Mobility of a Young Kyrgyz Woman

Abstract. This article follows the life-story of Ainura, a Kyrgyz female in her late 20s, in order to discuss the intertwinement of spatial and social mobility in contemporary Kyrgyzstan. It sets off by describing how Ainura's decision to learn English as a teenage girl opened up relevant educational opportunities for her, all of which were sponsored by US civil-society engagement in Kyrgyzstan. Seizing these opportunities led Ainura from her rural home to obtaining a Master's degree from an American university. Along these waypoints and further into her time as an employee of different international organizations operating in Kyrgyzstan's capital Bishkek, the article traces both Ainura's professional development and the evolvement of her social relations. In particular, I depict how Ainura 'manages' her personal network's two most significant segments: the ties to her rural kin group and those to her urban friends with whom she shares a similar 'US-background'. These reveal that Ainura's longing for individual freedom and her social leverage, which she especially uses to subdue traditional expectations of a speedy marriage, are strongly related to her success as a young professional, i. e. as a potent earner and potential creditor for her extended kin group.
[youth, Kyrgyzstan, education, social network, gender]

Einleitung

„Hätte ich nicht Englisch gelernt, würde ich wohl immer noch in diesem Dorf wohnen und wäre mit Sicherheit schon lange verheiratet. Und alles was ich zwischendurch erlebt habe, hätte es dann nicht gegeben. Erstaunlich, oder? Aber ich war mir damals schon sicher, dass Englisch der einzige Weg aus dem Dorf war. Damit hat es angefangen."[1]

---

[1] Doppelte Anführungszeichen („") geben grundsätzlich Ainuras Aussagen wider. Im Gegensatz dazu sind einfache Anführungszeichen (,') entweder Literaturzitate oder Kommentare des Autors. *Kursiv* geschriebene Wörter sind, wenn nicht anders gekennzeichnet, aus dem Russischen übersetzt und nach dem Standard ALA-LC (American Library Association and Library of Congress) ohne diakritische Zeichen transkribiert.

Dies ist die autobiographische Zwischenbilanz einer jungen Kirgisin, Ainura.[2] Im Jahr 2008 ist Ainura 28 Jahre alt und arbeitet bei einer internationalen Organisation als lokale Fachkraft im Bereich Öffentlichkeitsarbeit. Sie wohnt zu dieser Zeit in einer Ein-Zimmer-Wohnung in einem Plattenbauviertel in Bischkek, der Hauptstadt der Republik Kirgistan.

Ainuras Zwischenbilanz berührt sämtliche Themen, die für diesen Beitrag relevant werden. Ainuras Verweis auf „das Dorf", gepaart mit der Tatsache, dass sie ihrer Arbeit in Bischkek nachgeht, deutet ihren ‚Migrationshintergrund' an. Ihre Vermutung, sie wäre beim Verbleib im Dorf sicherlich bereits verheiratet worden, eröffnet das Spannungsfeld zwischen Verwandtschaft, sozialem Druck und ‚agency'. Ainura stellt hier unzweideutig heraus, dass die Kenntnis der englischen Sprache ihr „Ausweg" aus dem Dorf war. Im persönlichen Rückblick auf ihre Lebensgeschichte sieht Ainura vor allem diese Sprachfähigkeiten als Schlüssel an für weitere internationale Bildungsoptionen und ihre damit verbundene berufliche wie soziale ‚Karriere'[3] in der Stadt.

Anhand von Ainuras Lebensgeschichte diskutiert dieser Aufsatz das Zusammenspiel zwischen räumlicher und sozialer Mobilität. Räumliche Mobilität verstehe ich dabei allgemein als Ortswechsel, was im Ainuras Fall sowohl interne wie internationale, temporäre und permanente Migration beinhaltet (Strasser 2009:18; Agadjanian et al. 2008). Unter sozialer Mobilität möchte ich, neben dem klassischen Verständnis von beruflichen Aufstiegschancen, auch den damit verbundenen Handlungs- und Verhandlungsspielraum eines Akteurs gegenüber den Erwartungen anderer Akteure verstehen.

In der Beschreibung der Konstituierung und Nutzung von Ainuras sozialem Netzwerk wird das Zusammenspiel dieser beiden Verständnisse von Mobilität in einem lokal-globalen, translokalen Kontext deutlich (Hermann & Röttger-Rössler 2003:3; Smith 2011:192; Pilkington et al. 2002). Situationen in denen sie ihre sozialen Beziehungen aktiviert, verdeutlichen Ainuras räumlich-sozialen Spagat, den situationsabhängigen Wechsel zwischen Netzwerksegmenten von Freunden in der Stadt und Verwandten auf dem Land (Mische & White 1998; Knox et al. 2006:131). Mit dessen Bewältigung ist für Ainura im Vergleich zu anderen jungen Frauen in Zentralasien ein relativ breiter Handlungsspielraum beschrieben[4], der jedoch kontinuierlich ‚gemanagt' werden muss und dessen letztendliche Fragilität in bestimmten Lebenssituationen deutlich aufscheint.

Im Zusammenhang damit illustriert der Aufsatz die spezifische Verflechtung von internationaler Bildungsmigration mit lokalen, jedoch ‚westlich' finanzierten Karriere-

---

[2] Für sämtliche Personen in diesem Aufsatz benutze ich Pseudonyme.
[3] In Anlehnung an Hannerz (1980:270) verstehe ich den Begriff ‚Karriere' nicht nur als beruflichen Aufstieg, sondern umfassender als ‚sequentielle Organisation von Lebenssituationen', d. h. also auch in der Verschränkung mit der Entwicklung eines sozialen Netzwerks wie es in Ainuras Fall hier angesprochen wird.
[4] Einblicke in stärker eingeschränkte Handlungsräume junger Frauen in Zentralasien liefern etwa McBrien (2009:137) für Kirgistan oder Harris (2006:63–80) für Tadschikistan.

optionen und diskutiert dies in der konkreten Wirkung auf eine einzelne Biographie. In Anlehnung an Brettell (2003:26 f.) soll so Ainuras ‚Migrationsgeschichte' umfassend in ihren entscheidenden, auslösenden Momenten und den komplexen Folgewirkungen dargestellt werden. Die ethnographischen Daten hierfür entstammen meiner Feldforschung[5] in Bischkek, wo ich in den Jahren 2007 und 2008 mehrere narrative Interviews mit Ainura führte. Darüber hinaus konnte ich jedoch, begünstigt durch die Tatsache dass wir in dieser Zeitspanne die gleiche Nachbarschaft in Bischkek bewohnten, auch kontinuierlich an Ainruas Alltagsleben teilhaben, sei dies durch informelle Gespräche oder eigenes Erleben.

Wie im Verlaufe dieses Beitrags deutlich werden wird, ist Ainuras Lebensgeschichte weder repräsentativ für eine Mehrheit junger Kirgisinnen, noch stellt sie ein absolutes Einzelschicksal dar. Was etwa ihre Bildungssituation anbelangt, ist Ainura einerseits Teil einer für die Region vergleichsweise großen Gruppe weiblicher Studierender: Während in Kirgistan im Jahr 2008 54 % der jungen Frauen an einer Hochschule eingeschrieben sind, sinken diese Zahlen in den Nachbarländern Tadschikistan (16 %) und Usbekistan (8 %) deutlich ab.[6] Auf der anderen Seite gilt die Universität an der Ainura in Bischkek studieren wird besonders aufgrund der umfassenden finanziellen Unterstützung aus den USA als lokale Elite-Schule, die es sich zum Ziel gesetzt hat eine ‚New Generation of Leadership' hervorzubringen.[7]

Ainuras Fall einer erfolgreichen ‚Bildungsrückkehrerin aus dem Westen' ergänzt bestehende Studien zur transnationalen Arbeitsmigration, die von Kirgistan ausgehend vor allem nach Russland verläuft und den Niedriglohnsektor betrifft.[8] In Bezug auf Untersuchungen zu den internationalen Bemühungen um Kirgistans ‚zivilgesellschaftliche Entwicklung'[9] geht es in diesem Artikel weniger um die Evaluierung der Breitenwirksamkeit oder Angemessenheit von ‚donor-funded projects', sondern um die individuellen Chancen die sich dadurch für eine junge Person vor Ort ergeben.[10]

---

[5] Aus dieser Feldforschung sind weitere Veröffentlichungen zu den Themen Jugend, Stadt-Land-Beziehungen sowie Identität und Integration in Kirgistan hervorgegangen (siehe Schröder 2010, 2011, 2012).
[6] Siehe die ‚Gender Statistics' der World Bank: http://databank.worldbank.org/ (Zugriff: 29. 11. 2013).
[7] Siehe weiter unten und: https://auca.kg/en/20/ (Zugriff: 29. 11. 2013).
[8] Siehe z. B. Ruget & Usmanalieva (2008); Abazov (1999); Schmidt & Sagynbekova 2008; Marat 2009; Reeves 2011, 2012; Isabaeva 2011.
[9] Siehe z. B. Pétric 2005; Roy 2005; Anderson 2000; McMann 2003; Mendelson & Glenn 2002; Wilkinson & Kirey 2010.
[10] Kirmse liefert hierzu eine aktuelle Fallstudie mit Fokus auf Freizeitaktivitäten und Weiterbildungsmaßnahmen unter Studenten in Südkirgistan und beschreibt die entsprechende Perspektive wie folgt: ‚Young people re-appropriate donor-funded spaces and use them for their own purposes. A focus on opportunities thus helps us to see that donors fulfil important functions even if these opportunities have little to do with the donors' own terms of reference.' (2009:90).

Ziel: „Raus aus Naryn"

Ainura wurde 1980 in Naryn geboren. Die Stadt Naryn liegt etwa 400 km südöstlich von Bischkek und fungiert als Hauptstadt des gleichnamigen *oblast* (Verwaltungsbezirk). Ainuras Vater arbeitete bis zu seinem Tod im Jahr 2002 als Ingenieur in einem der Wasserkraftwerke dieser ländlichen Region Kirgistans, während ihre Mutter bis ins Jahr 2008 als Bibliothekarin an der staatlichen Universität der Stadt Naryn angestellt war. Ainuras ältere Brüder (einer Jahrgang 1971, der andere Jahrgang 1973) wurden ebenso in Naryn geboren. Nach ihren Studienabschlüssen in Bischkek entschieden sich beide Brüder für Karrieren im öffentlichen Dienst und wurden im Rahmen dessen in verschiedene Regionen Kirgistans versetzt. Im Jahr 2008 lebt der ältere von Ainuras Brüdern in Naryn, zusammen mit der gemeinsamen Mutter, seiner Frau und seinen vier Kindern. Der andere Bruder wurde in den benachbarten Issyk-Kul *oblast* abkommandiert und lebt dort mit seiner Frau und Tochter.

Ainura beschreibt ihre Kindheit und frühe Jugend in Naryn als glückliche Zeit, welche jedoch in Folge des Zerfalls der Sowjetunion auch von zahlreichen, besonders ökonomischen Unsicherheiten geprägt war. Für Ainuras Familie bedeutete die Unabhängigkeit Kirgistans im Jahr 1991 eine Verschlechterung, sowohl für ihre damalige Lebenssituation wie auch für ihre bis dato antizipierte Zukunft. Dennoch traf die Transformationsperiode Ainuras Familie weniger hart als viele andere Einwohner der ländlichen Gebiete Kirgistans. Ainuras Eltern konnten ihre Arbeitsstellen beibehalten und bezogen auch weiterhin größtenteils ihre Gehälter.[11] Nach diesen ersten post-sozialistischen Erfahrungen urteilten Ainuras Eltern, dass sich die Lage der Familie durch einen Umzug nach Bischkek nicht zwingend verbessern würde. Sie entschieden in Naryn zu bleiben und reihten sich damit nicht in die Abwanderungswellen derer ein, die in einem Umzug vom Land nach Bischkek[12] oder ins Ausland die einzige Chance auf eine Verbesserung ihres Lebens sahen.

Obwohl Ainura sich zu dieser Zeit in einer Situation eingebettet sah, die sie als emotional, sozial und ökonomisch befriedigend beschreibt, malt sie sich ihre individuelle Zukunft nicht im ländlichen Kontext von Naryn, sondern in Kirgistans Hauptstadt aus. Als junges Mädchen verbindet Ainura die Attraktivität Bischkeks besonders mit einer besseren infrastrukturellen Einbindung und Versorgung. „Wir hatten ja keine Dusche in unserem Haus in Naryn. Wir sind nur einmal die Woche ins türkische

---

[11] Wie Hilgers zeigt, kann dies als glücklicher Ausnahmefall gelten: ‚Die ökonomische Situation im Kirgistan der 1990er Jahre, verbunden mit steigender Arbeitslosigkeit, erschwerte jedoch Frauen den Zugang zu regulärer Lohnarbeit. Vor allem die von Frauen dominierten Bereiche Gesundheit und Bildung sind von staatlichen Einsparungen betroffen ...' (2002:40).

[12] Um eine Nahrungsgrundlage aufrechtzuerhalten und trotzdem das Problem des Bargeldmangels und der Versorgungsengpässe mit bestimmten Gütern in ländlichen Regionen anzugehen, war es eine weitere Strategie lediglich einzelne Mitglieder eines Haushalts zur Arbeitssuche nach Bischkek zu entsenden (Hilgers 2002:66). Siehe auch Kostyukova (1994).

Bad gegangen. Das war entweder am Samstag oder am Sonntag. Und sonst, unter der Woche, konnte ich mir zuhause nur zwei- oder dreimal die Haare waschen." Aus solchen kleinteiligen Alltagserfahrungen generierte sich Ainuras Zukunftsvorstellung: „Mein Traum war immer eine Wohnung in der Stadt zu haben, also in Bischkek. Mit Fließendwasser, Strom und Heizung."[13]

Trotz ihres damals noch sehr jungen Alters bildet sich für Ainura Mitte der 1990er Jahre zunehmend noch eine weitere Erkenntnis heraus, welche im Verlauf der nächsten Jahre immer bedeutsamer werden wird. Diese Erkenntnis betrifft auch konkrete Lebensumstände, jedoch weniger materielle als soziale. Ainura denkt ihr Lebensweg wäre eindeutig vorherbestimmt, sollte sie in Naryn bleiben. „Ich wäre mit 18, spätestens mit 20 verheiratet worden. Das ist dort eben so. Ich wäre schnell Mutter geworden und hätte mein Leben zuhause verbracht." Ainura bewertet einen solchen Verlauf keineswegs negativ, sondern betont lediglich, dass es in dieser Situation für eine Frau eben keine andere realistische Option gegeben hätte. „Es klingt vielleicht simpel, aber für mich war das einfach nichts ... also musste ich es irgendwie schaffen aus Naryn rauszukommen."

Mit dieser Aussage drückt Ainura die Erkenntnis aus, dass mit einer räumlichen Distanzierung oftmals auch eine Ablösung von bestehenden Beziehungen einhergeht, wodurch sozialer Druck abgemildert werden kann und sich neue Lebensoptionen ergeben (Guichard 2007:338). Zu dieser früheren Zeit in ihrem Leben ist jedoch der Anfangserfolg von Ainuras Vorhaben aus Naryn wegzukommen abhängig von Faktoren außerhalb ihres direkten Einflussbereichs. Als minderjähriges Mädchen aus dem ländlichen Bereich einer patriarchalisch geprägten Gesellschaft ist Ainuras individueller Handlungsspielraum gegenüber dem Willen ihrer Eltern eingeschränkt (siehe auch Harris 2006:151). Hätte Ainuras Vater auf eine frühe Hochzeit seiner Tochter gedrängt und alternative Lebenswege kategorisch ausgeschlossen, hätte sich Ainura diesem Verlauf der Dinge wohl nur durch den Bruch mit ihrer Familie (und erweiterten Verwandtschaft) entziehen können.[14] In Anbetracht dieser Alternative ist Ainuras tatsächliche familiäre Konstellation aus ihrer Sicht ein früher Glücksfall, der ihren wei-

---

[13] Finke gibt eine eindrückliche Beschreibung der Situation in vielen ländlichen Regionen zu dieser Zeit Mitte und Ende der 1990er Jahre: ‚Der Ausbau von Infrastruktur reichte in sowjetischer [sic] bis in die fernsten Dörfer hinein. Auch auf den hoch gelegenen Sommerweiden in den Bergen gab es Stromanschluss, Geschäfte, öffentliche Bäder, zum Teil Diskotheksveranstaltungen für Jugendliche. Auch in den Dörfern ist die Versorgung drastisch zurückgegangen. Busverbindungen sind seltener geworden, die Versorgung mit Elektrizität ist nicht mehr durchgängig, und die früher von allen verwendete Kohle zum Beheizen der Wohnungen ist für viele unbezahlbar geworden. Auch fließendes Wasser ist in den meisten Häusern nicht mehr vorhanden. Schulische und medizinische Versorgung sind ebenfalls schlechter geworden.' (2002:143).
[14] Neben arrangierten Hochzeiten ist auch die nicht-konsensuale ‚Brautentführung' eine weitere in der Region verbreitete patriarchalische Praktik, die den Handlungsspielraum junger Frauen, ihre Mobilität und Sexualität ‚männlicher Kontrolle' (Werner 2009:315) unterordnet. Siehe hierzu auch Kleinbach und Salimjanova (2007); Kleinbach et al. (2005); Kleinbach (2003).

teren Weg begünstigt. Ainura behauptet, sich bereits zu dieser Zeit bewusst gewesen zu sein, dass Bildung der Schlüssel zu mehr sozialer Selbstbestimmung ist. Dabei profitiert sie vom Werdegang ihrer Eltern, die beide während der Sowjetzeit durch Aus- und Weiterbildungen in ihre jetzigen, angesehenen Positionen im Ingenieurswesen und dem Wissenschaftsbereich gelangten. Die zu dieser Zeit zwar angespannte, jedoch nicht aussichtslose ökonomische Situation der Familie erlaubt es Ainuras Eltern das sowjetisch geprägte Ideal von Bildungschancen für Frauen (Humphrey 1983:288) und deren Integration in den Arbeitsmarkt[15] weiter zu tragen. Für Ainura bedeutet dies Freiraum zu haben, um sich schulisch entfalten zu können.[16]

Damit jedoch Ainura ihren Weg weiterverfolgen kann, müssen im post-sowjetischen Kirgistan Mitte der 1990er Jahre ihre Entschlossenheit und die wohlwollende Perspektive der Eltern auf einen weiteren Umstand treffen, der außerhalb beider dieser Einflussbereiche liegt. Zu dieser Zeit ist der staatliche Bildungssektor stark unterfinanziert und kämpft mit strukturellen Problemen, welche besonders die Schulen in ländlichen Regionen benachteiligen (DeYoung 2006:502; Shamatov 2005; Mertaugh 2004). In Naryn ist es für Ainura daher eine herausragende Gelegenheit am kostenlosen Englischunterricht teilzunehmen, der an ihrer Schule von einem Freiwilligen des amerikanischen ‚Peace Corps'[17] angeboten wird. Aus analytischer Perspektive tritt Ainura mit dieser Entscheidung in ein Beziehungsgeflecht ein, aus dem sich in ihrem weiteren Lebensverlauf zusätzliche Chancen und Vorteile ‚akkumulieren' werden.[18]

Dieses Geflecht aus internationalen und nationalen NGOs und staatlichen ‚Entwicklungsagenturen', das für Kirgistan auch als ‚globales Protektorat' (Pétric 2005:331) bezeichnet wurde, definiert individuelle Aufstiegschancen anhand der Elemente englische Sprache, international finanzierte Bildung und Beschäftigung im Bereich der Zivilgesellschaft. Erfolg wird Ainura in diesem Geflecht allerdings nicht automatisch zuteil. Die vorhandenen Chancen müssen in einer Verbindung aus Leistungswillen und (sozialer) Intelligenz aktiv genutzt werden, wobei auch der Konkurrenzdruck durch andere junge Kirgisinnen mit ähnlichen Ambitionen eine Rolle spielt. Ainura beginnt also während ihrer Schulzeit intensiv Englisch zu lernen. Mit inter-

---

[15] Auf der anderen Seite dieses sozialistischen Strebens das Potential von Frauen als Arbeitskräften zu erschließen, stand deren unveränderte Beanspruchung für Haushalts- und Erziehungsaufgaben. Dieser ‚sozialistische Paternalismus' wurde in post-sowjetischer Zeit umgekehrt in Richtung einer kulturell-nationalistisch verstandenen männlichen Dominanz (siehe Kandiyoti 2007:613; auch McBrien 2009:137).

[16] In Haushalten mit schlechterer ökonomischer Ausgangslage führten in dieser Zeit der Wegfall kostenfreier Bildung und der Einbezug Jugendlicher in alltägliche Haushaltspflichten zu sinkenden Anwesenheitszeiten in Kindergärten und Schulen (siehe Howell 1995; Kuehnast 1998:651).

[17] Der Peace Corps ist eine unabhängige Behörde innerhalb des Außenministeriums der Vereinigten Staaten von Amerika. ‚Peace Corps Volunteers' sind seit 1993 in Kirgistan aktiv.

[18] Merton nennt dies im Bezug auf das Matthäusevangelium (25, 29) den ‚Matthew Effect': ‚For unto every one that hath shall be given, and he shall have abundance: but from him that hath not shall be taken away even that which he hath.' (1968:3). Siehe auch Gladwell (2009:33).

nationaler Unterstützung erarbeitet sie sich damit eine zweite Option für ihren Lebensweg, neben der, wie sie es nennt, „traditionellen Variante" einer Hochzeit um die Zeit der Volljährigkeit herum.

Illinois, American University in Bischkek, Hawaii: „Integration auf Amerikanisch"

Nach der 11. Klasse und dem Abschluss der Mittelschule (*srednaia shkola*) in Naryn erfüllt sich Ainuras Hoffnung. Sie kann Kirgistan verlassen und ihr Bildungskapital weiter ausbauen. Dabei ist Ainuras nächstes Ziel jedoch nicht wie anfangs erträumt Bischkek. Während des Englischunterrichts im Rahmen der Peace Corps Initiative wurden Ainura und die anderen Teilnehmer über eine ganze Reihe weiterführender Bildungsoptionen aufgeklärt. Das ‚Future Leaders Exchange (FLEX) Program' ist eines davon. Es wurde im Jahr 1992 in Kirgistan eingeführt und ermöglicht es kirgisischen Schülern ein Jahr an einer High-School in den USA zu verbringen, inklusive der Unterbringung in einer lokalen Gastfamilie. Die finanzielle Unterstützung für diese Stipendien wird vom US-Außenministerium bereitgestellt. Nach ihren ersten positiven Erfahrungen mit dem Peace Corps bewirbt sich Ainura für dieses Programm, „gewinnt" eines der Stipendien, und verbringt so das Jahr 1997/1998 im US-Bundesstaat Illinois.

Bereits von dort aus plant Ainura ihre Rückkehr nach Kirgistan, dieses Mal tatsächlich auch nach Bischkek. Sie bewirbt sich um einen Studienplatz an der ‚American University of Kyrgyzstan' (AUK), welche 1997 als unabhängige Universität in Bischkek etabliert wurde.[19] Unter anderem zählen zu den Unterstützern dieser Universität das ‚Open Society Institute' sowie die Behörde zur Koordinierung der amerikanischen Entwicklungszusammenarbeit ‚USAID'.[20] Nach einem Englischsprachtest und weiteren Aufnahmeprüfungen, auf die Ainura durch ihr Schuljahr in den USA bereits vorbereitet war, wird sie dort als Studentin im Fach ‚Business Administration' angenommen.

Ab 1998 studiert Ainura vier Jahre in diesem Bachelor-Programm. Zur Finanzierung ihres Studiums und des Lebensunterhalts in Bischkek will sie möglichst nicht auf ihre Eltern zurückgreifen, die ohnehin kaum in der Lage gewesen wären Ainuras

---

[19] Die AUK nennt sich seit dem Jahr 2002 ‚American University of Central Asia' (AUCA). Vor der Zeit als unabhängige Universität bestand seit 1993 eine ‚Kyrgyz-American School' unter dem Dach der Kirgisischen Staatlich Nationalen Universität. Siehe: https://auca.kg/en/museum_20/; Zugriff: 29. 11. 2013.

[20] Cooley und Ron geben im Rahmen einer kritischen Auseinandersetzung mit den Zielen und Beschränkungen des ‚transnationalen Sektors' in Kirgistan an: ‚Per capita, Kyrgyzstan has received the second-most USAID technical assistance of all the post-Soviet States, with disbursements totaling $ 42 million in 1997, $ 36.5 million in 1998, and $ 30 million in the years since.' (2002:19).

Studiengebühren in Höhe von über $ 1000 pro Jahr aufzubringen.[21] Ainura bewältigt diese finanzielle Herausforderung nur mit Hilfe eines Stipendiums. Dieses wird ihr, wie anderen Studenten in ähnlicher Lage, von der Universität zugesprochen aufgrund guter akademischer Leistungen, aber auch weil ihre Familie nachweislich nicht über ausreichend eigene finanzielle Mittel verfügt (Reeves 2003:369). Im Rahmen dieses Stipendiums werden Ainura große Teile der Studiengebühren erlassen. Um über diese Einsparungen hinaus ihre Lebenshaltungskosten in Bischkek aufzubringen, arbeitet Ainura in einem Nebenjob. Dieser wiederum ist mit der ‚westlichen', zivilgesellschaftlichen Unterstützung für Kirgistan und mit Ainuras inzwischen ausgezeichneten Englischkenntnissen verbunden. Bei einer internationalen NGO beginnt sie als Projektmitarbeiterin zu arbeiten, wobei sie vor allem mit Übersetzungsaufgaben beschäftigt ist.

In ihrem ersten Jahr in Bischkek wohnt Ainura zunächst beim jüngeren Bruder ihres Vaters. In diesem Haushalt lebt sie ohne Miete zu bezahlen, beteiligt sich aber an den gemeinsamen Lebenshaltungskosten und sieht sich in der Pflicht ihren geringeren materiellen Beitrag durch größeren Arbeitseinsatz bei den täglichen Haushaltsaufgaben auszugleichen. „Nach einiger Zeit aber habe ich entschieden, dass sie es auch schwer haben, wenn ich noch zusätzlich dort wohne. Also habe ich mich entschieden umzuziehen."

Dieser Auszug bedeutet, dass Ainura zum ersten Mal eine Mietwohnung in Bischkek mit anderen Studenten teilt. Bereits seit ihrer Immatrikulation, nun aber noch verstärkt durch diese Wohngemeinschaft, beginnt sich Ainuras zweites ‚soziales Standbein' zu entwickeln: ein Netzwerk aus Studenten der Amerikanischen Universität, die aus verschiedenen ländlichen Regionen Kirgistans nach Bischkek gekommen sind.

Eine Gemeinsamkeit, die Ainura mit ihren Kommilitonen teilt, ist der Wunsch nach einem sozialen Neuanfang in der Hauptstadt. „Wir waren alle neu hier, Zugezogene. Alle kamen wir aus verschiedenen Regionen nach Bischkek, und alle hatten wir niemanden hier außer ein paar Verwandten. Und man kann ja nicht seine ganze Zeit mit Verwandten verbringen."[22] Diese Konstellation unterscheidet sich von derjenigen der anderen studentischen Hauptgruppe an Ainuras Universität, denjenigen die bereits ihre Kindheit und Schulzeit in Bischkek verbracht haben. „Die wollten nicht viel mit uns Zugezogenen zu tun haben", erinnert sich Ainura. „Warum auch, sie hatten ja ihre

---

[21] Diese Studiengebühren stiegen kontinuierlich. Im Jahr 2010 betrugen sie ungefähr $ 2100. Für das Jahr 2011 wurde eine Erhöhung auf $ 4900 angekündigt (http://www.neweurasia.net/ru/kyrgyzstan/ucheba-v-autsa-podorozhaet/; Zugriff: 14. 02. 2011).
[22] Das komplementäre Zusammenspiel von Freundschaften und näheren Verwandten stellt auch Finke fest: ‚Unseren Erfahrungen nach scheinen weniger postulierte Verwandtschafts- oder Regional-Identitäten für die Organisation von Zusammenleben entscheidend zu sein, sondern individuell geknüpfte Netzwerke – die etwa auch frühere Parteizugehörigkeit oder ein gemeinsames Studium an einer Hochschule zur Grundlage haben können.' (2002:147).

Freunde und alles ja schon hier. Uns fehlte eben die Schulzeit hier in Bischkek, um als Städter zu gelten."

Mit dieser Trennlinie zu den Städtern verstärkt sich für Ainura der Fokus auf die Selbstwahrnehmung als Zugezogene und die Integration innerhalb dieser Gruppe. Im Gegensatz zu den Städtern, die oftmals verächtlich auf die ‚Dörfler' herabschauen[23], kümmern sich Ainura und ihre Kommilitonen nicht darum, aus welchem von Kirgistans ländlichen Bezirken der jeweils andere stammt. Dass sie neu sind in Bischkek, viele der alten Freundschaftsbeziehungen aus der Schulzeit zurücklassen mussten, und sich ihre bisherigen Sozialkontakte in der Stadt auf Verwandte beschränken, schafft die soziale Ausgangslage für die Integration der Zugezogenen untereinander.

Nach diesem ersten Studienjahr und dem Auszug aus dem Haushalt ihrer Verwandten entwickeln sich Ainuras Freundschaften weiter. Während ihrer verbleibenden drei Jahre Studienzeit ist Ainura aktiv an der Universität und fungiert unter anderem als Präsidentin im „students' government". In dieser Zeit lernt sie diejenigen Personen kennen, die sie auch noch im Jahr 2008 als ihre „engsten Freunde" (*samyie blizkie druz'ia*) bezeichnet. Bis auf eine (ethnisch) russische Freundin die in Bischkek geboren wurde, sind diese Freundinnen sämtlich Kirgisinnen, die wie Ainura selbst aus einer ländlichen Region in die Hauptstadt kamen.

Neben dem Status als Zugezogene und den deprimierenden Anfangserfahrungen als Fremde in der Stadt gibt es einen weiteren, ideellen Aspekt dieser Integration zwischen Ainura und ihren Freundinnen. In der Rückschau aus dem Jahr 2008 beschreibt Ainura dies wie folgt: „Wir sind Freunde geworden und geblieben, weil wir alle diesen US-background [in Englisch] haben. Alle von uns haben etwas mit den USA zu tun ..."

Diese Verbindung mit den USA ergibt sich für Ainura und ihre Freundinnen besonders über das Selbstverständnis als Studenten der American University, einer englisch-sprachigen Universität mit internationaler Studentenschaft, die im Zeichen der amerikanischen ‚liberal-arts'-Tradition für „westliche, moderne Werte" wie Freiheit, kritisches Denken und Individualität steht (Reeves 2005:13 f.; Werner 2009:328; Kandiyoti 2007:615).[24] Weiter verstärkt wird dieser „US-background" durch die Tatsache, dass die meisten dieser Freundinnen, ebenso wie Ainura, vor dem Studium ein Jahr an einer amerikanischen High-School verbracht haben und inzwischen auch in „Projekten" (*proekty*) internationaler NGOs arbeiten.

---

[23] Ich diskutiere die andere Seite dieser identitären Grenzziehung, die Sichtweise der Städter auf die ‚Dörfler' in Bischkek an anderer Stelle (siehe Schröder 2010, 2012).
[24] Auch wenn Ainura es nicht in diesen Worten fasst, so lebt sie damit doch eine von ‚multiplen Modernitäten', die im nach-sowjetischen Kirgistan für junge Frauen möglich sind. Während sich Ainuras gegenwärtige Moderne aus der beschriebenen Orientierung „am Westen" generiert, beschreibt McBrien (2009) einer andere solche Moderne unter jungen Kirgisinnen, die sich mit einem Fokus auf Islam, Verschleierung und religiöse Praxis abspielt.

Direkt nach ihrem Bachelor-Abschluss im Frühjahr 2002 wird Ainura von derselben NGO übernommen bei der sie bereits als Studentin ihren Nebenjob hatte. Sie bleibt dort noch einige Zeit beschäftigt, bis sie eine Stelle als Projektassistentin bei einer anderen internationalen Organisation annimmt. Dort ist Ainura zunächst Koordinatorin der Weiterbildungs- und Trainingsmaßnahmen, wird aber im Jahr 2004 zur „Regionalkoordinatorin" für das gesamte zentralasiatische Gebiet befördert.

Obwohl Ainura dies als gute Stelle ansieht und auch mit dem Gehalt zufrieden ist, verlässt sie Mitte 2004 diese Organisation. „Ich habe einfach die Situation abgeschätzt und den Markt beobachtet. Mir wurde klar: Wenn ich eine gute Arbeit haben will, dann muss ich mindestens einen Master [Abschluss] haben. Überall haben sie einen Master verlangt."

Diesen Schritt zur weiteren Ausbildung will Ainura jedoch nicht mehr an der American University in Bischkek tun, sondern will „… den Master an einer echten [sic] westlichen Universität bekommen." Ainura bewirbt sich und wird für ein Stipendium an der Universität von Hawaii akzeptiert. Sie verlässt Bischkek, diesmal für zwei Jahre, und kehrt Mitte des Jahres 2006 mit einem Master-Abschluss zurück. Ainura verbringt daraufhin einige Monate bei ihrer Mutter in Naryn bevor sie eine Kurzzeit-Stelle in Projekt der ‚Asian Development Bank' aufnimmt. Anfang 2007 findet Ainura dann eine langfristige Arbeit bei einer anderen internationalen Organisation, wo sie als lokale Fachkraft in der Öffentlichkeitsarbeit tätig wird.[25]

Ainuras engste Freundschaften, die zu ihren früheren Kommilitoninnen aus Zeiten der American University, überdauern auch diesen vorerst letzten langjährigen Auslandsaufenthalt. Entlang der Stationen ihres Lebenswegs seit ihrer Immatrikulation an der American University haben sich für Ainura neben diesen engen Freundschaften zahlreiche weitere Kontakte zu Personen herausgebildet, die sie als „nicht nahe Freunde" (*neblizkie druz'ia*, plural) oder Bekannte (*znakomyie*, plural) bezeichnet. Zu diesem erweiterten Freundes- und Bekanntenkreis zählt Ainura im Jahr 2008 über 600 Personen. Ungefähr 50 von ihnen identifiziert sie als „alte Freunde aus Schulzeiten in Naryn". Die anderen Kontakte entstammen zwar verschiedenen Kontexten – der Studienzeit, verschiedenen Arbeitsstellen, Freizeitaktivitäten und dem Internet – werden aber letztlich ausnahmslos getragen von einem gemeinsamen „US-background".[26]

---

[25] Ainura gilt in Kirgistan als gefragte Spezialistin, weil sie an Bildungseinrichtungen studierte, die im Vergleich zu den lokalen Universitäten als qualitativ hochwertiger eingestuft werden; die vor allem aber nicht belastet sind von Korruptionsverdächtigungen (DeYoung 2010).

[26] Neben ihre engsten kirgisischen Freundinnen finden sich in Ainuras weiterem Bekanntenkreis Männer und Frauen verschiedener Ethnizitäten, solche aus der näheren regionalen Umgebung (Russen, Kasachen, Koreaner) wie auch aus Europa, Indien oder den USA. In Anlehnung an Handrahan lässt sich somit sagen, dass Ainura nicht nur eine ‚gender identity einer ethnischen Identität bevorzugt' (2001:70), sondern der Identitätsmarker „US-background" noch einen darüber hinaus reichenden Integrationsrahmen beschreibt und Männer wie Frauen verschiedener Ethnizitäten einschließt.

Managerin des Sozialen

An diesem Punkt in ihrem Lebensweg lerne ich Ainura kennen. Mit dem vorherigen Absatz wurde klar, dass sich ihre nicht-verwandtschaftlichen Sozialkontakte zu Freunden und Bekannten entlang eines gemeinsamen „US-background" integrierten. Das entsprechende Zitat wurde oben aber nur verkürzt wiedergegeben. In voller Länge sagte Ainura in diesem Gespräch: „... weil wir alle diesen ‚US-background' [in Englisch] haben. Alle von uns haben etwas mit den USA zu tun ... oder mit diesem Lebensstil." Was unter diesem „Lebensstil" (Kirmse 2010; Habeck und Ventsel 2009:4) zu verstehen ist, den Ainura und ihre Freundinnen in Bischkek teilen, will ich nun ausführen.

Der ‚US-marker' ihrer Identifikation (Donahoe et al. 2009:15) wirkt auf die Ausprägung bestimmter Werte in Ainuras alltäglicher Lebenspraxis. Sprache ist hierbei eines der offensichtlichsten Elemente. Ainura beherrscht Englisch ausgezeichnet und streut in ihre Konversationen treffgenau amerikanisch-umgangssprachliche Redewendungen und Slang ein. Sie wechselt ins Englische wie zwischen ihren „beiden Muttersprachen Kirgisisch und Russisch". Wenn Ainura sich mit ihren Freundinnen trifft oder sie sich am Telefon unterhalten, werden in den meisten Sätzen alle drei Sprachen verwendet. „Ja, irgendwie ist das komisch", sagt sie, „aber ich benutze eben die Sprache in der mir das Wort am schnellsten einfällt. Und das geht ja unter uns, wir können ja alle alle Sprachen." Zudem empfindet Ainura den Wechsel ins Englische vor allem dann angenehm, wenn sie sich dadurch „frei" unterhalten kann; das heißt die Gewissheit hat, dass nicht alle in ihrer näheren Umgebung den Inhalt eines Gesprächs vollständig nachvollziehen können. „Zum Beispiel wenn ich unter meinen Verwandten bin und es ruft eine Freundin an. Sagen wir, sie will meinen Rat wie sie sich gegenüber einem Verehrer verhalten soll. Dann wechsle ich natürlich ins Englische. Die Verwandten müssen ja nicht mitkriegen, dass wir so über unsere Beziehungen reden ... oder [lachend] besser gesagt sie überhaupt haben."

Wie und wo Ainura ihre Freizeit verbringt, ist ein weiterer Aspekt in diesem Zusammenhang. Ainura, ihre Freunde und Bekannten bevorzugen Cafés und Diskotheken in Bischkek, die dafür bekannt sind vor allem von „Westerners", also europäischen oder nordamerikanischen „expats", besucht zu werden. „Wir haben gute Jobs, also können wir uns den Eintritt und die Preise dort ja leisten. Außerdem gefällt es uns dort besser. Dort ist man sicherer als an anderen Orten, vor allem wird man dort nichts so plump angemacht."

Mit ihren Monatsgehältern von bis zu 1000 Euro (50 000 ‚Som')[27] ist es Ainura und ihren Freundinnen möglich bei ihren Freizeitaktivitäten nicht sparsam sein zu müssen. Für ihre Mitgliedschaft in einem Fitness-Studio bezahlt Ainura 900 Som pro

---

[27] ‚Som' ist die nationale Währung Kirgistans. Im Dezember 2007 lag der Wechselkurs zwischen Euro und Som bei ungefähr 1:50.

Monat. „Ich weiß, dass das für Kirgistan sehr viel Geld ist. Aber sie haben auch gute Geräte, saubere Umkleiden und es gibt heißes Wasser zum Duschen." Insgesamt verwendet Ainura einen großen Teil ihres Monatsbudgets für derlei Hobbys und Unternehmungen mit Freunden und Bekannten. Insgesamt 17 000 Som gibt Ainura aus, um mit ihren Freunden per Mobiltelefon oder über das Internet in Kontakt zu bleiben, um gemeinsam Auszugehen und Einzukaufen, Urlaub zu machen und um Geschenke für Geburtstagsfeiern zu kaufen. Im Vergleich dazu nehmen die Kosten für ihre Unterkunft (8000 Som) und Verpflegung (6000 Som) einen weitaus geringeren Stellenwert ein.[28]

Im Verlauf ihrer Auslandsaufenthalte in den USA und ihrer Studien an amerikanisch geprägten Bildungseinrichtungen hat sich Ainura, wie sie es ausdrückt, „typisch amerikanische Werte" angeeignet. Individuelle Freiheit und der „pursuit of happiness" sind für Ainura daher nicht nur Rhetorik, sondern können als gelebte Werte in ihrer Alltagspraxis wiedererkannt werden.

Beispielsweise manifestiert sich dies in ihrem Umgang mit dem anderen Geschlecht. Ainura hält nichts von kollektiven Verständnissen, die ihre Jungfräulichkeit als Gradmesser der Ehre ihrer Familie und Verwandtschaft auffassen oder die Wahl ihres zukünftigen Ehemannes als Entscheidung außerhalb ihres eigenen Einflussbereichs verstehen (vgl. Harris 2006:70 f.). Ainura stellt diesem konservativen Verständnis selbstbewusst eine auf Individualität ausgerichtete Perspektive entgegen und sagt: „Es ist doch mein Körper, nicht der meiner Verwandten oder meines Mannes. Also entscheide ich was mit ihm passiert."

Ainura nimmt somit die Partnerwahl als ihre alleinige Angelegenheit wahr und hat sehr konkrete Vorstellungen von ihrem zukünftigen Eheleben: dass es eine „Partnerschaft unter Gleichen" sein sollte und, dass ihr Ehemann sie nicht daran hindern sollte weiterhin ihre berufliche Karriere zu verfolgen, die ihr ein eigenes Einkommen sichert.

Ainura bringt damit zum Ausdruck, dass ihre Lebensmaxime eine möglichst umfassende finanzielle, berufliche, sexuelle und soziale Unabhängigkeit ist. Es ist das Streben nach diesen verschiedenen Ausprägungen von Unabhängigkeit das es für Ainura, wie sie es in Englisch ausdrückt, „zu managen gilt". Dies muss nicht in Bezug auf ihren Freundes- und Bekanntenkreis geschehen, im Rahmen dessen Ainura versucht ein unbeschwertes Freizeitleben zu gestalten, sondern gegenüber denjenigen sozialen Beziehungen, die stärker von traditionellen Erwartungen und Verpflichtungen geprägt sind: Ainuras Verwandtschaft.

---

[28] Dieses Konsumverhalten unterschied sich deutlich von dem der Hauptgruppe meiner Interaktionspartner während der erwähnten Feldforschung in Bischkek in den Jahren 2007 und 2008. Ein typisches Monatsbudget eines solchen Informanten betrug unter 250 Euro. Im Vergleich kennzeichnet dies Ainuras Lebensstil und Konsumverhalten als teuer und exklusiv, was Habeck und Ventsel für ihren sibirischen Kontext als ‚bohème' (2009:9) kategorisieren.

Neben ihren langjährigen engen Freunden ist Ainuras Kontakt zu ihrer Verwandtschaft die andere soziale Konstante in ihrem von räumlicher Mobilität und oftmaligen Ortswechseln geprägten Leben. Ainura stellt die Beziehungen zu ihrer Verwandtschaft nicht als einschränkende Altlasten dar, die sie in ihrem gegenwärtigen Leben in der Stadt und ihrer Unabhängigkeit behindern würden. Ganz im Gegenteil präsentiert Ainura die Verbindungen zu ihrer Mutter, ihren Brüdern und deren Familien in die ländlichen Regionen von Naryn und Issyk-Kul als bereicherndes Gegengewicht zu ihrem sonst so anderen Lebensstil. Sie beschreibt diese Beziehungen als „warm" und „intensiv". Ähnliches gilt für Ainuras „nahe Verwandte" (*blizkie rodstvenniki*), zu denen sie auch die Familien der jüngeren Brüder ihres verstorbenen Vaters zählt. Im Gegensatz zu Ainuras eigenen Eltern hatten diese bereits in den 1990er Jahre entschieden von Naryn nach Bischkek überzusiedeln, wo sie nun etwas außerhalb des Stadtzentrums leben.

Ebenso wie Ainura die individualisierten, „amerikanischen" Werte tatsächlich „lebt", lässt sich auch die verbal ausgedrückte Relevanz ihrer Verwandten in ihrem Lebensalltag beobachten. Ainura versucht ihre zeitlichen Ressourcen in gleichen Maßen auf ihre Freunde und Verwandten zu verteilen. Unter der Woche sieht Ainura ihre Verwandten kaum, sondern trifft sich beinahe täglich nach der Arbeit mit Freunden oder Bekannten. Die Wochenenden dagegen verbringt Ainura gewöhnlich im Wechsel zwischen Freunden und Verwandten. In der Zeit meiner Feldforschung bedeutete dies, dass Ainura in einem ‚durchschnittlichen Monat' zwei Wochenenden bei Verwandten verbringt und zwei Wochenenden mit ihren Freunden einplant.

Mindestens ein Mal pro Monat fährt Ainura nach Naryn oder an den Issyk-Kul, um ihre Mutter oder Brüder zu besuchen. Von diesen regelmäßigen Besuchen lässt sich Ainura auch ungeachtet mancher Widrigkeiten nicht abhalten. Unter Bedingungen in denen sie mit Verständnis rechnen könnte, würde sie einen geplanten Besuch in Naryn absagen, entscheidet sich Ainura trotzdem zu fahren. Auch wenn in den oft schneereichen Wintern Kirgistans besonders die Reise ins 2000 m hoch gelegene Naryn beschwerlich ist, fährt Ainura in der gleichen Regelmäßigkeit. „Neulich erst war ich wieder in so einem alten Taxi zu meiner Mutter unterwegs. Es ist auf dem Weg nach Naryn stecken geblieben, weil so viel Schnee war. Also mussten wir alle aussteigen, es war schon Nacht. Und dann haben wir alle geschoben, damit es weiter geht…und ich in so Hochhackigen [Schuhen; Ainura spreizt ihre Finger zielgenau auf 9 Zentimeter]. Das war ein Bild."

Ein Wochenende pro Monat verbringt Ainura in der Regel im Haus eines ihrer beiden Onkel in Bischkek. Neben ihren zeitlichen Investitionen in diese Besuche bei ihrer Mutter, den Brüdern und Onkeln bringt sich Ainura auch auf andere Weise innerhalb ihrer Verwandtschaft ein. In Bezug auf ihre Mutter und die Brüder besteht dies vor allem in der Bereitstellung von Wohnraum, wenn diese in regelmäßigen Abständen nach Bischkek kommen. Als während der Sommerferien die Tochter ihres Bruders zu einem Englisch-Intensivkurs nach Bischkek geschickt wird, lebt sie für insgesamt vier Wochen bei Ainura. „Ich mag dieses Familiengefühl", sagt Ainura. „Auf dem Weg nach Hause kaufe ich noch Lebensmittel ein und dann koche ich was zusammen mit ihr. Für mich selbst mache ich das fast nie. Ich gehe lieber mit Freunden was essen, wenn ich hier alleine in Bischkek bin."

Wichtig ist für Ainura auch die Beziehung zur Tochter ihres älteren Onkels. Diese Beziehung zu ihrer *ezhe* (kirgisisch für ‚ältere Schwester') stellt Ainura als besonders freundschaftlich und intim dar. Trotz ihres relativ geringen Altersunterschieds, die *ezhe* ist drei Jahre älter als Ainura, verliefen die Lebenswege dieser beiden kirgisischen Frauen sehr unterschiedlich. Während Ainura den ihrigen in der beschriebenen internationalen und individualisierten Weise beschreibt, ist das Leben der *ezhe*, wie Ainura es bezeichnet, „klassisch kirgisisch". Dies bedeutet nicht, dass Ainuras *ezhe* gänzlich von Bildungsmöglichkeiten ausgeschlossen wurde oder etwa das „Schicksal" erlitt, dem Ainura in ihrer Jugend aus Naryn entfliehen wollte. Wie Ainura kam auch ihre *ezhe* als junges Mädchen nach dem Abschluss der 11. Klasse nach Bischkek, um dort zu studieren. Dies tat sie jedoch nicht an einer internationalen Universität mit Englisch als dominanter Unterrichtssprache, sondern an Kirgistans Staatlich-Nationaler Universität, in der die meisten Fächer in Russisch unterrichtet werden. In Bischkek lernte Ainuras *ezhe* auch ihren zukünftigen Ehemann kennen, ebenso ein Kirgise aus Naryn. Kurze Zeit nach ihrem Studienabschluss heiratete Ainuras *ezhe* und brachte im Jahr 2001, mit 24 Jahren, ihr erstes Kind zur Welt. Zwischen dieser Geburt und der eines zweiten Kindes im Jahr 2003 war Ainuras *ezhe* vor allem Mutter und Hausfrau. Weniger als ein Jahr danach jedoch nahm sie wieder eine neue Beschäftigung auf und begann an einer Universität in Bischkek zu arbeiten. Vor allem ist für Ainura bei den Gesprächen mit ihrer *ezhe* der Erfahrungsaustausch wertvoll, „weil meine *ezhe* so ein anderes Leben hat als ich und meine Freundinnen. Sie ist die einzige aus meiner Verwandtschaft mit der ich mich auch über meine männlichen Bekannten unterhalten kann. Ihre Ratschläge sind mir wichtig, weil sie weiß wie unsere Verwandten denken."[29]

Diese Situationen aus Ainuras Leben vermitteln den Eindruck, dass sie nicht in besonderem Maße in die Interaktionen mit ihrer Verwandtschaft gezwungen wird, sondern diese aus einer zumindest finanziell-materiell unabhängigen Position heraus selbst wählt. Ainuras Leben ist jedoch nicht frei von verwandtschaftlichen Verpflichtungen und sie fühlt sich auch nicht in der Position, dass sie Unterstützungsanfragen aus dem Verwandtenkreis einfach ablehnen könnte. Ainura ist überzeugt, dass ihre Verwandten enttäuscht wären, würde sie ihnen ohne zwingenden Grund für längere Zeit keinen Besuch abstatten. Da es sie aber offensichtlich keine große Überwindung kostet diese Erwartungen zu erfüllen und regelmäßig an den verwandtschaftlichen Aktivitäten teilzunehmen, ergibt sich für Ainura auf der anderen Seite auch Handlungsspielraum

---

[29] Diese Solidarisierung und Empathie aufgrund einer geteilten Position in einer sozialen Struktur zeigt das freundschaftliche Element in Ainuras Beziehung zu ihrer *ezhe* (siehe Heady 2007 und Guichard 2007).

in Form einer ‚exit-Option'. Ainura hat die Möglichkeit ein geplantes Treffen mit den Verwandten zu versäumen, ohne dass sie dabei einen Bruch in diesen Beziehungen zu riskieren glaubt: „Weißt Du, es dauert schon eine halbe Stunde dorthin zu fahren, dann eine halbe Stunde zurück; und dann muss ich ja dort auch ein paar Stunden sein. Alles in allem wären das 4–5 Stunden gewesen ... und heute hatte ich diese Zeit einfach nicht."

Anhand solcher Einschätzungen scheint es, dass Ainura ein akzeptables Maß an sozialer Nähe und Distanz gegenüber ihren Verwandten gefunden hat. Dies jedoch ist keinesfalls eine statische Situation in ewiger Balance, sondern muss kontinuierlich bearbeitet werden. Das „typisch kirgisische Leben" ihrer *ezhe* dient dabei als Kontrastfolie vor der Ainuras Lebensweg aus Sicht der meisten, vor allem der entfernten Verwandten begutachtet wird. Mit fortschreitendem Alter, und besonders nach ihrer Rückkehr von der Universität in Hawaii, hat die einzig deutlich erkennbare Spannung zwischen Ainura und ihren Verwandten stetig zugenommen: der soziale Druck auf ihre baldige Hochzeit.

Als Ainuras Mutter in Anerkennung ihrer professionellen Laufbahn an der Universität von Naryn eine Ehrenurkunde in Bischkek überreicht bekommt, ist dies für die gesamte Verwandtschaft ein besonderer Anlass. Nach der Zeremonie der Urkundenüberreichung in Bischkek fährt Ainura gemeinsam mit ihrer Mutter in die Issyk-Kul Region zu ihrem älteren Bruder. Im Kreis der erweiterten Verwandtschaft wird dann auch über Ainuras Zukunft gesprochen: „Es waren sehr viele Leute da, manche Verwandte hatte ich schon ewig nicht mehr gesehen, manche habe ich kaum wieder erkannt. Und jeder zweite Trinkspruch ging dann auf meine zukünftige Hochzeit. Am Anfang dachte ich noch es werden nicht mehr als ein, zwei solcher Trinksprüche werden. Aber dann war es wirklich jeder Zweite!" Ainura versucht gelassen darauf zu reagieren. „Nun, ich habe es eben witzig genommen und gesagt, ‚ja, ja'. Aber aufgeregt hat es mich schon ... obwohl ich mich eigentlich nicht wirklich unter Druck gesetzt fühle, ich bin das Gerede ja schon gewohnt."

Im Jahr 2008 ist Ainura 28 Jahre alt. Damit liegt sie knapp fünf Jahre über dem durchschnittlichen Heiratsalter für Frauen in Kirgistan (Nedoluzhko & Agadjanian 2010). Ihre Verwandten sehen daher die Gefahr, dass Ainura bald keinen geeigneten Partner mehr finden könnte. „Meine Verwandten sagen mir schon, dass ich mir doch einfach irgendeinen netten Mann nehmen soll, den könnte ich ja dann immer noch während der Ehe formen, also das heißt seinen Charakter."

Derartige Versuche der Beeinflussung in einer so existentiellen Lebensentscheidung stehen im Konflikt mit dem Grad der Unabhängigkeit und Selbstbestimmung in dem Ainura es gewohnt ist ihr Leben zu gestalten. Diesen Hochzeitsdruck zu „managen" ist ihre gegenwärtige Hauptaufgabe. Ainura reagiert darauf in zweierlei Weise. Zum einen gibt sie dem Druck teilweise nach, indem sie nicht offen gegen die Bemühungen der Verwandten rebelliert, sondern sich zu Kompromissen bereit zeigt.

Ainura berichtet, dass sie einmal ihre Tante, die Schwester ihres verstorbenen Vaters, angerufen hat. „Sie sagte, dass sie eine Liste mit Jungs hat. Und dann hat sie mich gebeten, dass ich mich doch mal mit ihnen treffe und schaue, ob da nicht einer dabei wäre." Einen der Männer von dieser Liste traf Ainura während sie mit einigen ihrer Freundinnen in einem Café saß. Ihre Tante rief an und bat sie zumindest kurz mit dem jungen Mann zu sprechen. Ainura antwortete, dass sie jetzt nicht könne, weil sie unterwegs sei und, dass der Kandidat doch um 22 Uhr noch mal anrufen solle. „Meine Tante war verzweifelt und sagte, dass sie ihm doch nicht sagen könne, dass er erst um 10 Uhr abends zurückrufen könne. Das wäre nicht höflich." Ainura willigt also ein und spricht mit dem Mann. „Er hat gefragt, ob es uns nicht stören würde, wenn er kurz bei uns in diesem Café vorbeikommen würde. Das fand ich eigentlich ganz mutig und ich habe zugestimmt ... Als er dann aber kam ... naja ... ich will ja nicht sagen, dass er dick war, aber er war so klein ... Und außerdem saßen er und sein Freund nur stumm mit am Tisch ... Und weißt Du was am Komischsten war: als die Rechnung kam, haben diese Männer sie von sich weggeschoben und gesagt: Ihr seid doch AUCA-Mädchen [Absolventinnen der American University in Bischkek]; ihr seid es doch gewohnt selber zu bezahlen. Da war er schon weg von der Liste, das habe ich meiner Tante auch gesagt."

Ainura kann sich nicht vorstellen, dass einer der Kandidaten, der aus ihrer Verwandtschaft an sie herangetragen wird, auch für sie interessant sein könnte. Ainuras Kompromissbereitschaft besteht darin, dass sie trotzdem auf derartige Vermittlungsversuche eingeht und sie nicht offen zurückweist. Durch dieses nach außen hin kooperative Verhalten kann Ainura den Druck von Seiten der Verwandtschaft abmildern, selbst wenn die verwandtschaftlichen Bemühungen bis dato ergebnislos verliefen. Ainura gewinnt damit Zeit, die sie entweder verwenden will, um weiter ihr Singledasein zu genießen oder selbst die Augen für einen Kandidaten ihrer Wahl offen zu halten.

Ainura nimmt den Druck, der auf sie bezüglich ihrer Hochzeit ausgeübt wird differenziert war. Sie sagt, dass ihre Hochzeit im Kreis der engen Verwandten, zu denen sie neben der Mutter, ihren eigenen Brüdern, den Brüdern des Vaters auch ihre oben erwähnt *ezhe* zählt, kein brennendes Thema ist. „Meine engen Verwandten kennen mich, deshalb finden sie es ok, dass ich noch nicht geheiratet habe." Stärker als von diesen engen Verwandten wird der Druck auf eine Hochzeit Ainuras aus den Reihen der entfernten Verwandtschaft herangetragen, entweder an Ainura direkt oder aber an ihre Mutter. „Besonders wenn sich zu bestimmten Anlässen eine größere Gruppe von Verwandten trifft, dann wird am meisten über solche Dinge geredet. Irgendwelche Tanten, nicht nur die Schwestern meines Vaters, sagen immer was in diese Richtung."

An dieser differenzierten Wahrnehmung setzt auch Ainuras zweite Herangehensweise an, um den Druck in Richtung ihrer baldigen Hochzeit zu mildern. Dafür reinvestiert Ainura Teile ihres sozialen Aufstiegs in ihre verwandtschaftlichen Beziehungen. Durch ihre gut dotierten bisherigen Arbeitsstellen ist Ainura nicht nur finanziell unabhängig von verwandtschaftlichen Unterstützungsleistungen, sondern wurde im Laufe der Zeit vielmehr als potentielle Gläubigerin identifiziert. Innerhalb ihrer Verwandtschaft sind die 700–1000 Euro, die Ainura seit ihrer Rückkehr aus den USA monatlich verdient eine bedeutende Summe. Entsprechend sind es teilweise auch entfernte Verwandte, die Ainura um einen persönlichen Kredit bitten. In manchen dieser Fälle entscheidet sich Ainura nicht nur aus rein verwandtschaftlich-altruistischer Verbundenheit, sondern auch im Hinblick auf die Rückwirkungen mit einem Betrag auszuhelfen. „Manchmal gebe ich einem Verwandten etwas und weiß, dass dadurch weniger darüber geredet wird, dass ich noch nicht verheiratet bin." Ainura sendet mit dem Geld die subtile Botschaft, dass sie nur in der Lage ist zu helfen, weil sie sich eben bislang für eine Karriere und gegen ein Familienleben entschieden hat. Damit befriedigt Ainura direkt die unmittelbaren Bedürfnisse derjenigen Verwandten, die sie um Hilfe bitten. Indirekt aber, so sagt sie, kann sie damit diejenigen Verwandten bezüglich ihrer Hochzeit ruhigstellen, die eventuell schon darauf hoffen Ainuras nächste Schuldner werden zu können.

Solange Ainura der soziale Spagat zwischen den beiden Segmenten ihres Netzes gelingt, verfügt sie über ein hohes Maß an individueller Freiheit, die sie mit Freunden genießen kann; ebenso versichert sie, dass ihr die intakten Beziehungen zu Verwandten eine emotionale Stabilität geben würden. Im Sommer 2008 wird jedoch für kurze Zeit nachvollziehbar wie schnell dieser Spagat aus der Balance geraten und Ainura an Spielraum einbüßen könnte. Zu dieser Zeit beginnt Ainura darüber nachzudenken, ob es nicht an der Zeit wäre sich eine eigene Wohnung zu kaufen. Ihre Mutter rät Ainura zum Kauf, weil sie der Meinung ist, dass die Immobilienpreise in Bischkek weiter steigen werden und eine Wohnung daher eine gute Wertanlage sei. Ainura rechnet damit insgesamt $40.000 aufbringen zu müssen für eine durchschnittliche Zwei-Zimmer-Wohnung. „Ich selbst habe ungefähr 10.000. Na und den Rest könnte ich entweder über einen Kredit oder über meine Verwandten besorgen." Ainura geht davon aus, dass ihre Mutter und ihre Brüder ihr nach Kräften helfen würden, „zur Zeit aber sicher nicht mit mehr als 10.000". Aus den Reihen der entfernten Verwandtschaft erwartet Ainura eine Gesamtsumme von unter $10.000. „Sie schulden mir zwar Geld, ich habe in den letzten zehn Jahren sicher 20.000 Dollar an solche Verwandte verliehen. Aber sie sind nicht reich, sie könnten kaum mehr als zweihundert bis fünfhundert Dollar pro Familie geben."

Ainura muss daher die Entscheidung treffen, entweder ihre erweiterte Verwandtschaft nicht zu involvieren und einen Kredit über $20.000 aufzunehmen oder mit Hilfe dieser Verwandten lediglich $10.000 von einer Bank zu benötigen. Wie sie diese Restsumme für den Wohnungskauf aufbringen könnte, spiegelt Ainuras grundsätzliche Handlungsoptionen wider, genauso wie die Implikationen, die sie von der entsprechenden Wahl erwarten würde. Ein Bankkredit würde durch die anfallenden Zinsen finanzielle Mehrbelastungen für Ainura bedeuten. Demgegenüber wäre der Kredit aus Reihen der Verwandtschaft zinslos, hätte jedoch moralische und soziale Folgen, die Ainura gerne vermeiden würde. „Auch wenn ich ihnen nach einiger Zeit alles zurückgezahlt hätte, jeden Dollar, hätten sie immer noch gedacht, ihnen würde diese Wohnung auch gehören ... Sie würden immer denken, dass sie immer bei mir wohnen können wenn sie in Bischkek sind. Und sie hätten mich stets daran erinnert, auch noch in vielen Jahren, dass sie mir ja damals geholfen haben diese Wohnung zu bekommen." Darüber hinaus ist sich Ainura sicher, dass dem Druck auf ihre Hochzeit mehr Gewicht verliehen worden wäre, würde sie in der Schuld dieser entfernten Verwandten stehen. „Dann hätten sie es leichter sich in mein Leben einzumischen." Ainura tendiert also dazu einen größeren Kredit aufzunehmen und sich durch eigenes Wohneigentum, erworben ohne Beteiligung entfernter Verwandter, weiter deren sozialem Druck zu entziehen.

In dieser bereits relevanten Lebenssituation trifft Ainura eine Entscheidung, die sie kurzfristig aus ihrer sozialen Balance bringt. Nachdem Ainura bereits seit mehreren Wochen über die gegenwärtig schlechte Arbeitsatmosphäre im Büro geklagt hat, entschließt sie sich kurzfristig ihre Stelle zu kündigen. Ainura bringt dies in eine für sie ungewohnte Situation. Sie hatte bereits zuvor Arbeitsstellen gewechselt, jedoch waren diese Übergänge stets nahtlos gewesen, weil Ainura die alte Arbeitsstelle erst kündigte nachdem sie die Zusage für die neue hatte. Nun aber war Ainura arbeitslos und dies eröffnet den Blick darauf, wie sehr Ainuras Unabhängigkeit von den Verwandten von ihrem professionellen Erfolg abhängt.

Ainura aktiviert umgehend ihr Netzwerk aus Freunden und Verwandten „in guten Positionen" und schafft es so, bereits einige Tage nach ihrer Kündigung mehrere Jobangebote vorliegen zu haben. Diese Angebote entsprechen jedoch sämtlich nicht Ainuras Vorstellungen, denn sie will „in die Privatwirtschaft wechseln, vielleicht zu einer der internationalen Firmen die hier in Kirgistan Gold abbauen." Sie lehnt diese Angebote also ab und hält weiter Ausschau.

In dieser nur wenige Wochen anhaltenden Periode nimmt der verwandtschaftliche Druck, dass Ainura bald heiraten sollte zu. Neben den üblichen, jedoch nun häufiger geäußerten Kommentaren von Seiten der entfernten Verwandtschaft, wird nun auch Ainuras Mutter konkreter: „Auf einmal hat sie mir gesagt, ich könne doch auch statt nach dem nächsten Job mal nach einem Mann suchen." Ainura sieht ihren Spielraum schwinden. Ohne Arbeitsstelle, die nicht nur ihren finanziellen Status, sondern auch ihren sozialen Freiraum gegenüber den Verwandten mitdefiniert, will sich Ainura durch den Wohnungskauf nicht in irgendeine Abhängigkeit begeben. Sie verwirft also diese Pläne vorerst und intensiviert ihre Arbeitssuche. Den entscheidenden Tipp erhält sie dann von einer jungen Frau aus ihrem Bekanntenkreis. „Sie arbeitet schon in der Gold-Branche", sagt Ainura „und daher wusste sie frühzeitig, dass bei dieser einen Firma eine Stelle frei werden würde."

Obwohl die dort angebotene Position als Assistentin der Geschäftsführung nicht ihren Vorstellungen entspricht, bewirbt sich Ainura. „Ich war überzeugt von der Firma und wollte dort arbeiten. Und ich wusste, dass wenn ich die Chance zu einem persönlichen Gespräch bekomme, dann kann man noch mal verhandeln." Ainuras Rechnung geht offensichtlich auf, denn kurze Zeit später tritt sie, in einer neu geschaffenen Position als „International Buyer", den einträglichsten Job ihres bisherigen Lebens an, mit einem nochmals höheren Gehalt und einem umfassenden „Sozialpaket".

Schluss

In diesem Beitrag habe ich den Lebensweg einer jungen Kirgisin bis zu ihrem 28. Lebensjahr verfolgt. Ich habe beschrieben wie Ainura als junges Mädchen die Entscheidung traf, dass Bildung und die englische Sprache ihr Ausweg aus der ländlichen Heimat und einer für sie ungewollten frühen Ehe waren. Im Zusammenhang mit dieser Entscheidung ergaben sich in Ainuras Lebensverlauf Optionen für den weiteren sozialen Aufstieg, die in ihrem Fall sämtlich mit der starken Aktivität internationaler, vor allem US-amerikanischer, zivilgesellschaftlicher Entwicklungsbemühungen in Kirgistan verbunden waren.

Ich habe daraufhin die Entwicklung von Ainuras sozialen Beziehungen nachverfolgt und dargestellt wie sie zwei separate, für sie jedoch komplementäre Segmente ihres Netzwerks „managt". Im Rückgriff auf einen „amerikanischen" Identitätsmarker entwickelte Ainura einen neuen Freundes- und Bekanntenkreis in der Stadt, der Wert auf individuelle Freiheit und Unabhängigkeit legt. Damit konnte gezeigt werden, wie sich im gegenwärtigen Kirgistan soziale und räumliche Mobilität mit international finanzierten Bildungs- und Karriereoptionen verbinden; genauso jedoch, dass deren individuelle Realisierung abhängig ist von Zufall, Wohlwollen, Geschick und Eigenantrieb.

Grundlegende Erkenntnisse der klassischen Beschäftigung mit dem Thema Migration in einen urbanen Kontext können anhand von Ainuras Fall auch für den zentralasiatisch, post-sowjetischen Raum wieder entdeckt werden. Durch ihre deutliche Zuwendung zu „westlichen Werten" ist Ainura ein ‚marginal woman' im Sinne Parks und der Chicagoer Stadtsoziologen der 1920er Jahre, d. h. eine ‚kulturelle Hybride' und damit in gewissem Maße randständig bezüglich zweier ‚Kulturen' (siehe Ackermann 1997:6). Trotz der Ablösung vom ländlichen Kontext ihrer Jugend und der teilweisen ‚Emanzipierung' von traditionellen Erwartungen an einen weiblichen Lebenslauf droht Ainura jedoch keineswegs der Verlust ihrer ‚kirgisischen Kultur'. Vermittelt über ihre intensiven und emotional bedeutsamen Bindungen nach Naryn und in die Issyk Kul-Region integrieren sich für Ainura die ‚dualen Sphären' Stadt und Land in ein gemeinsames ‚soziales Feld', wie dies bereits Gluckman und andere Vertreter der Manchester School für das sich ‚modernisierende Süd-Zentral Afrika' in den 1950/60er Jahren beschrieben haben (Werbner 1984:168).

Jenseits einer solchen Land-Stadt-Dynamik innerhalb Kirgistans ist Ainuras soziales Feld als Folge ihrer internationalen Bildungskarriere auch in räumlich weiter gespannte transnationale Kontexte eingebettet (Glick Schiller & Fouron 1999). In diesen grenzüberschreitenden Dimensionen geht es für Ainura zwar auch um die ‚Imagination' einer möglichen Lebenswelt (Appadurai 1996). In ihrem Fall ist diese jedoch nicht nur medial vermittelt, sondern speist sich kontinuierlich aus eigenen Erfahrungen im ‚westlichen' Ausland sowie dem persönlichen Kontakt mit westlichen Ausländern in Kirgistan (McBrien 2007; Kuehnast 1997:385).

Anhand der ethnographischen Details aus ihrem Lebensalltag konnte somit herausgearbeitet werden inwiefern Ainuras Netzwerk lokal verortet ist und wie genau durch eine initiale, zeitweise Entlokalisierung die Konstellation ihrer sozialen Bindungen verändert wurde. Ainuras partielle, jedoch dauerhafte Relokalisierung – die Rückkehr aus Chicago und Hawaii nach Bischkek, aber nicht nach Naryn – wurde möglich, weil die ‚international (donor) community', Ainuras prädestinierter lokaler Ausbilder und späterer Arbeitgeber, sich seit dem Ende der Sowjetunion ‚nachhaltig' in ihrer kirgisischen Heimat niedergelassen hatte.

Ainura gehört damit zu einer gegenwärtigen Generation junger Kirgisinnen, die als Reaktion auf einschneidende gesellschaftliche Übergänge eine spezifische Form multipler Identität und Lebenspraxis ausgebildet haben. Zu Beginn des 20. Jahrhunderts war für Ainuras Vorfahren der Eintritt in die ‚sowjetisch-sozialistische Moderne' verbunden mit signifikanten Veränderungen ihrer Alltagskultur und institutionellen Kontrolle (Fitzpatrick 1992), etwa im Zuge der Kampagne zur „Entschleierung" zentralasiatisch-muslimischer Frauen in den 1930er Jahren (Northrop 2004). Später, nach über 70 Jahren als Teil der Sowjetunion, stand eine andere Generation von Kirgisinnen vor der Herausforderung ihre sozialistische Sozialisation zu vereinbaren mit den neuen Realitäten eines unabhängigen Kirgistans, beispielsweise mit der Einführung einer kapitalistischen Marktwirtschaft und dem global vermittelten Streben nach individuellem Erfolg (Kuehnast 1998).

Für Ainura, Jahrgang 1980, und ihre Generation ist diese sowjetische Periode in der Geschichte ihrer Heimat nur noch am Rande erwähnenswert, da sie einen Großteil ihrer Lebenserfahrungen während und nach den 1990er Jahren gemacht hat. Dennoch lässt sich in Ainuras Lebenspraxis ein ähnlicher *modus operandi* erkennen wie ihn Kuehnast (1997: 372 f.) für die Generation ihrer Vorgängerinnen beschrieben hat: ein ‚collaborative conservatism', bei dem das kontinuierliche Einbeziehen des ‚kirgisischen Traditionalismus' allerdings nicht zu einem ängstlichen Zurückschrecken führt, und so dem simplen, dichotomischen Zusammenspiel von Dominanz und Unterordnung weicht, sondern zu einer pragmatischen ‚Offenheit' wird gegenüber sozialem Wandel.

Danksagung

Ich danke dem Max-Planck-Institut für ethnologische Forschung in Halle/Saale, das meine Feldforschung in Kirgistan und somit das Zustandekommen dieses Beitrags zwischen November 2006 und Januar 2011 unterstützt hat. Für wertvolle Kommentare und Anregungen danke ich besonders Peter Finke, Rita Sanders und Manja Stephan sowie den TeilnehmerInnen des Workshops ‚Mobility and Identity in Central Asia', der im Mai 2012 an der Universität Zürich stattfand.

Literatur

Abazov, R. 1999: Economic migration in post-Soviet Central Asia: The case of Kyrgyzstan. *Post-Communist Economies* 11:237–252.

Ackermann, A. 1997: Ethnologische Migrationsforschung: ein Überblick. In: P. Bräunlein (Hrsg.), *Ethnologie der Migration*. kea – Zeitschrift für Kulturwissenschaften (Vol. 10), pp. 1–28.

Agadjanian, V.; Nedoluzhko, L.; Kumskov, G. 2008: Eager to leave? Intentions to migrate abroad among young people in Kyrgyzstan. *International Migration Review* 42,3:620–651.

Anderson, J. 2000: Creating a Framework for Civil Society in Kyrgyzstan. *Europe-Asia Studies* 52,1:77–93.

Appadurai, A. 1996: *Modernity At Large: Cultural Dimensions of Globalization*. Minnesota: University of Minnesota Press.

Brettell, C. 2003: *Anthropology and Migration. Essays on Transnationalism, Ethnicity, and Identity*. Walnut Creek: AltaMira Press.

Cooley, A.; Ron, J. 2002: The NGO Scramble: Organizational Insecurity and the Political Economy of Transnational Action. *International Security* 27,1:5–39.

DeYoung, A. J. 2010: Embracing globalization: university experiences among youth in contemporary Kyrgyzstan. *Central Asian Survey* 29,4:421–434.

DeYoung, A. J. 2006: Problems and trends in education in Central Asia since 1990: the case of general secondary education in Kyrgyzstan. *Central Asian Survey* 25,4:499–514.

Donahoe, B.; Eidson, J.; Feyissa, D.; Fuest, V.; Hoehne, M. V.; Nieswand, B.; Schlee, G.; Zenker, O. 2009: *The Formation and Mobilization of Collective Identities in Situations of Conflict and Integration*. Max Planck Institute for Social Anthropology Halle/Saale, Working Paper No. 116.

Finke, P. 2002: Wandel sozialer Strukturen im ländlichen Mittelasien. In: A. Strasser, S. Haas, G. Mangott, und V. Heuberger (Hrsg.), *Zentralasien und Islam/Central Asia and Islam*. Hamburg: Deutsches Orient-Institut, pp. 137–149.

Fitzpatrick, S. 1992: *The Cultural Front. Power and Culture in Revolutionary Russia*. Ithaca und London: Cornell University Press.

Gladwell, M. 2009: *Outliers. The Story of Success*. London: Penguin Books.

Glick Schiller, N.; Fouron, G. E. 1999: Terrains of blood and nation: Haitian transnational social fields. *Ethnic and Racial Studies* 22,2:340–366.

Guichard, M. 2007: Hoch bewertet und oft unterschätzt: Theoretische und empirische Einblicke in Freundschaftsbeziehungen aus sozialanthropologischer Perspektive. In: J. F. K. Schmidt, M. Guichard, P. Schuster und F. Trillmich (Hrsg.), *Freundschaft und Verwandtschaft. Zur Unterscheidung und Verflechtung zweier Beziehungssysteme*. Konstanz: UVK, pp. 313–342.

Habeck, J. O.; Ventsel, A. 2009: Consumption and Popular Culture among Youth in Siberia. *Zeitschrift für Ethnologie* 134,1:1–22.

Handrahan, L. M. 2001: Gendering Ethnicity in Kyrgyzstan: Forgotten Elements in Promoting Peace and Democracy. *Gender and Development* 9,3:70–78.

Hannerz, U. 1980: *Exploring the City. Inquiries toward an Urban Anthropology*. New York: Columbia University Press.

Harris, C. 2006: *Muslim Youth: Tensions and Transitions in Tajikistan*. Boulder, Colorado: Westview Press.

Heady, P. 2007: Kameraden und Geschwister: Sympathie, Solidarität und Identität in sozialen Netzwerken. In: J. F. K. Schmidt, M. Guichard, P. Schuster und F. Trillmich (Hrsg.), *Freundschaft und Verwandtschaft. Zur Unterscheidung und Verflechtung zweier Beziehungssysteme*. Konstanz: UVK, pp. 343–367.

Hermann, E.; Röttger-Rössler, B. 2003: *Lebenswege im Spannungsfeld lokaler und globaler Prozesse: Person, Selbst und Emotion in der ethnologischen Biografieforschung*. Münster: LIT.

Hilgers, I. 2002: *Transformationsprozesse im Norden Kirgistans. Sozio-ökonomischer Wandel am Beispiel eines Dorfes*. Kölner Ethnologische Beiträge, Heft 3.

Howell, J. 1995: Household Coping Strategies in Kyrgyzstan. *Development in Practice* 5:361–364.

Humphrey, C. 1983: *Karl Marx Collective*. Cambridge: Cambridge University Press.

Isabaeva, Eliza 2011: Leaving to enable others to remain: remittances and new moral economies of migration in southern Kyrgyzstan. *Central Asian Survey* 30, 3–4:541–554.

Kandiyoti, D. 2007: The politics of gender and the Soviet paradox: neither colonized, nor modern? *Central Asian Survey* 26,4:601–623.

Kirmse, S. 2010: In the marketplace for styles and identities: globalization and youth culture in southern Kyrgyzstan. *Central Asian Survey* 29,4:389–403.

Kirmse, S. 2009: Leisure, business and fantasy worlds: exploring donor-funded 'youth spaces' in southern Kyrgyzstan. *Central Asian Survey* 28,3:289–301.

Kleinbach, R. 2003: Frequency of Non-Consensual Bride Kidnapping in the Kyrgyz Republic. *International Journal of Central Asian Studies* 9:108–128.

Kleinbach, R.; Ablezova, M.; Aitieva, M. 2005: Kidnapping for marriage (ala kachuu) in a Kyrgyz village. *Central Asian Survey* 24,2:191–202.

Kleinbach, R.; Salimjanova, L. 2007: Kyz ala kachuu and adat: non-consensual bride kidnapping and tradition in Kyrgyzstan. *Central Asian Survey* 26,2:217–233.

Knox, H.; Savage, M.; Harvey, P. 2006: Social networks and the study of relations: networks as method, metaphor and form. *Economy and Society* 35,1:113–140.

Kostyukova, I. 1994: The towns of Kyrgyzstan change their faces: rural-urban migrants in Bishkek. *Central Asian Survey* 13,3:425–434.

Kuehnast, K. 1998: From pioneers to entrepreneurs: young women, consumerism, and the 'world picture' in Kyrgyzstan. *Central Asian Survey* 17,4:639–654.

Kuehnast, K. 1997: *Let the Stone lie where it has fallen: Dilemmas of gender and generation in Post-Soviet Kyrgyzstan*. PhD thesis, University of Minnesota.

Marat, E. 2009: *Labor Migration in Central Asia: Implications of the Global Economic Crisis*. Central Asia-Caucasus Institute. Silk Road Studies Program: Silk Road Paper.

McBrien, J. 2009: Mukadas's struggle: veils and modernity in Kyrgyzstan. *Journal of the Royal Anthropological Institute* 15,1:127–144.

McBrien, J. 2007: Brazilian TV and Muslimness in Kyrgyzstan. *ISIM Review* 19:16–17.

McMann, K. M. 2003: The Civic Realm in Kyrgyzstan: Soviet Economic Legacies and Activists' Expectations. In: P.J. Luong (ed.), *The Transformation of Central Asia: States and Societies from Soviet Rule to Independence*. Ithaca: Cornell University Press, pp. 213–245.

Mendelson, S. E.; Glenn, J. K. 2002: *The power and limits of NGOs: a critical look at building democracy in Eastern Europe and Eurasia*. New York: Columbia University Press.

Mertaugh, M. 2004: Education in Central Asia, with Particular Reference to the Kyrgyz Republic. In: S. P. Heyneman (ed.), *The Challenges of Education in Central Asia*. Greenwich, Connecticut: Information Age, pp. 153–180.

Merton, R. K. 1968: The Matthew Effect in Science. The reward and communication systems of science are considered. *Science* 159,3810:56–63.

Mische, A.; White, H. 1998: Between conversation and situation: public switching dynamics across network domains. *Social Research* 65:695–724.

Nedoluzhko, L.; Agadjanian, V. 2010: Marriage, childbearing, and migration in Kyrgyzstan: Exploring interdependencies. *Demographic Research* 22,7:159–188.

Northrop, D. 2004: *Veiled Empire. Gender & Power in Stalinist Central Asia*. Ithaca und London: Cornell University Press.

Pétric, B.-M. 2005: Post-Soviet Kyrgyzstan or the birth of a globalized protectorate. *Central Asian Survey* 24,3:319–332.

Pilkington, H.; Omel'chenko, E.; Flynn, M.; Bliudina, U.; Starkova, E. 2002: *Looking West? Cultural Globalization and Russian Youth Cultures*. University Park: Pennsylvania State University Press.

Reeves, M. 2012: Black Work, Green Money: Remittances, Ritual, and Domestic Economies in Southern Kyrgyzstan. *Slavic Review* 71,1:108–134.

Reeves, M. 2011: Staying put? Towards a relational politics of mobility at a time of migration. *Central Asian Survey* 30,3–4:555–576.

Reeves, M. 2005: Of Credits, Kontrakty and Critical Thinking: encountering 'market reforms' in Kyrgyzstani higher education. *European Educational Research Journal* 4,1:5–21.

Reeves, M. 2003: Cultivating ‚Citizens of a New Type'. The Politics and Practice of Educational Reform at the American University in Kyrgyzstan. In: S.P. Heyneman (ed.), *The challenges of education in Central Asia*. Greenwich, Connecticut: Information Age, pp. 365–385.

Roy, O. 2005: The Predicament of 'Civil Society' in Central Asia and the 'Greater Middle East'. *International Affairs* 81,5:1001–1012.

Ruget, V.; Usmanalieva, B. 2008: Citizenship, migration and loyalty towards the state: a case study of the Kyrgyzstani migrants working in Russia and Kazakhstan. *Central Asian Survey* 27,2:129–141.

Schmidt, M.; Sagynbekova, L. 2008: Migration past and present: changing patterns in Kyrgyzstan. *Central Asian Survey* 27,2:111–127.

Schröder, P. 2012: *From Shanghai to Iug-2: Identification and Integration among and beyond the Male Youth of a Bishkek Neighbourhood*. Dissertationsschrift, Martin-Luther-Universität Halle-Wittenberg.

Schröder, P. 2011: Der Alltag der 'revolutionären' Jugend Kirgistans. *Zentralasien-Analysen* 48:2–5.

Schröder, P. 2010: 'Urbanizing' Bishkek: interrelations of boundaries, migration, group size and opportunity structure. *Central Asian Survey* 29,4:453–467.

Shamatov, D. 2005: Challenges of Education and History Teaching in Kyrgyzstan. In: M. Gervers, U. E. Bulag und G. Long (eds.), *History and Society in Central and Inner Asia*. University of Toronto, Toronto Studies in Central and Inner Asia, pp. 275–295.

Smith, M. 2011: Translocality: A Critical Reflection. In: K. Brickell and A. Datta (eds.), *Translocal Geographies. Spaces, Places, Connections*. Surrey: Ashgate, pp. 181–198.

Strasser, E. 2009: Was ist Migration? In: M. Six-Hohenbalken and J. Tosic (Hrsg.), *Anthropologie der Migration. Theoretische Grundlagen und interdisziplinäre Aspekte*. Wien: Facultas, S. 15–28.

Werbner, R P. 1984: The Manchester School in South-Central Africa. *Annual Review of Anthropology* 13,1:157–185.

Werner, C. 2009: Bride abduction in post-Soviet Central Asia: marking a shift towards patriarchy through local discourses of shame and tradition. *Journal of the Royal Anthropological Institute* 15,2:314–331.

Wilkinson, C., und A. Kirey. 2010: What's in a name? The personal and political meanings of 'LGBT' for non-heterosexual and transgender youth in Kyrgyzstan. *Central Asian Survey* 29,4:485–499.

Labour Migration and the Ritual Economy of the Uzbek Extended Family

Alisher Ilkhamov

Centre of Contemporary Central Asia and the Caucasus, School of Oriental and African Studies (SOAS), University of London, Thornhaugh Street, Russell Square, London GB–WC1H 0XG

Abstract. Of all aspects of labour migration in Central Asia, one of the least studied is the impact of cross-national mobility upon the migrants' home societies, particularly the daily life style of individuals and families. This essay focuses less upon how and under what conditions the labour migrants make their income, but upon how they and their families spend it, how patterns of consumption are affected by customs of ritual life and the role structures characteristic to extended families and whether these customs and role structures are being affected by the process of labour migration. The essay establishes that in a significant number of cases, the migrants' experiences abroad not only refrain from leading to an erosion of the patriarchal family order and ritual economy, but actually reinforce them. The large proportion of remittances committed to ritual obligations is explained by two kinds of calculations and motivations: 1) consideration by migrants' families of ritual life as a kind of investment into solidarity networks that indeed often help the migrants survive and succeed in their foreign odyssey; and 2) families' desire to maintain their own social status and prestige among the local community. These expectations often prove to be illusory and drive already poor families into greater poverty.
[*labor migration; extended family; ritual economy; family budget; remittances*]

Introduction

The growth of labour migration

Although a great deal has been written on labour migration from Central Asia, the impact of this phenomenon on the fabric of society and family life in particular has been neglected. During Soviet times, the indigenous population of Uzbekistan (ethnic Uzbeks, Tajiks, Karakalpaks, and others) had among the lowest rates of mobility/migration among the Soviet republics. These populations tended to refrain from leaving its homeland, preferring to seek a livelihood in the country. From 1968–1970, only 1.4 % of ethnic Uzbeks were migrating from the republic, while among ethnic Russians of Uzbekistan labour migrants constituted 6.7 %.[1] Most of the labour migration took place between provinces of Uzbekistan, from villages to cities, from provinces to

---

[1] *Itogi vsesoyuznoi perepisi naselenia 1970 g.* V. VII, Moscow: Statistika, p. 84.

the capital, or from the over-populated Fergana Valley to the newly irrigated *virgin lands* in Djizakh and Syrdarya oblasts. This intra-republic migration, driven mostly by the lack of living space in densely populated areas, had a limited impact on the patterns of Uzbek family and social life.

Uzbekistan had been a destination country for immigrants from other parts of the Soviet Union, with migrants coming mainly from Russia, Ukraine, and Belarus. It should be noted that in Uzbekistan there was an ethnic division of labour whereby the European populations were mainly urban and employed in technical industrial occupations whereas a majority of Uzbeks were occupied in rural economy. The immigration significantly increased the ratio of the Russian-speaking population in Uzbekistan, and this change in the ethnic composition of the republic had deep social and cultural impacts on the local societies, such as the expansion of the Russian language and the adoption of elements of "European" lifestyles and habits by the local populations.

The Uzbeks' low geographical mobility continued after the dissolution of the USSR. However, by the end of the first decade of Independence (1999–2000) the situation changed dramatically. Forced by the steady decline in living standards, Uzbek citizens turned to a new kind of nomadic lifestyle after centuries of being a sedentary, settled people, to cope with the new economic reality.

The broken social contract between the government and population that took place at the end of 1990s[2] was the push factor for labour migration. This occurred together with the government's crackdown on bazaars and petty cross-border trade, which were the main sources of livelihood for hundreds of thousands of people as the country's industry and welfare system fell into decline. This needs some clarification. Among the Soviet republics Uzbekistan was always a labour surplus country where rural underemployment was endemic. The labour surplus was absorbed by a combination of a public sector and various petty business activities, mainly in the household economy and petty trade. What broke down with so-called agrarian reforms of de-collectivization was the capacity to keep this labour on the land plus a crackdown on informal sector activities that had become a last refuge for the post-Soviet new poor. At the same time and in contrast to Uzbekistan, Russia and Kazakhstan experienced remarkable economic growth, driving Uzbeks and other Central Asians to these two relatively wealthy countries for work. On top of that, prospective migrants enjoy the visa-free regimes and can use their Russian language skills (at least part of the older population of Uzbeks can speak fluently Russian).

According to estimates cited by Konstantin Romodanovsky, head of the Russian Federal Migration Service, as for January 2013 there were around 2 mln Uzbek citizens in Russia[3]. 760 thousand had work permits, while 885 thousand arrived with in-

---

[2] See: Deniz Kandiyoti, Andijan: prelude to a massacre, 13 May 2009, http://www.opendemocracy.net/globalization-institutions_government/Andijan_2527.jsp.
[3] *Interfax, 21 January 2013,* http://www.interfax.ru/txt.asp?id=286161 (retrieved on 23 November, 2013).

Table 1 Money transfers from Russia to Uzbekistan, 2007–2012.

Years	Transfers, US$ bln
2007	1,666
2008	3,007
2009	2,071
2010	3,834
2011	4,692
2012	6,241

Source: Central Bank of Russian Federation, 2013[4]

tention to work but didn't have necessary documents for that. The rest had arrived with other visit purpose. In other words, almost 900 thousand Uzbeks live and work in Russia without the required residence registration and work permits. Some independent experts, such as Moscow-based Valentina Chupik, show even higher figures, with two-thirds of Uzbek migrants preferring Russia to other countries.[5]

The scale and dynamics of migration can be assessed indirectly, by looking at remittances. Table 1 shows the growth of remittances from Russia to Uzbekistan, most likely a result of the increase in the number of migrants rather than the growth of average individual incomes.

The discourse of tradition and social change

How does this increased out-migration affect society in Uzbekistan? Certainly, the dramatic shift in attitudes of Uzbeks toward migration has inaugurated significant social changes. The question is, however, whether this shift triggers a series of social changes in Uzbek society, apart from its socio-economic impacts. This paper will explore whether the experiences and ventures of Uzbekistanis in foreign countries, their encounter with cultures more affected by industrialization than the Uzbek society, shakes Uzbeks' common, traditional worldviews, which will be addressed below. To what extent does migration change their life goals, priorities, needs, and how they live their daily lives when they eventually return back home? This paper seeks to answer this by exploring the institution of the Uzbek family and how its consumption patterns are affected by these migration trends. Consumption will be examined through family budget, its priorities, management, and rules driving income and benefits distribution among family members.

---

[4] http://www.cbr.ru/statistics/CrossBorder/print.asp?file=Personal_Remittances_CIS.htm (retrieved on 23. 11. 2013).
[5] Source: Valentina Chupik, NGO 'Tong Jahoni', Uzbekistan, 2005.

Family life in Uzbekistan is diverse, ranging from families more affected by a modern, late-Soviet or western style worldview to those more dedicated to Uzbek ethnic customs and traditions. To find out the extent of the social and cultural impact of labour migration on Uzbek society, one needs first to look to which extent the categories of family most resistant to social change and modern industrial life are affected. That is why the so-called "traditional family" and its strategic priorities and consumption patterns are the main focus of this essay.

But what can we say about this category of the Uzbek family? We use the term "traditional" with the understanding expressed by Eric Hobsbawm and Terence Ranger (Hobsbawm & Ranger 1992), of it having been "invented" as an opposition to "modern". Nevertheless, we can legitimately use this term to describe the reality in Uzbekistan if we regard tradition and modernity not as 'natural' or primordial entities, but as beings subject to contestation and bargaining by various individuals, families and communities. We can define, for the purpose of academic inquiry, a "traditional family" as one that is guided by a shared understanding of traditions and customs. Such traditional families have their own social and geographical coordinates and can be found in rural areas and small towns, rather than in cities whose population is characterised by relatively larger ethnic, cultural, and occupational diversity and respective inter-cultural borrowings and assimilation.

Methodology and References

This essay is based on materials from three separate studies in which I also took part in the planning and analysis.

The first of the three was conducted in 2001[6] as part of "Social Development Research Cooperation Project", and henceforth will be referred to as "SDRC 2001." The results of this research are based on 51 individual household interviews and eight focus group discussions held in Ferghana oblast, in Ferghana city and a few surrounding rural areas.

The second study, to be referred to as "Migration Survey 2007", was implemented by the Petersburg Centre for Independent Sociological Research in 2007 and focused on the processes of Uzbek labour emigration.[7] 64 interviews with labour migrants from Uzbekistan in Petersburg, Kazan (Russia), Almaty and Shymkent (Kazakhstan), as well as with former migrants and their families living in two areas of Uzbekistan (in

---

[6] The Project Director was Dr. Deniz Kandiyoti. The fieldwork research was performed by two research centers, 'Expert' (coordinator and chief researcher Alisher Ilkhamov) and 'Sharkh' (coordinator Nadira Azimova).

[7] The Project Director was Dr. Sergey Abashin. I've been a member of the research group and assisted in the preparation of its program, methodology and instruments. The author had presented his own analytical findings at the project's working meeting held in London in November, 2007.

rural Andijan and in Samarkand city) were conducted. This paper will refer primarily to the ten interviews taken in Andijan oblast as representative of families exemplifying traditional Uzbek values.

The third study, "Migration Survey 2011", was conducted by the same Petersburg Centre in 2011 with the fieldwork having been carried out in Petersburg, Kazan, Pskov, and Samarkand. 43 migrants (and former migrants from Samarkand) were interviewed.[8]

Though none of these three projects were initially intended to be part of a comparative study, they all address comparable issues, relevant to the subject of the Uzbek family and, in the last two studies, labour migration. All of the studies used the methodology of qualitative research, employing in-depth, non-standardized interviews. Given the small number of interviews considered here, it is impossible to claim representativeness, from a statistical point of view, of data collected, but they are sufficiently representative of a significant part of a population, particularly those living in rural areas and small urban settlements (so called *posiolki*, in Russian). The ratio of rural population to the general population in Uzbekistan remained very high throughout the late Soviet period, at 60%, and has even increased since, reaching 64% in 2007.[9] When coupled with populations living in small towns, this figure would be even higher. This allows us to qualify the rural segments of the population as the mainstream of Uzbek Society, which is even more the case in some regions, where the ratio of rural population is even higher, as, for instance, in Fergana (71%, or 76% if coupled with those living in small towns) and in Andijan oblasts (65% and 83% respectively). Ethnically, the populations in villages and small towns tend to be less diverse than in cities making them correspondingly less affected by social and cultural influences of other ethnic groups, Russians in particular.

Uzbek extended family as bearer of 'tradition'

Extended Families and Tradition

As some scholars suggest, family, as an institution, provides structure and guidelines for behaviour, and shapes human interaction between its members (Martin 2004; North 1990; Scott 1995). This chapter explores the social positions and roles in the traditional Uzbek family, a social order driven by patriarchal norms which are not fixed properties but are often in reality negotiated, contested and bargained by various actors involved (Kandiyoti 1988). And this space for bargaining has its own limits safe-

---

[8] The project director was Elena Chikadze. I assisted in the preparation of its program, methodology and instruments.
[9] Uzbekistan in Figures, UNDP, http://statistics.design.uz/data_finder/2335/ (retrieved on 17. 05. 2012).

guarded by the local community. For the purpose of empirical verification, the term "extended family" will be used in this context to refer to the traditional family. By extended family, in its Uzbek context,[10] we mean families with more than one adult generation living together that can constitute a single household or extend beyond it comprising of more than one household. One of constituting features of such families is a united family budget. Even if the family consists of more than one household, its members earning income are expected to contribute to such a united budget, at least for certain spending targets defined as a rule by the family's patriarch, while other family members would benefit from the united budget depending on one's age, situational needs, and financial earning capabilities. Although not synonymous, the "extended family" and the "traditional family" are closely associated with each other, as the former often bears patriarchal traditions and customs, more so than nuclear families that are not members of tightknit patrilineal and patrilocal extended family networks.

Our observations suggest that relationships within extended families are often governed by traditional (read patriarchal) values and norms characteristic of a male-dominated social hierarchy. The extent to which the patriarchal values and norms influence the relationships within extended families varies from one family to another. This influence has also definitely waned to some degree during the Soviet era as a result of social and economic modernization policies of the Soviet regime, in particular, the process of urbanization and the creation of multi-ethnic settlements with a significant ratio of the Russian speaking population.

According to some Russian ethnographers (Sazonova 1952), the size of an Uzbek extended family forming a single household at the end of the 19th century could include 45–60 family members. During the Soviet era, the average size of extended families diminished dramatically. Field research by Tommaso Trevisani in Uzbekistan's Khorezm region between 2002 and 2005 detected households of extended families of six to seven members (Trevisani 2010: 46). This dramatic reduction of the size of a family (constituting a single household) over the last century has transformed it as a social institution. Yet, the traditional extended family has not disappeared as such.

One also should take into account existing family networks uniting more than one single household into a complex socio-economic unit. According to Trevisani's local informants, extended family networks still play crucial a role in the material lives and livelihoods of villagers (Trevisani 2010: 46). Therefore, for the purpose of this research, we will take into account not only extended families forming one single household, but also family networks that are split among more than one household; they share a combined family budget, in terms of income contribution and jointly plan expenses. All three studies shed light upon both forms of the extended family – those forming a single household and those formed of more than one household.

---

[10] I am not trying here to give a universal definition of the extended family, only the phenomenon observed in the field research referred to in this essay.

Normally, in such extended family units and networks, the elder male parent occupies the leading position, ruling over the most important family affairs, foremost the united family budget, regardless of his own contribution to it. For example, if he is already retired and contributes only his modest pension, and his children earn much more than he, the children are expected to yield at least part of their income and their right to make decisions over this joint family budget to the parents. This rule is observed not in all extended family units and networks, but quite common for rural Uzbek society.

Extended family's budget priorities

The 2001 SDRC survey concluded that the Uzbek traditional family, specifically its head, faces four overarching life goals and obligations, apart from daily breadwinning duties (such as food, clothes, medical, etc.): 1) marrying off of children as they come of age; 2) building new houses for married children; 3) celebrating traditional lifecycle events, including weddings (*nikokh toi*), funerals (*ma'raka*), births (*beshik toi*), circumcision of boys (*sunnat toi*); remembrance parties (*khudoyee*)[11]; and 4) providing education for children. Whereas the first, second, and fourth are common to many societies, not only traditional ones, the third task – the omnipresent custom of organizing large-scale, lifecycle ceremonies can be considered as something unique to communities guided by traditional values and norms. For the purpose of analysis, I will further focus on this allegiance of families to ritual life and examine how it is affected by labour migration, whether it continues or diminishes due to the experience of migrants' interaction with host societies.

Apart from ceremonial duties as one of budget spending priorities, another feature of traditional extended families is the strong commitment of their members to the united family budget that results in the redistribution of individual incomes for the benefit of those in the family most in need. Here is a typical example from the series of interviews conducted in 2007.[12]

> The Usmanovs are a three-generation multi-household family network living in a village in the Djalakuduk district of Andijan oblast: the head of the family, his wife, and four adult children, including three sons Tolib, Turghun, and Anwar, and one daughter, Rayhon, each of whom have their own families with young children. According to local traditions, as the Usmanovs said, as soon as the eldest son reaches the age when he is expected to create his own family, he becomes eligible for the creation of a separate household and applies to the local authorities for a land plot

---

[11] Strictly speaking, the remembrance ceremony belongs bot to life-cycle, but to propitiatory ceremonies, but closely related to them.
[12] The name is changed to meet the respondent's preference.

to build his own house.[13] This entitlement to a new land plot is enables him to separate from the parents' household. The youngest son, Anwar is supposed to live with the parents, even when he also reaches the age of marriage and creates his own family. At the time of the interview, Anwar was 29 years old and lived with his wife and children in the same household with his parents, while his brothers and sister lived in separate households. Anwar has a separate house in the same yard with his parents, yet his family creates with parents a united household as they share one cooking pot and share income and expenses on other daily needs.

Anwar's siblings who live separately meet their daily budgets independently from the parents and Anwar's family. However, in spite of having separate households, all of them, with the exception of Rayhon, are bound to each other by a mutual commitment to run the united budget aimed at the extended family's strategic priorities, that is, to conduct life-cycle ceremonies and build houses for any family member who starts a family. For instance, all brothers contributed financially and with labour to build a house for Anwar and arrange his wedding celebration and other associated ceremonies. The oldest brother had been the first beneficiary in queue to receive financial, material and labour contributions from other family members. As for Rayhon, she is not expected to contribute very much, as her life is now tied around another family network built around their own male lineage members. This feature, the family formation around the men, with sons and not daughters being considered as the holders of family blood and heritage, is an essential feature of these extended families. Daughters are considered by local traditions as a 'cut slice', or a loss to the expanded family's budget[14], rather than an asset as she, once joined to another family, is expected to follow her husband's kin interests. In cases of good and cooperative relationships between the daughters' birth and married families, both families may unite their resources and assets, but this is not so often the case. On the contrary, there are plenty of examples of feuds between the two parties.

Patriarchal "communism"

The system of intra-family commitments and support can be viewed as a sort of patriarchal "communism," to some extent akin to primitive communism, described by

---

[13] According to the law, each young family is entitled to get a land plot for creating a household, it is, however, a subject of land availability which varies depending up the density of population in the region in question. In rural areas and in provinces the might be more available lands for households, than in larger urban settlements.

[14] However, in some parts of the country, especially among Karakalpaks and Kazakhs, the family marrying off their daughter would expect from the groom's family a "ransom" (*kalym*) the amount of which can be substantial.

Friedrich Engels in his work "The Origin of the Family, Private Property and the State" (Engels 1884). In the societies of primitive communism all able-bodied persons would have been engaged in obtaining food, and everyone would share in what was produced by all of them. Members of today's extended family scrutinized here also can be considered as having subscribed to the principle "from each according to his ability, to each according to his needs". As such, this family constitutes, to a certain extent, the "communist" order of the redistribution of resources. At the same time it is patriarchal because the elder members in such a family have superiority towards the younger generation, and the men towards the women. The head of an extended family, usually the oldest male family member, assumes the role of the chief decision maker in governing the family's budgetary affairs, a role recognized and not challenged by others in the family and among the surrounding community in which the family is embedded. Thus the "communist" spirit of the family in question is belittled by its patriarchal order and not quite egalitarian as communist principles would imply. The family priority needs the family-owned resources to be redistributed for they are also defined not by their bearers, especially when they are younger family members, but imposed from above, i.e. decided by the elders who would say: "You, my son (or my little brother), have grown up and it's time to get married, so we're going organize a decent wedding party for you, and we'll need to observe all rituals according to our customs and traditions and our fathers' testaments". Indeed, such a family order is patriarchal also because it abides by rules, norms and traditions blessed and "bequeathed" by fathers in the past. At least, many bearers of tradition sincerely believe they are following the testaments of their patriarchs in the past. Such a belief is reinforced by various public narratives circulated on local and national levels.

In reality, there are some exceptions to the rule of man's superiority, such as in the case when the male head has died or earns considerably less than his wife. Unable to assert his role as a breadwinner, he may cede the role of decision maker to his wife. But such examples are rare. Here are several other examples of the patriarchal order of decision making in the expanded family:

> 'My father is steward of our budget.' (Man, 29, Aim village, Andijan, 2007)
> 'Everything we earn we gather in one common pool. We live in the following concert: elders help the younger; money I earn helps to solve our common problems: weddings, rites, clothes, home repairs. The pool is divided evenly between the brothers. Now the younger brother lives with our parents. I need to help him with home repairs, and the same with elder brothers. (Male, 34, Aim village, Andijan, 2007)
> I give all my earnings to my father and keep only pocket money for myself. That is the rule in our community: money is managed by the elders. .... My sister is with her husband in Russia, but they don't send money; they have their own family budget. (Male, 31, Aim village, Andijan, 2007).
> I've spent my son's earnings on house repairs and expansion (Father of the main informant, Male, 25, Aim village, Andijan, 2007).

As soon as the head of the family passes away, his wife or eldest son may take over as the head. The eldest son would be responsible not only for his own family and household, but for his brothers and sisters who constitute an expanded family.

Drawing parallels with the communist principle of the accumulation and redistribution of wealth, the other side of the coin is the lack of individual freedoms characteristic of patriarchal families. The younger the member of the patriarchal family, the less rights he or she is entitled to in many aspects, such as in selecting their spouses, which is particularly the case for young women. As a rule, parents select spouses for their children, although there are exceptions, i.e. numerous cases in Uzbekistan in which young couples find each other in love. Yet, the situation cited below is quite common:

- How did you meet your husband? Did you marry him because you liked him?
- No, that's not customary here for people to like each other. We marry the one who is chosen by our parents.

(Female, unmarried girl, Yaz'yavan, Ferghana oblast, SDRC 2001)

The lack of individual freedom does not mean that the rule of the elders is imposed by means of coercion. In distinction from state socialism, instead of coercion the power of local traditions, reinforced by the family and local community and by local public opinion, strictly define the distribution of roles within the family, so that the younger generation and the women, as a rule, do not question this patriarchal social order. Their obedience may often look voluntary, although in reality there are examples, not many, however, when this social order is challenged and disobeyed by the young and women.

Family's ritual economy

Rites of passage blessed by Uzbek customs

The family network of Usmanovs described above represents a remarkable example of solidarity network. It requires sacrifices from each family member, with the wealthier members contributing more than others, but at the same time, ensures the survival and wellbeing of the family as a whole by bestowing benefits to each of its members sometimes in a greater amount than their individual contributions to the joint pool. However, along with this seeming harmony, the traditional extended family bear some features that may outweigh the advantages of its communal character.

The problem arises when it comes to coming to consensus on how the united family budget is to be spent. Among the priority needs of the traditional family, costs associated with observing rites and ceremonies are significant, and this is how the family budget is spent. Both contributions to the united family budget and the way this budget is spent are to a large extent defined by tradition and national customs. The part of the family budget spent on ritual would be directly proportional to the extent of the family's susceptibility to pressure from the patriarchal authority represented by the older parents, older relatives, and the neighbourhood community. Kandiyoti and Azimova identified three types of ceremonies among the rites practiced by Uzbek women: sacred, lifecycle, and propitiatory (Kandiyoti & Azimova 2004). These types of rituals can be applied to the society at large regardless of gender, and for the purposes of the current analysis, the life-cycle, or rites of passage, according Van Gennep (Van Gennep 1960), and propitiatory ceremonies are directly related as they represent relatively expensive items of the family budget, in comparison with expenditures on other family needs.

Among the ritual events that are subjects for the family budget, some are more or less important from the point of view how the custom is understood and what is most endorsed by local public opinion. Many traditional families consider marriage and funeral celebrations as obligatory, whereas other rituals, like *beshik-toi*, or *sunnat-toi*, may be considered optional. But observation of even these less important rituals would serve families' prestige and respectability in their local community.

Local traditions and customs, and how they are understood and observed follow specific rules, which give rise to social expectations that traditional families, sensitive to local public opinion, try to meet. They do so by spending their family budgets on various ritual celebrations. The costs of these celebrations may vary depending on three major factors: the family wealth; how much prestige the head of the family seeks for the family; and the minimal requirements needed to receive the endorsement of the local community. The requirements for organizing a wedding are especially complex in Uzbek traditional society. In many regions of the country, they include the following sub-events and corresponding budget costs:

- Main wedding party (*nikoh toi*) – conducted in evening, usually done with a two-three course menu and entertainment (music and dance)[15]. Often the party is split into two parties, in the home of bride and in the home of the groom. All relatives, friends, and members of neighbourhood community are invited, and the number of invitees can reach more than a hundred people. This party can be organized either at home or by renting a restaurant or banquet hall. The latter has become quite fashionable recently, especially in Tashkent.
- *Osh* – a short party organized in the morning or daytime. All relatives, friends and members of neighbourhood community, often more than from one *mahalla*, are invited. The menu would be more modest than at the *nikoh-toi*, but it is supposed

---

[15] In the last several years, holding so-called Muslim wedding celebrations are becoming also prestigious, especially in the Ferghana valley. They are distinct by eliminating the entertainment program. Instead of it, an imam is invited. He reads a Muslim sermon. Men and women seating are separated stricter than in the usual *nikoh-toi*. The latter is also to observe Muslim tradition, but it is limited to visiting to the local imam for his blessing prior to the evening party.

to serve a greater number of people. Members of nearby neighbourhoods are also invited. Musical accompaniment is expected.

- *Chaqirdi* - a smaller party organized on the day following the *nikoh* party. Mainly closer relatives and friends are invited. It is organized by both families, one after another on different days.
- Apart from parties, the families of the bride and groom prepare a dowry. The bride's family prepares and presents to the newlyweds the *sep* (a set of clothes for the bride and groom, furniture, and other home furnishings). The groom's family presents the bride's family (*sarpo*) and provides a living space for the newlyweds. In some regions that have a nomadic tradition, the groom's family is expected to pay *kalym*, a "ransom" for the bride.
- *Challa* – a small party organized mainly for women of both sides during which they examine the content of *sep*, and sometimes the evidences of bride's virginity prior to the wedding celebration. *Challa* is organized on the following day after the *nikoh-toi*.

In terms of the costs of meeting these requirements, weddings turn out to be the most expensive among all life-cycle rituals. Funeral celebrations, *maraqa*, are also expensive, as they are not simply a one-off celebration, but a series of parties held over a period of time. The first of them is held on the seventh day of the death of a family member. The second is organized on the fortieth day, and called *qyrq*. The third is held on the first anniversary. Although after this series of events, the close relatives of the deceased may be considered to have paid their respects, they may also celebrate remembrance through the so-called *khudoyee,* the sacrifice parties dedicated to the memory of all family members who have passed away. *Khudoyee* is not strictly required by the customs but its celebration is endorsed by local public opinion and allows the family to gain greater respect among the local community.

The burden of ritual life

Needless to say, all of these celebrations place a significant burden on family budgets. Table 2 shows the estimated cost of a wedding party (*nikoh toi*) (which is only part of the marriage ritual), calculated on the basis of the 2001 SDRC survey. It shows that the cash expenses for the party varied from 170 to 3000 US dollars, a significant amount of money in 2001, when living standards hit bottom and labour migration only began to rise. For comparison, monthly individual cash income varied among the interviewed residents of Fergana oblast between 4.1 and 30 US dollars, thus making expenses for *niqoh toi* exceeding their monthly salaries by 3 to 373 times. Families could pay for these weddings only by dipping into savings accumulated over years. Table 3 shows that the average cost of the various ritual events most often exceeds the annual cash income of a nuclear family, and in the case of weddings, often five

Table 2 Households' expenses for wedding celebrations (nikoh-tois). 2001 SDRC survey data.

Infor-mants	Monthly cash income, US$	Expenses in cash on the wedding party (nikoh-toi), US$**	Ratio of expenses to per capita cash income, times	Disposal in kind (cattle and sheep mainly from own household economy)				Number of people invited
				Cattle	Sheep	Meat, kg	Rice, kg	
1	8.5	250.0	29					500
2	4.1	*	*		1		100	124
3	10.8	170.0	16					*
4	8.3	300.0	36					200
5	6.4	600.0	93					60
6	8.7	*	*					200
7	30.3	1,000.0	33				70	500
8	11.9	800.	67		1			*
9	6.3	3,000.0	473					*
10	7.9	*	*	2	5		30	*
11	9.9	400.0	40					140
12	8.3	310.0	37					200
13	4.1	185.0	45					15

* – Data not available
** – estimated by informants themselves

Table 3 Average cost per different types of ritual celebrations. 2001 SDRC survey data.

	Average cost, US$	Average number of guests invited	Average monthly per capita cash income (nuclear family), US$	Ratio of celebration cost to monthly per capita cash income	Average annual per capita cash income, US$	Ratio of celebration cost to annual per capita cash income
Nikoh-toi	530	223	8.4	63	101	5.3
Maraqa per event	93	161	8.4	11	101	0.9
A series of maraqa events (3 times)	279	161	8.4	33	101	2.8
Sunnat-toi	166	120	8.4	20	101	1.6

times more than an annual income, a *maraqa* party, three times, and *sunnat toi*, 1.6 times.

A single family can meet all of these requirements if its members accumulate resources far in advance before the planned or expected event is to be celebrated. The priority targets of the extended family's budgets are not ad-hoc, but long anticipated and predetermined by established rules and priorities require preparation, saving, and sacrifice over a long period of time. Most traditional Uzbek families are well aware of what age (or at, least, approximately) they will marry, start a family, have children.

Accordingly, it is possible to calculate resources an extended family would need to meet all of these expectations. Some families do such calculation with greater precision and others with less. What is curious, they make estimations in kind, for instance, in a number of sheep, cows, bulls, kilos of meat or rice, rather than in cash:

- When did you organize a *sunnat-toi* for him [son]?
- In 1995. We had been preparing for this event for 5–6 years, since our elder son was born.
- What did it cost for you?
- One bull that we bought two years before, in 1993 for 500 *soum*, and nurtured it. 20–30 kg of cotton seed oil, 50–60 kg of carrots, vodka for 300 *soum* (that time vodka costed 10 soums a bottle), etc.

(Male, Turkiravot, Ferghana oblast, 2001)

To afford such significant expenses, families sacrifice on their other needs, including nutrition, education, personal development. To some extent, the burden of ritual obligations is spread due to support from the broader family network and community. Mahalla committees have some equipment, furniture, and tableware that can be used by mahalla residents for a symbolic fee. Many mahallas in urban apartment building estates also jointly build buildings where families can hold events. Nevertheless, the costs of meals for a large number of guests, and for musicians (for wedding and *sunnat tois*) are so high that in many cases they have a devastating effect on the financial wellbeing of a family.

In any circumstance, each family goes through a sequence of long term accumulation of savings and one-off disposals of the accumulated wealth. This is characteristic of many families that strictly observe national customs and can be called the 'growth and busts' model, borrowing the terminology from the boom and bust model characteristic of capitalist societies. Indeed, after completing expensive events as wedding celebrations, a family may go bankrupt and acquire debts it will pay off for months and years to come.

It turns out that the zealous observation of national customs to some extent contributes to poverty. The solidarity networks of extended family, instead of working for the wellbeing of their members, often works counter to that if their needs and priorities are affected by traditional customs and consideration of their social status and prestige. One can argue, however, whether or not these costly ritual celebrations indeed can be attributed to national traditions and customs. There is a debate in the society around this question; Muslim clerics have spoken out against such expensive ceremonies and state authorities have several times condemned expensive wedding celebrations and other similar events.[16] In spite of that, the social norms established in

---

[16] On 28 October 1998 President Karimov signed a decree banning ostentatious ceremonies as 'offensive' to the general public (Arifhanova 2011; Kandiyoti & Azimova 2004:337). The last such campaign against the squander of resources in holding wedding and other kinds of ritual celebrations was launched by the government in 2003. It was accompanied by the *fatwa* by the mufti Abdurashid qori

many Uzbek communities, the norms of social prestige and respectability seem to be left unshakeable by these condemnations and administrative measures. Partly it is explained by the fact that many wealthy state officials and businessmen continue the tradition of lavish celebrations with the respective demonstrative effect for the rest of society, thereby reinforcing the norms of social prestige. Partly it is due to the fact that people are still influenced by widely circulated narratives that it is mandatory to follow what their fathers prescribed for them and the celebration has a blessing or "purifying" effect upon their families:

> In our Uzbek families, the son's wedding, the daughter's marriage, *sunnat* and *khudoyi*, are considered a tradition inherited from our ancestors. That's why I believe it is mandatory to organize these events. For example, *khatmi sunnat* is also considered important, because a boy who was born and brought up in this family is "purified." This rite is rooted in the wish of his parents to see their son grow up, get married, leave children behind, and be a continuer of the clan. If our son gets married, we shall soon (in nine months) have a grandson (granddaughter). After the baby is born, of course, a *beshik toi* should be organized. This event is essential to strengthen the family. It should be organized sooner, one year after the baby was born. The man's mother and 10–15 others goes to the wife's house. We spend 50 % and they, that is, the girl's mother, spends 50 %. The purpose and meaning of *beshik toi* is that the child growing up in the *beshik* [cradle] will become healthy and strong. We follow a saying of our ancestors: *beshik*'s baby is *bek*'s baby [meaning master's baby – A. I.]. In our family we often organize *khudoyee* - once or twice a year. This event is organized for remembering the souls of dead fathers, grandfathers, mothers. This is a honourable thing [to organize these events]. For *khudoyee* they invite 10–15 women from the *mahalla*, read the *Quran* and serve food. It lasts 2–4 hours, then everyone leaves (female, Turkiravot, Ferghana oblast, 2001).

The factor of labour migration

Remittances spending patterns

What has emerged from migration surveys in 2007 and 2011 is that the escape from hunger and extreme poverty isn't the main driving force behind migration. The survey of 2007 especially revealed that the families who sent members to Russia and Kazakhstan for work were able to survive financially without leaving their homeland. What forced them to go abroad was the lack of opportunities in the local job market to ex-

---

Bakhromov who called upon the Muslims to restrain from too lavish and pompous ceremonies and rites. (Fergananews.com, 1 April, 2003, http://www.ferghana.ru/article.php?id=1531).

pand their homes, build new homes for the younger generation, buy durable goods, and observe their customs-related obligations, i.e. to marry off their children or younger brothers and sisters and conduct wedding ceremonies by local standards. According to interviews conducted in 2007 among the residents of a small town in Andijan oblast, those who stayed home, while the main breadwinners went abroad, often were able to provide themselves with food and basic needs. Some of them benefited from their land that gave them some products, others received a salary or pension, albeit too small to cover durable goods or to pay for ritual celebrations. Thus, the main driving force of labour migration was to be able to fulfil the strategic priorities of their family budgets, rather than to meet daily needs and escape from starvation. Among these strategic priorities are expenditures for life-cycle ceremonies and dowries. Here are some examples:

> In 1998, there were many people willing to "buy" [ask in marriage – A. I.] my daughter. But I did not have enough money to organize the wedding. That year I took 20 thousand soum from my parents and left to Russia. (Male, Kuvasai, Ferghana oblast, 2001)
> Everything I earned during my trips I've spent for weddings and other [family] events. To earn enough for two weddings and *seps,* I travelled to Russia five times for three-to-seven months each time. A lot of money is spent on weddings. You have to provide a new wardrobe, and textile for clothes to the groom's side, then *dastarhans* (bundles of food), a lot goes to festivals, furniture – it should be provided by her father. Then there are parties after the wedding, such as the obligatory one on the second day, first *chaqirdy* (invitation by the groom's, then by the bride's family). Then the bride's family has to provide meals during the course of 20 – 40 days. Everything is about $2,000 [compared with the average cost of a wedding party of $530, reported by 2001 SDRC survey – see Table 2 and 3 – A. I.] [Thus] the most important reasons to go work abroad were weddings for daughters, then education (courses on sewing, medical care, and bookkeeping) (Female, 42, Kurgan-tepa, Andijan, 2007).
> Everything that Uzbeks earn [doesn't matter in migration or at home – A. I.] goes to weddings and food. Here's the priority of order: weddings, rites, clothes, home repairs (Male, 34, Aim, Andijan, 2007).
> After graduation from the university I could not find a job. My time to marry was coming, big expenses for the wedding were ahead." (Male, 25, Jalakuduk district, Andijan oblast, Migration survey 2007).

The accumulation of funds for life-cycle ritual ceremonies as the chief rationale for labour migration was identified by another survey conducted by Uzbek anthropologists in 2006 (Abdullayev 2008:183–185). According to that research[17], 18% of remittances were spent on life-cycle ceremonies, including 35% sent by migrants from

---

[17] In total, 51 in-depth interviews were conducted in several regions of Uzbekistan.

rural areas and 10% by urban residents. For rural residents this spending target was prioritized on the list of needs. If for urban residents, education was the third spending target (15%) after accommodation and nutrition, then for rural residents it was not among their priorities at all.

The second feature of Uzbek migrants' use of their income was their submission to the authority of their parents or elder brothers, and giving them their income with the strong belief that their parents would spend this income in the interests of the whole family. Even older men submit their income to the parents, if they are still alive. A 29-year-old man from Jalakuduk district of Andijan oblast told the interviewers that he gave over his entire income earned abroad to his father who runs the family budget. Another man from the same area, age 31, whose family lives with his parents, while he is working in Russia, said, "we have such an order: the elders in the family manage the family finances. If I had my own household, I would be the chief in the family and manage my own budget" (2007 Migration survey).

The third feature of migrants from extended families is the principle of solidarity they follow in the distribution of remittances and other incomes. The labour migrants themselves are not always the beneficiaries of the remittances that they are sending back home. Someone else from his or her household or family network could be the beneficiary. For instance, an elder brother may leave home to help his younger brother to get married, or, the reverse, the younger brother may sacrifice his time and efforts to help his older siblings build a house. Thus, labour migration has become not only a coping strategy employed by conjugal families to make ends meet. It is also a strategy for an extended family to fulfil its overarching strategic priorities, including building houses for a new family or meeting traditional and ceremonial duties. In other words, it is not only about practical, physical survival, but survival of an extended family as a social unit and member of the local community. Here is one example of such intra-family solidarity:

> For this money [remittance – A. I.] we completed the construction and did repairs on our parents' home. My younger brother got married in this home. The money that we made we pool together for all of the brothers. We all live together happily, especially after the death of our parents. The older help the younger get set up, and that's how it goes in our life. Those who remain here farm rice. And thus we live together. The earnings that I make, we use towards any of our common issues (weddings, ceremonies, clothing, construction, repairs, etc.). (Male, 34, Jalakuduk district, Andijan oblast, 2007 Migration survey).

What the migration experience command

From a cognitive perspective, what migrants learn about their host countries depends on where they find work and how they get there. If they come from urbanized areas and venture out on their own, then they risk not finding a decent job, not getting paid, and not securing registration. But, as a rule, they learn a lot more than those reaching their destination and living there through the support of a highly organized social network.[18] In the latter case, the risks are lower but the learning experience is minimized. As one migrant, a member of such a social network, witnessed: "At the time when we worked there [in Russia – A. I.], we didn't have any conflicts and we lived in peace. We all obeyed the elder in charge" (Male, 47, Jalakuduk District, Andijan oblast, 2007 Migration survey).

According to survey data, migrants from Uzbekistan appreciate and praise a number of features they observed in Russia: the honesty and kindness of ordinary people, the higher average living standards (in comparison with Uzbekistan) that allow even the rank-and-file to travel abroad, the easiness and affordability of bank loans and mortgages, greater freedom of enterprise and expression, and more entertainment options (Migration survey 2011). Some believe that all of these things can be adapted in Uzbekistan. At the same time, traditionally minded migrants reject other features of Russian life styles, for instance, sexual promiscuity and hard drinking habits.

The two surveys from 2007 and 2011 suggest that the socio-cultural impact of the migrant's experience in a foreign country on the traditional family is not as significant as one would expect. The reason is probably the fact that the interaction of migrants with host societies has been quite limited. Logistical issues such as finding accommodation and work, acquiring registration of residence and work permits, are in fact, in many cases, provided by brokers and intermediary parties so that the migrants are not required to come into contact with local institutions, except the employers and direct supervisors. As a result, the migrants' acquaintance with the social environment in the host country is often superficial. This social isolation in the host country is contributed by migrants' poor Russian language skills, especially if they are from rural areas, and if he or she works long hours with only one weekend day for rest. During the weekend, the migrant often prefers to stay at home to avoid encounters with the local police, notoriously known for abuses against migrants and the extortion of bribes, or to shop. Of course, this observation mirrors not the case with all labour migrants from Uzbekistan, but mainly those from Uzbekistan's rural districts, and those who work in construction and other low qualified jobs. The construction industry, which demands lots of low-qualification manpower, attracts the majority of labour migrants (which is also the case for other Central Asians). According to the Federation of Russia's Migrants (the association of national diasporas living in Russia), 40% of officially registered labour migrants in Russia work in the construction industry.[19] In reality, taking into

---

[18] According to an estimation of a Russian expert on labour migration, Sergey Ryazantsev, 80–90% of migrants from Central Asia arrive to and settle down in Russia through the informal mediation of brokers, and often find themselves being illegal migrants with forged registration documents. Sergey Ryazantsev, seminar presentation at the School of Oriental and African Study, London, 23 February 2012.

[19] http://www.fmr.su/news-view-158.html (data retrieved on 30. 04. 2012).

account non-registered migrants, the proportion of Uzbek migrants working in the construction sector might be even bigger, as many illegal migrants tend to be working in this sector. Often the construction gangs are formed by brokers, or so-called "brigadiers" who collect the teams in Uzbekistan and negotiate with future employers. Upon arrival in their destination country, the recruited migrants proceed directly to the construction site where they will work and even live. The following picture is quite common for the life style of migrant-builders: a construction site, migrant workers live on site in *vagonchiks* (trailers) with limited comfort, several people in one room. They communicate mainly with their teammates, usually from the same country, even from one province. Their awareness of Russian society is limited to watching TV and sometimes reading the tabloid press.

This arrangement of work and residence on one site limits the migrants' interaction with host societies. Correspondingly, the socio-cultural impact on the worldview of those Uzbek rural and semi-urban migrants is quite limited. They not only have few chances to learn about social life in Russia and juxtapose it with their own life, but often see the worst parts of Russian society, for instance, abusive and corrupted police, dodgy employers and brokers, hard drinking habits. Not surprisingly, they respond to these interactions with fear and repugnance, prompting them to express patriotism in the socio-cultural sense of this word, as for instance in the following case:

> "There are many things I don't like there [in Russia – A. I]. Their lifestyle. Ours is better … their young people don't know and follow rituals. In our society every child knows that one has to greet elders first. [In Russia they don't]. All in all, we're more adhered to religion. This is good." (Male, 47, Aim, Andijan, 2007).

Social-conservative trends and social stratification

Of course, there are plenty of examples of the opposite, when the migrants embrace the new socio-cultural environment and find many attractive features in it worth adopting and transferring into Uzbek society. Such positive attitudes toward the host societies can be more often found among female migrants, especially if they are single mothers and divorced women who have been forced to assume the role of breadwinner:

> I'm a breadwinner and therefore manage the family budget and all members give earnings to me … I wanted to reside in Russia, because in our country people are treated inhumanely, rudely (Female, 42, Kurgan-tepa town, Andijan, 2007).

Some women came to radically change their life priorities and vision of their roles within the family. For instance, this shift in worldview happened with a single mother who had found a job in Turkey and stayed there in a wealthy educated family. Being impressed by the lifestyle of that Turkish family that treated her humanely and with respect, she was convinced that priority must be given to education and the health of her children and that this should not be sacrificed for customary obligations and the narrow outlook characteristic of traditional families:

> In our Kurgan-tepa [a village in Andijan oblast] we still remain in the last century: we all stick to the duty to build a house, save for *sep* (dowry), marry off our children, spent a lot for celebrations ... all of our life revolves around this. People earn money only for this, nobody thinks of and cares for himself. They don't see what is going on around them (Female, 50, 42, Kurgan-tepa town, Andijan, 2007).

However, such cases are rather marginal in comparison to mainstream Uzbek provincial society. Besides, women constitute a small part of labour migrants from Uzbekistan, especially those from the rural and semi-urban countryside. The number of single mothers among them is even smaller. As for the majority of men from these areas, as a rule, they present themselves as righteous family men, firmly adhering to traditional values and customs. After returning home they change their life a little, still following the same social order dictated by customs.

What, however, changes is their social status. It is largely because they acquire more wealth and are able to demonstrate it to the surrounding neighbourhood, via renovation of their homes, buying cars, and other durable goods. The survey records suggest that, upon returning home, they enjoy more respect and attention from their neighbourhood. They often find themselves as counsel and advisers to local young people, sharing with them their knowledge of living and working in foreign countries. Not surprisingly, the migrants cherish their improved social status and are eager to reinforce positive opinion of them by more strict observation of local customs and ritual events. When they can afford to spend more on various ritual celebrations, they cannot do otherwise and as a result find themselves more obliged to act according to their new social status, i. e. present themselves as exemplary in allegiance to national customs.

As a result, the migrants' families are finding themselves trapped into a vicious circle of growing scale of re-investment into their raised social status. Thanks to income higher than the local standards labour migrants and their families are acquiring higher positions in the local social hierarchy, but along with that they are now expected to demonstrate generosity and honour by spending more lavishly for ritual celebrations. But the hierarchy of their family needs and budget priorities remain largely unchanged.

In some cases, labour migration can contribute even to greater influence of patriarchal and conservative values upon the families. It is particularly manifested in gender relations. As some published reports[20] and the fieldwork data cited in this

---

[20] See, for instance: *Abandoned Wives of Tajik Labor Migrants: IOM Study on the socio-economic characteristics of abandoned wives of Tajik labor migrants and their survival capabilities*, IOM Dushanbe, Tajikistan August 2009; Tajikistan: Divorce Spurs Female Labor Migration, *Eurasianet.org*, May 22, 2012, http://www.eurasianet.org/node/65441 (retrieved on 30 November, 2013).

essay suggest, there is a trend of male migrants having two families, one in the home country and another in the host country, with two wives. In such cases, they sometimes use references to the Koran to justify polygamy. Our data account for such cases of relatively well-to-do migrants who reside and live in Kazan and other areas of Russia that are witnessing an Islamic revival. Local communities in these areas are not hostile toward such practices. As an example, Kamil, 48, interviewed in Kazan in 2011, said that he has lived there already for 16 years and has settled into a second marriage there and has a child from his second wife, also Uzbek, 30, who is already a Russian citizen. At the same time, he did not divorce with the first wife with whom he has three children, two of whom are grown up. He says he visits his home in Bukhara 2–3 times a year and supports his first family financially, thus becoming a breadwinner of two households located in two different countries. Along with his two adult children he contributes to a united budget of an extended family network with such bizarre socio-geographical coordinates. According to him, his first wife has "accepted"[21] the existence of the second wife, and she even continues to live with his father in Bukhara.

It is worth noting that nowadays the practice of polygamy is already not uncommon in Uzbekistan and has become an attribute to prestige for those occupying higher ranks in the social hierarchy. The practice is taking root in spite of having been condemned officially and made into a criminal offence[22]. One of the reasons that polygamy is thriving in Uzbekistan has been the conservative public opinion more and more prevailing in the society, considering a woman remaining single as less acceptable than being the second or the third wife of a wealthy man (Hashimova: 2005; IWPR: 2010). Polygamy is serving the same end as ritual ceremonies, the attainment of social prestige and demonstration of one's social status.

Thus, one can ascertain the trend of the Uzbek traditional society as remaining immune to any modernizing or socially anomalous socio-cultural effect of labour migration. This immunity is demonstrated by the continued practice of revenue from labour migration being allocated to family life-cycle ceremonies, combined with a little cognitive effect of migrants' experience of living in host societies. In some cases one can even witness the increase of expenditures on ritual ceremonies, the trend associated with other forms of expansion of social conservatism in the Uzbek society.

This trend of social-conservative encroachment can also be linked to and be reinforced by the process of social stratification progressing in the post-Soviet societies. The representatives of the emerging class of wealthy people, including holders of pub-

---

[21] It is quite possible that she just didn't have other options but to embrace her new role as one of two wives of a single husband.
[22] According to the article 126 Criminal Code, polygamy in Uzbekistan is punished with fine from fifty to one hundred minimal monthly wages or correctional labor up to three years, or imprisonment up to three years., see: http://www.lex.uz/Pages/GetAct.aspx?lact_id=111457.

lic offices, are asserting their new social status by holding lavishly funded lifecycle ceremonies or acquiring second wives, thereby establishing norms of prestige consumption that spark envy and anxiety among the lower classes and desire to look not much worse. As a result, the poorer part of population finds itself trapped into this race for social prestige and being forced to spend their revenues and savings into the endless series of ritual ceremonies.

Investing into ritual: symbolic and practical meanings

External observers may find the dedication to ritual life by a considerable part of the Uzbek population, especially in rural and semi-urban areas covered by the study cited here, irrational. Yet this allegiance to ritual life does not totally lack in its own internal logic and rationale. If we consider ritual as a set of actions carrying a symbolic value for its performers and participants, then we should understand that this symbolic action is important to them, and this is why they invest so many resources into this symbolic aspect of their lives. Apparently, the bearers of the lifestyle that requires them to sacrifice for symbolic purposes are expecting to receive in exchange something important for them, not only respect among the society or at least being seen not worse than others.

For many, the wedding ceremony per se is a joyous moment, a great occasion they dreamed of for years, and worth sacrificing every penny of their savings for it. It would be also fair to suggest that they are expecting to get in return the sense of their identity that is associated, in their view, with the observation of customary rites and norms of conduct endorsed by their communities. To earn recognition of their identity by the members of their neighbourhood, they need to demonstrate certain virtues and endure sacrifices. Ritual ceremonies turn out to be one such occasion, a kind of a membership fee they are bound to pay to get community's acknowledgment.

One wonders then why membership in a given community is so imperative for them. Is it just a matter of self-esteem? And does it have some practical meaning? The answer is yes, to some extent. The community membership can be practical as it can in some cases secure support and solidarity. The hour of getting paid back comes, for instance, when members of the local community decide to embark on a venture to foreign countries to find jobs, an endeavour where mutual trust is especially important. As the survey data suggest, the Uzbek migrants manage to solve many problems of logistical, legal, and security character by engaging in social networks. But the latter are being nurtured for years, with ritual life probably playing a role of glue helping to stick network members together. Below is an eloquent example of such social networks in action narrated by a labour migrant:

– Meaning, when you started out, your acquaintance found work and board [in a host country – A. I.] for you?

– In a general sense, yes. If someone brings him with you [to a host country – A. I.], then he's responsible for you; otherwise he would be a traitor. He has to find you work, find you a place to live. He won't leave you out in the streets. He also helps you register and with your documents. You need money for everything, but for now, you don't have money. For a year you will need help. In short, no one is going somewhere that doesn't have anything; you have to go with someone, who will help you out when you are starting out. (Sahrof, 23, Samarkand oblast, 2011 Migration Survey).

Symbols and rituals turn out to be an entry pass allowing families to join and maintain solidarity networks. Van Gennep considered rites of passage as rituals marking the transitional phase between childhood and full inclusion into a social group (Van Gennep: 1960). Being outside of the group one cannot count on its solidarity, which is true especially for pre-modern societies (whereas in a modern society the solidarity can more often be expressed out of political conviction and shared groups interests).

The value of and demand for these neighbourhood community originated solidarity networks has increased in the post-Soviet period (Trevisani: 2010), due to the hardships following the degradation of the welfare state and the break of the social contract between the state and society (Kandiyoti 2002, 2009). However, one should not overestimate the economic benefits of these social networks. They may have effect in a limited number of cases, for instance in labour out-migration. They indeed play a crucial role in finding job and solving various problems related to accommodation, registration, works permits and the like in destination countries.

What then is more important to families in following ritual life: its symbolic meaning or its practical utility? From a theoretical perspective, to adequately reflect on ritual life and ritual economy, in the context of Central Asian labour migration, one should embrace both of two paradigms of understanding the phenomenon of ritual, the approaches often regarded as opposing to each other. The first paradigm, represented by the school of symbolic anthropology (Van Gennep 1960; Turner 1969; Geertz 1973, 1974), stresses the interpretive approach, while the adherents of the second one argue that "human social life is a response to the practical problems of earthly existence" (Harris 2001:XV). Indeed, the ritual life Uzbek traditional families are dedicated to can be conceived of as activity bearing symbolic and, at the same time, some practical values. The extent to which either of these two aspects of ritual life prevails can be defined only in a specific situational context.

From the macro-societal perspective, we can also consider ritual life as a means of social integration both into the local community and the nation. It was already noted by a number of students of Soviet and post-Soviet studies that the persistence in observing rituals and customs has been the way for the Uzbeks (and for other nationalities in the region) to preserve their national and cultural identity and self (Kandiyoti & Azimova 2004). This resilience of the indigenous population in Central Asia to the systematic efforts by the Soviet regime to eradicate everything standing on its way to communist society, is truly remarkable. Nowadays, the state comes as the sponsor of Uzbek nationalism, but this nationalism appears to have a tint of patriarchal values. The accommodation of patriarchal values has become a deliberate state policy quite recently,[23] beginning from the end of the first decade of Independence, when the state became their sponsor contributing to the resurrection of social conservatism.

Both the state and families have their respective calculations and expectations regarding conservative values and ritual life. The state expects to reinforce the established social order and political control over society. As for families, the question whether the economic return from "investing" into ritual economy is sufficient enough and satisfies their needs, depends very much on social circumstances, especially the position of a family in a social and class stratification. As our observations suggest, those belonging to the wealthy class are right to consider the observance of ritual celebrations as a kind of investment in social capital: a membership fee they are ready to pay allows them to join certain social clubs of wealthy or influential people. These investments eventually pay off both in terms of material benefits and political clout.

But for a poor family, such a disposal of their wealth may not always pay back, because poor families are not usually involved in commercial business and have little access to state offices, and they are likely to marry into similarly poor families. Very often the only positive effect of ritual life for them is the moral satisfaction of gaining the respect of the neighbourhood, and avoiding the shame of abandoning tradition:

> Among us, the Uzbeks, this is the way it should be. Perhaps, it is impossible not to organize weddings. People will talk (female, Yaz'yavan village, Ferghana oblast, 2001).

Normally, for poor families, this respect can be hardly converted into other material forms of capital (with the exception of solidarity networks that play a role in some cases such as labour migration as discussed earlier) and often only supports the illusion that the family in question is on a higher level in the socio-economic hierarchy than it does in reality. Strict observance of ritual life thus may serve interests of wealthier fa-

---

[23] Since independence, the Karimov regime has undertaken systematic efforts to promote the patriarchal nationalism and did it in several campaigns. The last campaign was launched in 2008 with attacks against critics of excesses of patriarchal social norms and practices and using legal action as the method of persuasion. Feminist documentary filmmaker and photographer, Umida Akhmedova, was charged for alleged distortion in her film and photography of national customs.[See: Rachel Aspden, Uzbek documentary maker found guilty of slander, *The Guardian*, 11 February 2010, http://www.theguardian.com/film/2010/feb/11/uzbekistan-umida-akhmedova-slander). Maksim Popov, HIV outreach worker, was sentenced to seven years for "promotion of homo-sexuality" (See: Anti-AIDS Campaigner Serving 7-Year Sentence In Uzbekistan, Radio Free Europe/Radio Liberty, 24 February, 2010, http://www.rferl.org/content/Uzbeks_Give_AntiAIDS_Campaigner_SevenYear_Sentence/1967550.html), and the public information about condoms as the means of tackling HIV/AIDS and reproduction health was banned.[See: Uzbekistan favours forced sterilisation over condom promotion, Uznews.Net, 3 March, 2010, http://www.uznews.net/news_single.php?lng=en&cid=30&nid=12706).

milies, but may have rather a devastating effect upon poor families, unless the latter find the way to transform the value of ritual economy into something tangible, in terms of their material well-being, which is unlikely to happen.

* * *

Uzbek society finds itself on the crossroads of contradictory tendencies. On the one hand, Uzbekistan is involved in the process of globalization with increasingly cross-national and geographical mobility of its population. This engagement in globalization was supposed to bring about some socio-cultural changes. However, the coincidence of market driven social stratification with the ideological climate fostered by the authoritarian state seems to work towards reinforcing social conservatism, with ritual economy, as one of its manifestations, getting entrenched in the society. We see that at least part of labour migrants from Uzbekistan and other Central Asian countries remain committed to conservative values and traditional ritual life, even if this allegiance requires from them enormous financial contributions and the sacrifice of individual needs and interests.

References

Abashin, Sergey 2003: *Vopreki "zdravomu smyslu"? K voprosu o ratsionalnosti/irratsionalnosti" ritualnyh raskhodov v Srednei Azii* (In spite of "convention wisdom" – to the question of "rationality/irrationality" of ritual spending in Middle Asia). Evrazaia: Lyudi I Mify, Moscow: Natalis.
Abdullayev, Yevgeny V. (ed.) 2008: *Trudovaya migratsia v respublike Uzbekistan*. Tashkent: UNPD.
Arifnanova, Zoia 2011: *Sovremennaya obryadovo-ritualnaya zhizn' uzbekov Tashkenta*. (Contemorary ritual life of Tashkent Uzbeks), Tashkent Islamic University's website, http://www.tiu.uz/index.php?option=com_content&view=article&id=108:2011-06-13-18-12-56&catid=12:articles&lang=en&Itemid= (retrieved on 24 November, 2013).
Engels, Friedrich 1972[1884]: *The Origin of the Family, Private Property and the State*, London: Penguin Books.
Geertz, Clifford 1973: *The interpretation of cultures*. New York: Basic.
Geertz, Clifford (ed.) 1974: *Myth, symbol, and culture*. New York: W. W. Norton and Co.
Hobsbawm, Eric J.; Ranger, Terence O. 1992: *Invention of Tradition*. Cambridge: Cambridge University Press.
Harris, Marvin 2001[1979]: *Cultural Materialism: the Struggle for a Science of Culture*. Updated ed., Walnut Creek, California: AltaMira Press.
Hamidova, Muhsina 2005: Uzbekistan's Trophy Wives, *Institute of War and Peace Reporting*, 21 February: http://iwpr.net/report-news/uzbekistans-trophy-wives (retrieved on 6 May, 2012).
IWPR 2010: Uzbek Officials Fall Foul of Polygamy Ban. *News Briefing Central Asia*, Institute of War and Peace Reporting, 11 August: http://iwpr.net/report-news/uzbek-officials-fall-foul-polygamy-ban (retrieved on 6 May, 2012).
Kandiyoti, Deniz 1988: Bargaining with Patriarchy, *Gender and Society*, Vol. 2, No. 3, Special Issue to Honor Jessie Bernard, pp. 274–290.
Kandiyoti, Deniz 2002: Agrarian Reform, Gender and Land Rights in Uzbekistan. United Nations Research Institute for Social Development. *Social Policy and Development Programme Paper* 11.

Kandiyoti, Deniz; Azimova, Nadira 2004: The Communal and the Sacred: Women's World of Ritual in Uzbekistan. *Journal of the Royal Anthropological Institute* 10,2:327–349.

Kandiyoti, Deniz 2009: Andijan: Prelude to a Massacre, *Open Democracy*, 13 May 2009, http://www.opendemocracy.net/globalization-institutions_government/Andijan_2527.jsp.

Martin, Patricia Y. 2004: Gender as a social institution. *Social Forces* 82:1249–1273.

North, Douglass C. 1990: *Institutions, institutional change and economic performance*. Cambridge: Cambridge University Press.

Sazonova, Maria V. 1952: K etnografii uzekov iuzhnogo Khorezma. In: S. P. Tolstov and T. A. Zhdanko (eds.), *Trudy Khorezmskoy arkheologo-etnograficheskoi ekspeditsii*. Moscow: Izdatel'stvo Akademii nauk SSSR, pp. 247–318.

Scott, Richard W. 2001: *Institutions in organizations*. Thousand Oaks, CA: Sage Publications.

Trevisani, Tommaso 2010: *Land and Power in Khorezm: Farmers, Communities, and the State in Uzbekistan's Decollectivisation*, Berlin: LIT Verlag.

Turner, Victor 1969: *The Ritual Process: Structure and Anti-Structure*. London: Routledge & K. Paul.

Van Gennep, Arnold 1960: *The Rites of Passage*, London: Routledge & K. Paul.

Asianizing Russia after 'The Friendship among Peoples'

Russell Zanca

Department of Anthropology, Northeastern Illinois University, 5500 N. St. Louis Avenue, Chicago, USA-IL 60646

Abstract. With a degree of hindsight, the exodus of millions of people from Central Asia to Russia in search of work appears predictable. Conversely, contemporary scholars would be hard pressed to find such academic soothsaying published in the mid-1980s. Arguably, the labor migration phenomenon of Central Asians working in and actually settling parts of Russia looks to be something of an irony in the Soviet political economy context but indicative of a general trend if we view contemporary Russia in its Soviet guise as a European colonial power. At any rate, the foreignness of Central Asian people working and living in Russia has heightened during the past 15 years, and along with a retrenchment of policies akin to ethnic/national equity among (Soviet) citizens, the early effects of 21st century globalization are resulting in greater structural inequalities and othering of those rapidly moving into Russia from Central Asia. The movements themselves largely are a product of distinctively retrograde nationalist politics that foster uncooperative and unfriendly relations among Central Asian states as well as between given Central Asian governments and the Russian government. This essay aims to consider two matters: (1) taking stock of the trends that have recently emerged because of Central Asian labor migration; and (2) propose an approach to fieldwork study among Central Asians who are connected directly and indirectly to migration that emphasizes their own outlooks about experiencing Russia and what we could call the *anthropology of socio-economic relations* – the tolerable and the intolerable.
[labor migration, Central Asia]

With a degree of hindsight, the exodus of millions of people from Central Asia to Russia and Kazakhstan since the mid-1990s in search of work appears predictable. After all, what other alternatives emerged from the Soviet Union's disintegration and the rapid impoverishment and violence that resulted partly from sovereignty and independence politics in the countries of Kyrgyzstan, Tajikistan, and Uzbekistan? Conversely, contemporary scholars would be hard pressed to find such academic soothsaying published in the mid-1980s. And to be fair, Russia itself seems stunned at the influx of temporary migration that since the mid-late 1990s has surpassed even the United States in terms of being a recipient country of temporary workers from abroad (Vlasov 2013).

I first began to think seriously about studying what I think of as Central Asia's great globalizing experience some seven or eight years ago. Obviously, media reporting that I read about, learned from colleagues, or occasionally heard about over the radio influenced me. Those colleagues and friends who were returning from Uzbekistan, for example, started remarking that they could sense various effects of migration in town and country. Like many things, my first feeling was that I was engaging the phenomenon a bit late, but then I realized that while journalists, some Central Asian and other post-Soviet scholars, and a few westerners were studying migration seriously, there was little literature out there, and most of it pertained to the Tajiks or Kyrgyz. During the past few years I've asked myself, and, occasionally, the odd, indulgent conference panel audience a few questions that seem worthwhile, but that remained largely lacking for research. Remarking on these past five or so years helps get us a lot closer to my theme and argument.

Arguably, the labor migration phenomenon of Central Asians working in and actually settling parts of Russia looks to be something of an irony in the Soviet political economy context but indicative of a general trend, if we view contemporary Russia in its previous Soviet guise as a European colonial power. At any rate, the foreignness of Central Asian people working and living in Russia has heightened during the past 15 years, and, along with a retrenchment of policies akin to ethnic/national equity among (Soviet) citizens, the early effects of 21st century globalization are resulting in greater structural inequalities and *othering* of those rapidly moving into Russia from Central Asia. The movements themselves largely are a product of distinctively retrograde nationalist politics that foster uncooperative and unfriendly relations among Central Asian states as well as between given Central Asian governments and the Russian government from time to time (O' Suilleabhain 2013). Generally, it bears mention that Central Asia's poorest countries and Russia must work to resolve the damaging dualism of labor surfeit and labor shortages (Anichkova 2012). Ideally, it is not unreasonable to imagine enlightened policies that serve the entire former U.S.S.R. well with labor migration as a basis (World Bank 2009). Conversely, this is nothing other than a modular ideal belied by such basic issues as the inherent inequalities of capitalism, unmediated inter-ethnic relations left over from the Soviet period, and virulent nationalisms-cum-racisms of the period coinciding with sovereignty and these large-scale movements of poorer peoples moving into relative richer areas – countries, actually.

The title for this essay plays on the theme, of course, of the kind of inter-ethnic or inter-nationalities harmony that supposedly guided the internal politics of the Soviet Union for decades, especially in the post-World War II period. The effort here is neither to mock or denigrate the old concept, but rather to showcase its failure in one sense, which is that as more and more Asians, especially Central Asians move into Russia – still mainly temporary and for economic purposes – Russia itself increasingly acts unwelcome and unfriendly towards the millions, who not only fulfill important roles in the workforce, but who once, not so long ago, were considered to be fellow citizens.

This essay aims to consider two matters: (1) taking stock of the trends that have emerged recently because of Central Asian labor migration; and (2) propose fieldwork studies among migration-connected people who are directly and indirectly a part of the process. Perhaps this has not been so simple a topic and field of investigation for anthropologists in recent years because it requires us to be almost as mobile and multi-sited as informants themselves are. Naturally, this has practical concerns and constraints; monetary resources would be a major consideration in this regard. Lastly, it could nag at researchers that the subjects of the very cultural areas that they have been trained to study are not staying put.

Such studies should emphasize migrant-connected people's own outlooks about experiencing Russia and Kazakhstan as well as what we might call the anthropology of socio-economic relations – the tolerable and the intolerable.

In Morgan Liu's recent review article (2011) concerning the anthropology of Central Asia, he discusses many of the themes of anthropologists' research during the past 20 years, such as the perduring Soviet legacy, religion, nationalism and identity, etc. Surprisingly, he does not discuss labor migration. After all, Central Asians have been working outside of their own countries in earnest for at least 15 years now. However, perhaps Liu was right not to discuss the phenomenon in his review because, with a few noteworthy exceptions, there really has not been much of a western anthropology of Central Asian labor migration. In fact, interested parties and those who have actually researched and published on this topic are remain uncommon (Doolotkeldieva 2008; Hegland 2010; Reeves 2011).

Those who follow the trends have been content with labor migration stories coming out of Central Asia for the drama, for their occasional aspects of grotesqueness, and, really, as newsworthy reporting of current events. Maybe many also think that it sort of does and does not make for ethnographic grist because it involves Central Asians leaving Central Asia, and anthropologists wish to work with people who are in Central Asia. Moreover, it might be difficult to reconcile ourselves to the fact that Central Asian migration probably is much less temporary – in terms of affecting Central Asian societies and cultures – than we could have realized by the late 1990s when those of us working in rural Central Asia began realizing it was something germane. Too, Central Asian people themselves tended to downplay it, as if in traveling to work in Omsk, or Almaty, or the Moscow suburbs, they expected to be gone but just a few weeks, and only to sell produce, or help on a construction project, etc. Truthfully, why should they have seen it as anything more important than that? And if the person were to return in a few weeks time, then one could just see it as yet another income-maximizing strategy in the ensuing and prolonged rough patch that marked the end of the Soviet system, helping people to supplement their costs of living expenses and often grossly diminished wages.

Now, while it may be conjectural to assert that we came to the study of labor migration sluggishly, it also may have something to do with the fact that the voluminous data and literature on international labor migration during the course of the past thirty years or so are not always very theoretically satisfying or creatively fashioned. Far more able and engaged scholars of anthropology and migration (Silverstein 2006) have sketched the various theoretical approaches to how these studies have been carried out in places such as Europe, North America, and Australia, so that a re-hashing would be both dull and barely competent. Furthermore, because of our daily readings on

Central Asian affairs and events, many of us vaguely interested in the topic are familiar with all manner of official and semi-official statistics about, let's say, how many Tajiks work in Russia, what percentage of Uzbekistan's GDP derives from migrant remittances, and what are the typical labor categories for Central Asians, whether working in rural or urban areas of Russia and Kazakhstan. And knowing these things makes less for intellectual excitement and more for considering oneself to have a robust, professional understanding of who migrates where, why, and for how long.

While fieldworkers realize that answering the questions about why Central Asians migrate to work can be more surprising than we might assume, such answers typically are not terribly complicated and the consideration forms part of the baseline level of inquiry. Also, it is equally fitting and social scientific to take stock of trends showing the kinds of effects that Central Asian peoples and countries will experience in another decade as a result of the mass movements of their populations both permanently and transnationally. And this leaves us with an approach to meaningful research as anthropologists that remains sound and continues to provide the basis for writing that both can engage wider scholarly audiences and help us settle on helpful theories. Essentially, we have to continue conducting and initiating fieldwork projects that may be either quantitative or qualitative depending on personal, methodological preferences – but that should engage labor migration from the perspective of living human experiences, especially what those experiences of migration mean to people who undertake it as well as those who are left back home. Combined with the individual's thoughts and emotions centered on migration, we would do well to utilize those comparative perspectives that we gain from reading cases, again, with regard to North America, Europe, and Australia. After all, we know of the similarities among postcolonial experiences, contemporary demographic shifts and the needs of powerful capitalist- producing states, and also situations of people who are migrating because of insatiable consumer demands of commodities considered essential to industrial development and growth, such as China (Ryzhova & Ioffe 2009).

By bringing together the basic research approaches just suggested, it should be obvious that there are then myriad social phenomena of Central Asian labor migration that will not only serve our scholarship for years to come, but that will also allow us whichever professional roles as anthropologists we choose to play that may have practical consequences and outcomes for people with whom we work and processes that we study – to wit, policy prescriptions for states that send and receive, improved quality of health and wellbeing for migrants, multi-lingualism, and cross-cultural understanding among migrants and host country residents, and, realistically, tens of other such applied outcomes of contemporary research. Of course, there's no requirement that an anthropologist undertake migration study in order to devise an applied outcome, however this phenomenon lends itself to such a field because of much migration writing in comparative contexts.

We know that readers share the deep concern for the chaotic and violent conditions that engulf the world of migrants whenever they travel to other parts of the former

Soviet Union in search of work. Hardly a week or so passes that we don't read about the abuse of some migrant at the hands of authorities – bribery, at the hands of landowners or building site managers (withholding of wages, confiscation of official documents, virtual enslavement), and the inter-ethnic gang fights, horrible housing conditions and tragedies associated therewith, and racist murders that we know occur for Central Asians within Russia, and in Kazakhstan to a much more limited degree. It goes without saying that migrants globally face similar dangers in other settings, such as the border between Mexico and the U.S., within European cities, including Athens, Rome, London, and Paris, and for people from Bangladesh working in Syria's textile industry (Wilson 2000; McLaren 2003; Jureidini 2010). In focusing our research, analyses, and perhaps eventual recommendations vis-à-vis Central Asian migrants, we are joining an established and engaged field of anthropology that concentrates on migrants and their socially networked communities – ever changing, ever hybridizing communities.

While many untoward happenings were predicted with Soviet dissolution, one would be hard pressed to find predictions about massive labor migration to Russia, and the consequent alienation of Central Asians within Russia. Whereas few are so naïve to think that "friendship among peoples" meant that prejudices and superiority-inferiority complexes of members from a given ethnic group towards others had been eliminated, few would have considered the reality that Central Asians could be made to feel as aliens in Russia and feel themselves so utterly other there. But this has come to pass. Now, of course, we understand factors that have contributed to growing xenophobia and racism – part and parcel of a pronounced Russian nationalism. Indeed, there also are politics and economics, there's some sense that Russia always has to help a backward, underdeveloped and overpopulated Asia, but that Russia gets next to nothing in return (stoked recently by Solzheitsyn, Zhirinovsky, and Yeltsin), now considered a classic white man's burden, now a *mission civilisatrice*. And then there are the increasingly resented markers of difference – physical appearance, sounds and fragrances of Asia. There is also the perception that either Asians are taking over good Russian land and city spaces, or that Asians just want Russia's wealth without imparting any loyalty to her; the latter is a frequent sort of *racializing* technique or trope throughout Europe, too (Fireside 2002; Sevortian 2009).

In all this some may suggest, fairly or unfairly, that Russia reaps what it sows, that such a phenomenon is blowback, and that all colonizers have learned or are learning to face these human intrusions in their 20th and 21st centuries scapes. One must hope that we as anthropologists, endeavoring to be mindful of our own biases and prejudices, also make time somewhere along the way to acquaint ourselves with Russia's history. The notions or ideas, to say nothing of experiences, of the fear of being taken over and ruled from outside, whether from Russia's east, north, or south (Mongols, Swedes, Ottomans w/ Crimean surrogates) is not something that we should either ignore or treat with insensitivity. It also appears worth remarking that for the better part of a century now, it is not necessarily the case that a whole lot of Russians have lived a whole lot better than millions of Central Asians over the past four generations (Hauner 1992).

The point, on the whole, is that if we are to have any type of problem-oriented ethnography connected to labor migration from Central Asia, we will acquit ourselves well not to see it as a Manichaean battle. One issue that clearly exacerbates tensions for receiving and sending countries is language. Unlike representatives of earlier generations of visitors and workers who arrived from non-Slavic or non-European parts of the U.S.S.R. to the Russian Federation, more and more younger Central Asians are coming with so low a competency level of literary Russian that the linguistic element alone is mentioned as a significant cause of resentment (Eurasianet 2012). Given this matter, accounting for the loss of Russophonic abilities or arguing for culpability in having enabled this to happen will not necessarily lead to much in the way of changes that will do any concerned parties a great deal of good. And given the likelihood that Russian will remain Central Eurasia's *lingua franca* for years to come – obviously within Russia (a very multi-ethnic country in its own right that now experiences the influx of millions of new non-native Russian speakers in its country) – resources and time must be devoted to basic, effective, and practical courses in Russian with particular emphasis on job-specific language training; many immigrant sending and receiving countries – Philippines and Australia have developed programs.

As my thesis declaims, an Asianizing of Russia proceeds in an explosive and reactive fashion, and the states concerned substitute policies based on a familiarity of the past rather than a vision of a planned future (including making careful and humanitarian policies for migrants themselves). This article advocates that anthropologists begin thinking about and accounting for these processes. There is little doubt that the Russian people and the Russian government now favor a much more old-fashioned, assimilationist model to the situation. Such attempts, however, could be undermined in consideration of anthropology's and sociology's understanding of transnationalism insofar as people who migrate do not necessarily invest themselves mentally in becoming what me might term newly identified persons (Bloemraad et al. 2008). Some of the ethnographic research that people here have done, in concert with journalists' reports, show us that immigrants in large cities tend typically to live in enclaves, and perhaps in less urbanized areas we are getting something akin to Central Asian settlements –in parts of Siberia, the Volga region, and in areas of the Urals.

What we need to learn in more exacting detail is how and to what extent Central Asian migrants either are interested in or trying to make their living spaces Central Asian. This includes their living, working, recreating and consuming areas. And along with the mundane spatio-cultural areas, what are they doing linguistically and socially to create Central Asian space? We might make such studies that emphasize all five senses of what I will call "cultural capture." My notion of cultural capture is not only empirical, but should seek to maximize a cultural anthropology of the senses, including the tactile and tasteful. Naturally, this can be captured in prose, but anthropologists should seek to apprehend culture of Central Asian migration the film, photography, and audio recordings. It is simply an effort to make the ethnography as vivid and voluble as possible.

Although it may not strike readers as especially insightful on my part to point out that it is to a degree very human – as in human nature – to be conflictual wherever and with whomever we live in our groups, including families, neighborhoods, work places and social gathering sites. People in such settings really don't require much ethnic, linguistic, or confessional markers of identity to find causes of conflict with others. Nevertheless, when we consider the immigration experiences for Central Asians, conflictual relations in numerous settings with numerous identities form a substantial realm of discourse. As anthropologists of labor migration in fledgling settings (compared to Western Europe), we have unique opportunities to probe established hypotheses and common assumptions (such as postcolonialism), about what we ordinarily consider to be ethnic conflict, whether from Barthian, multiculturalist, or even primordialist/essentialist understandings. This could involve everything and anything from prejudicial schema in the minds of those who discriminate to the reinforcement of cultural evolutionist sentiment about "superior" European culture as opposed to "inferior" Asian or Asiatic culture still lingering from the Soviet past. Thus in asking people why they do not or cannot force themselves to get on with migrants generally, or with people representing a given group, we have the ability to discern reasons for or sources of antagonism – namely, their deep-rootedness, situationality, or perhaps even something as potentially temporary as an immediate materialist cause. In investigating prejudices, xenophobia, etc., we can focus on situations and places where people of varying backgrounds do get on with one another and even cooperate for a common purpose Outside of Barcelona, for example, Brad Erickson has investigated the situation for labor migrants and has been struck by the notion of "convivencia," a uniquely Spanish way of accommodating migrants, especially through public rituals and festivals with further expectations of all who wish to become part of civic life (2011). If nothing else, research results in such a context well may provide a more balanced analysis of what drives and brakes conflicts based on a kind of scaled graph, marking intolerable and tolerable otherness. Naturally, these processes may be sui generis and attitudinal based on all manner of diverse historical processes.

During the last 20 years, middle aged and older Central Asians have been wont to remark that until the Soviet collapse they never thought seriously of factual borders among the republics of the U.S.S.R., or between their republics and Russia. We should continue to think about the degree to which borders themselves gave rise to greater intolerance and the reifying of **personhoods** (I use this fraught term in an anthropological sense with a due nod to its culture-specific connotations) to be feared and distrusted rather than welcomed or embraced. And while the Russian government and state obviously seem to have a lot to do with contemporary understandings and opinions, its administering and decree making cannot be cause alone. For years scholars of the Soviet Union have discussed the considerable ironies with regard to the promotion of unity despite the promotion of defined identities. Furthermore, in concert with awesome efforts to forge territorial nationalities, is there any irony greater – to say nothing of sudden – for this unitary state than (in formation for at least 75 years) the fact that it is now wracked with conflicts and resentments given the movements of a variety of people throughout what was once a somewhat non-internally bordered polity?

That Russia will continue to become a more Asian country by dint of people living, working, and being born there in coming decades seems beyond any doubt. Obviously, part of the labor migration phenomenon ties into capitalism, ties into the demographic decline (being experienced similarly in parts of Europe and the U.S.), and increasingly ties into political dictatorships with their attendant stagnant and jobless economies. Joining these objective factors are those that shape human consciousness and attitudes toward what we might think of as poles of seamless integration or relative harmonious progress and chaos resulting from jealousies, corruption, mismanagement of human flows, perceptions of loss, theft, etc. In sum, we will do well to tap into all sorts of perceptions and feelings along with the important macro-data of migrations' quantifications.

We anthropologists may or may not succeed in making recommendations based on applied studies, but we maintain success at interviewing as well as conversing with people who ordinarily remain faceless and disregarded/excluded when laws, regulations, and policies are enacted. And since labor migration involves not just proverbial social networks, but people who leave, stay, live near, or participate in migrants' activities, we should consider expanding our objects to include a very wide range of people to understand the migration phenomenon in this context.

Lastly, I will suggest that in the past decade anthropologists and sociologists have published considerably on a host of human dimensions of migration that go creatively, thankfully beyond the nuts and bolts enumerations of education levels, remittance figures, number of work permits issued, types of jobs, etc (Grey 2002; Rudnyckyj 2004; Silverstein 2005; Trager 2005). Thus we can fruitfully take this domain of area studies and move it on to equivalent, disciplinary planes when we consider materials published on Mexico, China, Australia, and Europe broadly.

Whereas empirical data in the short term may reveal to us that aspects of what we might term traditional or long-established society and culture in Central Asia are not changing because of labor migration, and in fact are being solidified through it, we should make no bones about the fact that labor migration is a new phase of culture change throughout the former Soviet space. We anthropologists are here to figure out how this is unfolding as well as use whatever degree of detachment we do have to suggest ways that the migrant process and condition not be reduced to living perhaps materially better yet also living with and enduring fear, resentments, and racializing violence.

References

Anichkova, Daria 2012: *Central Asia's Migrant Headache, International Economic Bulletin*, June 21, Carnegie Endowment for International Peace. http://carnegieendowment.org/ieb/2012/06/21/central-asia-s-migrant-headache/c41a.

Bloemraad, Irene; Korteweg, Anna; Yurdakul, Gokce 2008: Citizenship and Immigration: Multiculturalism, Assimilation, and Challenges to the Nation-State. *Annual Review of Sociology* 34:153–179.

Doolotkeldieva, Asel 2008: Conducting Interviews with labor migrants in Moscow. *Central Eurasian Studies Review* 7(2):29–33.

Erickson, Brad 2011: Utopian Virtues: Muslim Neighbors, Ritual Sociality and the Politics of *Convivencia*. *American Ethnologist* 38(1):114–131.

Eurasianet.org 2012: *Russia: Moscow Toughens Rules for Labor Migrants.* http://www.eurasianet.org/print/65561.

Fireside, Harvey 2002: The Demographic Roots of European Xenophobia. *Journal of Human Rights* 1(4):469–479.

Grey, Mark A. 2002: Unofficial Sister Cities: Meatpacking Labor Migration Between Villachuato, Mexico and Marshalltown, Iowa. *Human Organization* 61(4):364–376.

Hauner, Milan 1992: *What is Asia to Us? Russia's Asian Heartland Yesterday and Today.* New York: Routledge.

Hegland, Mary Elaine 2010: Tajik Male Labour Migration and Women Left Behind: Can They Resist Gender and Generational Hierarchies. *Anthropology of the Middle East* 5(2):16–35.

Jureidini, Ray 2010: Trafficking and Contract Migrant Workers in the Middle East. *International Migration* 48(4):142–163.

Liu, Morgan 2011: Central Asia in the Post-Cold War World. *Annual Review of Anthropology* 40:115–131.

Mclaren, Laura M. 2003: Anti-Immigrant Prejudice in Europe: Contact, Threat Perception, and Preferences for the Exclusion of Migrants. *Social Forces* 81(3):909–936.

O' Suilleabhain, Andrea 2013: *Discrimination, Often Violent, Impacts Thousands of Central Asian Migrants in Russia, Global Observatory Analysis on Global Issues.* http://theglobalobservatory.org/analysis/440-discrimination-often-violent-impacts-thousands-of-central-asian-migrants-in-russia.html.

Reeves, Madeleine 2011: Staying Put? Towards a Relational Politics of Mobility at a Time of Migration. *Central Asian Survey* 30(3–4):555–576.

Rudnyckyj, Daromir 2004: Technologies of Servitude: Governmentality and Indonesian Transnational Labor Migration. *Anthropological Quarterly* 77(3):407–434.

Ryzhova, Nataliya; Ioffe, Grigory 2009: Trans-border Exchange between Russia and China: The Case of Blagoveshchensk and Heihe. *Eurasian Geography and Economics* 50(3):348–364.

Sevortian, Anna 2009: Xenophobia in Post-Soviet Russia. *The Equal Rights Review* 3:19–27.

Silverstein, Paul A. 2005: Immigrant Racialization and the New Savage Slot: Race, Migration, and Immigration in the New Europe. *Annual Reviews of Anthropology* 34:363–384.

Trager, Lillian (ed.) 2005: *Migration and Economy: Global and Local Dynamics.* Lanham, MD: AltaMira Press.

Vlasov, Alexei 2013: *Russia and Central Asia: Missed Opportunities and New Prospects.* Valdai Discussion Club: http://valdaiclub.com/near_abroad/54980.html.

Wilson, Tamar Diana 2000: Anti-Immigrant Sentiment and the Problem of Reproduction/Maintenance in Mexican Immigration to the Unites States. *Critique of Anthropology* 20(2):191–213.

World Bank 2009: *A Catalyst for Labor Migration Discussions* (Report). http://web.worldbank.org/WBSITE/EXTERNAL/COUNTRIES/ECAEXT/0,,contentMDK:22865040~pagePK:146736~piPK:146830~theSitePK:258599,00.html.

Buchbesprechungen

Thomas Bierschenk, Matthias Krings und Carola Lentz (Hg.): Ethnologie im 21. Jahrhundert. 288 Seiten. Berlin: Dietrich Reimer Verlag 2013. ISBN 978-3-496-02863-5.

Reading this book I could not help getting jealous. It would be wonderful to have a book like this on Dutch anthropology, stating so clearly and honestly the discipline's position in a rapidly changing environment with new challenges that raise doubts about its very right of existence. This book's strength is that the authors are never apologetic – convinced of the value of new beginnings in German anthropology over the last decades, but also not ashamed to express doubts and uncertainties. The introduction by Bierschenk, Krings and Lentz, offering a clear overview of major trends, firmly sets the tone. A central theme is the nachholende Modernisierung of German anthropology that they justly see as succeeded: since about the 1970s German anthropologists did catch up with global trends in the discipline. However, the authors add that this hat einen Preis (p.26/7). And, indeed, there are several costs. A practical one is that publishing in an international context – notably in leading Anglo-saxon journals – decides about the career of German anthropologists. In Germany also academics seem also to be haunted by the decreasing value of publishing in one's own language. One of the charms of the book is the firm but open way in which the authors position German ethnology in German and within their own society. Again a reason for jealousy but also concern: if the Germans stop publishing in their own language any hope for a more diversified global academy that is not dominated by English only seems to be lost.

A related question about costs is whether this Modernisierung is threatening specific achievements of German anthropology. On this point the authors offer different suggestions. A common theme in many contribution is a certain dissatisfaction with the 'writing culture debate' as it was waged in America. USA anthropology seems to be 'the other' against which these German anthropologists define themselves (I am wondering though whether a powerful trend in recent British anthropology, the celebration of 'ontology' might not have offered an at least as productive counterpoint).. Several authors see as an objection of the USA debate that it risks to lead to a bashful distancing from das Fremde, which to most remains the hallmark of anthropology. Bernhard Streck proposes the idea of a Perspecktivenwechsel as crucial to the discipline. And, from a more methodological perspective, Matthias Krings agrees with him: it is precisely in this respect that anthropologists have something to offer in interdisciplinary collaboration. Karl-Heinz Kohl admonishes German anthropologists to take the rich ethnographisches Archiv from explorers, missionaries, artists and others more seriously without being bashful about possible exoticizing tendencies. Richard Rottenburg pleads for eine Ethnologie der Kritik in which what seems to be exotic becomes part and parcel of globalisation processes so that the anthropologist can be liberated of the guilty duty to protect the local. Carola Lentz offers a spirited defense of the notion of Kultur that many see lately as a ballast rather than a support; indeed, it is in relation to this (and other) notions that the German tradition can prove to be a still inexhaustible Fundgrube. Thomas Bierschenk's analysis of Zidanes Kopfstoss – the famous

French footballer's faux pas in his last international match – seems to be the exception: here das Fremde is only appearance, Bierschenk's explanation is rather in terms of rough talk of male friendship. But the point of convergence with the other contributions remains the emphasis on field-work whether in Marseille or in Africa. In his historical overview of German anthropology Dietrich Haller arrives at the same emphasis.

The collection is enriched by a series of contributions by non-anthropologists. From Kultursoziologie, Stefan Hirschauer gives an original twist to the emphasis on das Fremde, by opposing the anthropologists' struggle to relate to the other, despite cultural differences, to the Befremdungstechniken of the sociologists with which they try to distance themselves from their research topic, thus robbing the obvious from its self-evidence. The political scientist Klaus Schlichte contrasts anthropology's look from outside to the political science perspective from inside. Michael Bollig offers a rich overview of German anthropology now – of its central topics and research regions – that graphically confirms the success of this nachholende Modernisierung.

However, the consistent emphasis on das Fremde and on field-work in an other environment feeds also into an undercurrent of discomfort (luckily so, it makes the collection all the more convincing): what about the danger of 'othering,' of excluding the people studied from one's own world? For ethnological museums, Larissa Förster also signals such Unbehagen; for her the solution is to transform museums into places of contact, or even into arenas for the negotiation of social values and identities. A very practical and all the more promising solution for such Unbehagen can be found in the shortest contribution by Judith Schlehe on Lehrforschung for students from Freiburg University and Gadjah Mada University in Djokja according to a 'transcultural tandem-model': one year in Schwaben, next year in Java; anthropology as wechselzeitige Übersetzung. Maybe it is in such concrete practices rather than in ever more complicated self-reflexive exercises that the solution of the eternal anthropological dilemma between encounter and strangeness has to be sought. The recent dynamics of German anthropology certainly offer powerful resources for this.

Peter Geschiere
University of Amsterdam

Jochen Bonz: Subjekte des Tracks. Ethnographie einer postmodernen/anderen Subkultur. 166 Seiten. Berlin: Kulturverlag Kadmos 2008. ISBN 978-3-86599-049-5.

Dieses Buch ist eine Studie über die elektronische Musikszene in Deutschland der 1990er Jahre. Es ist nicht das erste Buch in deutscher Sprache zu diesem Thema. Erwähnenswert ist hier die Dissertation von Ulf Poschard, die 1997 als Monographie unter dem Titel „DJ Culture. Diskjockeys und Popkultur" im rororo Verlag, Hamburg, erschienen ist. Seitdem gibt es mehrere Veröffentlichungen zur elektronischen Musikszene in Deutschland.

Auf der musikalischen Ebene beschäftigt sich der Autor mit der House-Musik-Szene, die er über mehrere Jahre hinweg beobachtet hat, bis er schließlich selbst Teil dieser Szene wurde. Das heisst, Jochen Bonz hat mehrere House-Veranstaltungen besucht, die er auch sehr ausführlich beschreibt. Außerdem führte er Interviews mit mehreren DJs und Musikjournalisten (die sehr oft auch DJs sind). Beachtenswert sind die langjährigen Interviews, die er mit der ein und derselben Person geführt hat. In dieser Weise werden hervorragend sowohl die Veränderungen innerhalb der Szene als auch die Veränderungen, die sich in den Einstellungen der DJs vollziehen, aufgezeigt. Des Weiteren diskutiert Bonz die Rolle der Medien für die House-Szene. So wird die Berichterstattung in großen Musikzeitschriften – zum Teil auch in Mainstream Zeitschriften – und in kleineren Szenezeitschriften (die als Fanzine bekannt sind)analysiert. Der Autor zeigt auf, dass die Underground-Szene von der Mainstream-(oder basalen) Kultur gar nicht so isoliert ist, und dass „normale" Medien häufiger Veränderungen in den Underground-Kulturen herbei führen, denn durch ihre zahlreiche Berichterstattung fühlen sich immer mehr Leute zur Underground-Szene hingezogen. Die ethnographische Darstellung legt dar, dass die Natur der elektronischen Tanzmusikszene schnell wechselnd ist. Bedeutungen, Orte, Leute und die Musik selbst sind einem stetigen Wandel unterworfen. Daher ist der Schlüsselbegriff des Buches „Track". „Track" bezeichnet ein Musikstück, das weniger Stabilität besitzt als ein „Lied". „Tracks" sind in der House-Musik (und im Allgemeinen in der elektronischen Tanzmusikszene) Musikstücke, die ständig kommen und gehen, durch Remixen verändert und mit unterschiedlicher Geschwindigkeit und Dauer gespielt werden. Der Autor hebt die Bedeutsamkeit der sich stets veränderbaren Atmosphäre in der „Kultur des Tracks" hervor. Diese Atmosphäre, die von unterschiedlichen Symbolen und Subjekten geprägt wird und immer wieder neue „Gestalt annimmt", ja immer wieder neu erfunden wird, ist das, was die House-Kultur ausmacht.

Auf der theoretischen Ebene bezieht sich Jochen Bonz auf Jacques Lacans Konzeptionen der strukturalen Psychoanalyse. Die „Kultur des Tracks" wird beschrieben als eine Kultur sowohl der Moderne als auch der Postmoderne. Überhaupt zeigt sich Jochen Bonz als begeisterter Anhänger der postmodernen Theorie. Diese Begeisterung schlägt sich auch in der Struktur des Buches nieder. Die theoretischen, ethnographischen und analytischen Passagen kommen unsystematisiert und unlogisch hintereinander gereiht daher. Manchmal hat man das Gefühl, eine schlechte Kopie von Derrida zu lesen. Der Leser ist öfters verwirrt darüber, wo genau sich der Autor mit seinem Buch positionieren will. Bonz verliert manchmal nicht nur die Distanz zu seiner Forschung – insbesondere an den Stellen, wo die Gegenüberstellung der House-Kultur und der basalen Kultur diskutiert wird –, sondern ist auch viel zu subjektiv und offensichtlich auf der Seite der House-Kultur (z. B. Seite 74). An diesen Stellen wäre es gut, sich als Szenemitglied hervor zu tun. Bis zum Ende wird nicht klar, ob das Buch den Cultural Studies oder der Soziologie von Subkulturen zugeordnet werden kann. Es ist gut, unterschiedliche Zugänge und Theorien zusammenzubringen, allerdings werden beide theoretischen Richtungen viel zu einfach und rudimentär diskutiert (z. B. S 85–86). Auf die Theorie der Subkulturen geht der Autor viel zu oberflächlich ein. Mit der Aussage, „[d]er Begriff Subkultur ist heute aus der Mode gekommen" (Seite 57), wird deutlich, dass er mit den neuesten Diskussionen in der englischsprachigen Literatur nicht vertraut ist. Es gibt eine Reihe an Veröffentlichungen, die sich genau mit diesem Thema beschäftigen, z. B. Andy Bennett, Alan O'Connor, Hilary Pilkington, David Muggleton. Das theoretische Hin und Her ist langwierig (und langweilig). Erst ab Seite 51 wird das Buch interessant, wo die *Club Culture* auf sehr elegante, spannende und lebendige Art und Weise ausgeführt wird. Man wünscht sich allerdings ein Sachregister, das bei einer solchen postmodernen Struktur des Buches sehr hilfreich wäre.

Die Interviews und die detaillierten Beschreibungen der „Track-Kultur" sind sehr interessant aber auch hektisch strukturiert. Z.B. befindet sich das Datum des Interviews mit Hans Nieswand – einer House Legende – auf Seite 145, das Interview selbst wird auf den Seiten 100–104 wiedergegeben. Der Leser erfährt nicht, wo und unter welchen Umständen der Autor die Interviews überhaupt durchgeführt hat. Es sollte schon am Anfang des Werkes betont werden, dass es sich hier um ein bestimmtes Zeitalter der deutschen elektronischen Musik handelt. Die langen Diskussionen über White Label und 12" Veröffentlichungen sind heutzutage gar nicht mehr relevant, da die meisten DJs mp3-s spielen und nur wenige DJs Vinylplatten benutzen.

Das Buch ist trotz allem ein wichtiger, ethnographischer Beitrag zu einer bestimmten Epoche der deutschen House-Szene. Es beinhaltet sehr originelle Ideen und theoretische Zusammensetzungen. Das Buch dürfte nicht nur für Leser interessant sein, die sich mit der reflexiven oder postmodernen Ethnologie auseinandersetzen, sondern auch für alle diejenigen, die sich für Jugendkulturen interessieren.

Literatur

Bennett, A. 1999: Subcultures or Neo-Tribes? Rethinking the relationship Between Youth, Style and Musical Taste. *Sociology* 33:599–617.
– 2002: Researching Youth Culture and Popular Music: A Methodological Critique. *British Journal of Sociology* 53:452–466.
Muggleton, D. (ed.) 2000: *Inside Subculture*. Oxford, New York: Berg.
O'Connor, A. 2002. Local Scenes and DangerousCrossroads: Punk and Theories of CulturalHybridity. *Popular Music* 21:225–236.
Pilkington, H. 1994: *Russia's Youth and its Culture. A Nation's Constructors and Constructed*. London and New York: Routledge.

Aimar Ventsel
TartuerUniversität/University of Warwick

Mirco Göpfert und Andrea Noll: Disziplin und Kreativität an ghanaischen Internatsschulen. 156 Seiten. Frankfurt am Main: Brandes & Apsel 2013. ISBN 978-3-95558-015-5.

„If you want to become somebody in the future, you have to be educated and you have to be disciplined" (S. 15). Mit diesem Schülerzitat beginnen Andrea Noll und Mirco Göpfert ihre ethnographische Studie zu *Disziplin und Kreativität an ghanaischen Internatsschulen*. Sie analysieren in ihrem Buch jedoch nicht nur die Bedeutung von Disziplin als Erziehungsideal in den Diskursen von Schülern und Lehrkräften, sondern zeigen darüber hinaus anhand von empirischen Beispielen aus dem Schulalltag eines Jungen- und eines Mädcheninternates im Nordwesten Ghanas die interaktive Disziplinierungspraxis, an der Schüler wie Lehrkräftebeteiligt kreativ beteiligt sind.

Bei der *St. Francis Girls' Secondary School* in Jirapa und der 20 km entfernten *Nandom Secondary School* für Jungen, handelt es sich um Sekundarschulen, die in den 1950er/60er Jahren als eine der ersten Internate in der *Upper West Region* Ghanas von katholischen Missionaren gegründet wurden. Trotz ihrer wenig später erfolgten Transformation in öffentliche Internatsschulen und dem damit verbundenen Anstieg der Schülerzahlen gelang es beiden Schulen ihren Ruf als „Eliteschmieden" (S. 15) zu bewahren.

Wie aber werden die Schülerinnen und Schüler in Jirapa und Nandom zu gebildeten und disziplinierten Personen? Was macht ihre Disziplinertheit aus? Worin unterscheiden sich die Erziehungsprozesse und -ideale in den beiden Internatsschulen? Diese Fragen stehen im Zentrum der von Göpfert und Noll vorgelegten Studie. Anders als Goffman, auf den sich die Autoren neben Foucault und Turner für ihre theoretische Rahmung maßgeblich beziehen, sehen sie Internate nicht als „Treibhäuser" oder „totale Institutionen" (Goffman 1972 zitiert auf S. 19), in denen Insassen von der restlichen Gesellschaft losgelöst als passive Objekte geformt werden; sie verweisen vielmehr auf die aktive Selbst-Arbeit der Schüler, auf die dynamische Produktion und Reproduktion von Disziplin als „gelebte Ordnung" (S. 149), auf die Schaffung und Nutzung von Freiräumen innerhalb dieser Ordnung und auf die identitätsstiftende Wirkung dieser Prozesse für die Akteure, sowie für die internatsschulischen Institutionen.

Wie andere Internatsethnographen vor ihnen (Kalthoff, Simpson) begreifen die Autoren die Internatsschule durch ihr Ineinandergreifen von außerschulischer und schulischer Bildung als einen besonders geeigneten Raum für eine dichte Beschreibung von interaktiven Erziehungsprozessen. Hier sind die Schüler, wie die Autoren in Anlehnung an Simpson mit Turner formulieren, in einer Übergangsphase des „betwixt and between" (S. 19): einer Phase, in der – wie es das eingangs zitierte Erziehungsideal vorsieht – aus einem seiner ländlichen Herkunftsregion verhafteten, kindlichen „nobody" ein gebildeter und disziplinierter, erwachsener „somebody" wird. Nun ließe sich argumentieren, dass dieser identitätsbildende Prozess auch an ‚normalen' Tagesschulen beobachtet werden kann, an denen eine Differenz zwischen den in der Schule vermittelten Verhaltenserwartungen und familiär/ gesellschaftlich geteilten Normen hergestellt wird. Während sich dieser Prozess für Schüler an nur tageweise frequentierten Schulen als ein ständiges Springen oder ein Spagat zwischen zwei Lebenswelten darstellt, ist der vom Internatsleben geforderte und von den Internatsschülern – zuweilen rituell – erzeugte Bruch mit ihrer Herkunftswelt umfassender, wie Göpfert und Noll eindrucksvoll schildern.

Das vorliegende Buch resultiert aus einer jeweils dreimonatigen Feldforschung, die Göpfert am Jungeninternat in Nandom und Noll am Mädcheninternat in Jirapa im Jahr 2006 im Rahmen ihrer Magisterarbeiten durchführten. Ausführlich gehen die Autoren auf die unterschiedlichen Rollenzuschreibungen und -erwartungen ein, die ihnen im Forschungsprozess als weder Schüler, noch Lehrer, noch Erzieher, zuteilwurden. Ihre Selbstwahrnehmung als „Lernende" und der geringe Altersunterschied zu den Internatsschülern führte im Verlauf der Forschung zu einer Privilegierung der Schülerperspektive.

Zum Aufbau des Buches: Nach einer Verortung der von ihnen erforschten Internate in der Bildungsgeschichte Nordghanas unter besonderer Berücksichtigung der Bildungschancen von Mädchen, widmen sich die Autoren in vier Kapiteln der Disziplinierung der Schüler, ihren Freiräumen, den Erziehungsidealen der Internatsschulen, und der Bedeutung von Schule als „Ort komplexer Liminalität" (S. 121).

Im Zentrum der Disziplinierungstechniken an der *Nandom Secondary School* sieht Göpfert in Anlehnung an Foucault die „Kontrolle der Körper" (S. 44) und die „Zuweisung einer sozialen Position" (S. 29), die durch die Prinzipien der Vereinheitlichung (das Tragen der Schuluniform, die zeitliche und räumliche Regelung des Tagesablaufs), der Klassifizierung (die Zugehörigkeit zu verschiedenen Jahrgängen, Klassen, Häusern und Schlafräumen), und der Hierarchie (in Jahrgangsstufen und Posten) sowohl von den Lehrkräften, wie von den Schülern überwacht, und gesichert wird. Freiräume, die sowohl eine Umgehung, wie eine Perpetuierung der Disziplinierungsprozesse zulassen, ergeben sich aus der Kontrolle von Lehrern durch die Schüler (bisweilen unter Zuhilfenahme externer Instanzen wie der *Parents Teacher Association*), durch die Aktivierung ‚außerschulischer' Klassifizierungsmerkmale wie Alter, Religionszugehörigkeit, regionaler und sozialer Herkunft, durch die (Aus)nutzung prestigeträchtiger Schülerposten wie der des *prefects*, und „im Lachen der Schüler" (S. 88), beispielsweise durch die Verwendung von Spitznamen. Disziplinierung und Freiräume sind somit eng miteinander verwobene Dimensionen der Schulordnung, der die Schüler nicht einfach unterworfen sind, sondern die sie aktiv mitgestalten.

Ebenso aktiv sind sie an der Produktion und Reproduktion der von den Internatsschulen propagierten Erziehungsideale beteiligt. In Nandom kreist dies Ideal vor allem um die Ausbildung von Führungs- und Folgequalitäten, wie Göpfert anhand einer Analyse des *prefect*-Systems, der Ausstattung einiger Schüler mit besonderer Verantwortung und Kontrollfunktion, zeigt. An der *St. Francis Girls' Secondary School* steht die Erziehung zu guten Staatsbürgerinnen und modernen Hausfrauen im Vordergrund, erläutert Noll basierend auf ihren Beobachtungen aus dem Hauswirtschafts- und Sozialkundeunterricht. Den Übergang, den die Internatsschulen zwischen der dörflichen Herkunft ihrer Schüler und einer modernen Zukunft markieren, analysieren die Autoren im letzten Kapitel ihres Buches, wobei sie sich insbesondere auf die in Jirapa beobachteten ‚partnerschaftlichen' Erziehungspraktiken unter den Schülerinnen, auf das Mobbing von Neuankömmlingen und auf das Initiationsritual der *Nino's Night* beziehen. Mit van Gennep und Turner stellen sie die Internatsschulen überzeugend als „Orte komplexer Liminalität" (S. 121) dar, als Schwellenphase, die in den Augen von Lehrern und Schülern nur durch Disziplinierung – als Prozess und Distinktionsmerkmal – durchschritten werden kann.

Bei ihrer Beschreibung der Disziplinierungspraktiken an der *Nandom Secondary School* und der *St. Francis Girls' Secondary School* tendieren die Autoren insgesamt zu einer Privilegierung der außerschulischen Sozialisation bzw. konzentrieren sich auf jene schulischen Aspekte, in denen die Vermittlung von Erziehungsidealen (wie im Hauswirtschafts- und Sozialkundeunterricht) im Vordergrund steht. Der Unterrichtsalltag und die „Fabrikation schulischen Wissens", die etwa in Kalthoffs (1997:150ff) Studie deutscher Jesuitenkollegs und Landerziehungsheime ausführlich behandelt wird, spielt bei Göpfert und Noll eine Nebenrolle, bedingt u. a. durch ihre schülerzentrierte Perspektive auf Selbstdisziplinierungsprozesse. Ihrem Anspruch, eine „umfassende Schulethnographie vorzulegen" (S. 17), können sie daher nur mit Abstrichen genügen. Eine dichte ethnographische Beschreibung und Analyse internatsschulischer Erziehungsprozesse, die sowohl die Bildungsforschung, wie die Forschungen zu Jugend und der Herausbildung von Eliten bereichert, ist ihnen allerdings hervorragend gelungen.

Literatur

Kalthoff, Herbert 1997: *Wohlerzogenheit: Eine Ethnographie deutscher Internatsschulen.* Frankfurt am Main: Campus Verlag.

Sarah Fichtner
LAM, Science Po Bordeaux

Bruce Kapferer (ed.): Legends of People, Myths of State. Violence, Intolerance, and Political Culture in Sri Lanka and Australia. New and revised edition. 446 pages. New York und Oxford: Berghahn Books 2012. ISBN 978-0-85745-436-2.

Angela Hobart and Bruce Kapferer (eds.): Contesting the State: The Dynamics of Resistance and Control. 297 pages. Wantage/Ascona: Sean Kingston Publishing/Centro Incontri Umani 2012. ISBN 978-1-907774-13-3.

Introduction[1]

> History, then, is very much a mythical construction, in the sense that it is a representation of the past linked to the establishment of an identity in the present. (Friedman 1992:195)

Anthropological interest in the states and state institutions goes back at least to Rivers' monumental *History of Melanesian Society*, published in 1914. In the Preface to the *African Political Systems*, Radcliffe-Brown famously declared: 'The task of social anthropology, as a natural science of human society, is the systematic investigation of the nature of social institutions' (Fortes and Evans-Pritchard 1940:xi). However, it was after the questioning of some colonial-era premises (in the Fortes and Evans-Pritchard volume), and following the horrors of the Second World War that the issue of political organization (and how people deal with it) gradually moved to the forefront of anthropological studies. The end of colonialism, post-colonial controversies, globalization, and bloody conflicts in Sri Lanka, former Yugoslavia and the Horn of Africa, along with some more recent global threats, only reiterated interest in what could loosely be labelled 'anthropology of the state.' The 'state,' of course, can also be used as a symbol, as demonstrated by Abélès (1990).

Issues like ethnicity came more recently into the focus of anthropological research (Schlee 2008:5; Eriksen 2010:4), with Barth stressing that ethnic groups are *constructed*, and that they serve as 'culture-bearing units' (1969:11–13). In his masterful overview, Eriksen points to the role that self-identification plays in many contemporary expressions of nationalism. Sometimes issues of identification and self-identification are related to 'cost-benefit' evaluation (Schlee 2008:27; Bošković and Ignjatović 2012:291–293). When it comes to relationship between ethnicity and identity, Schlee has drawn attention to the fact that conflicts often arise from the actual 'sameness,' so 'enemies become alike' (2008:11).

The books under consideration here present important contributions to contemporary anthropological attempts to understand the intricacies of political behaviour. They set out to explore the relationship between myth, ethnicity and violence (Kapferer), and resistance and control in state context (Hobart and Kapferer), and contributors to both of these volumes try to do it primarily through exploring different types of narratives.

---

[1] Acknowledgements. I am very grateful to Thomas Hylland Eriksen, Edward F. Fischer, and William H. Fisher for comments on an earlier version of this paper. The research for it was supported by the Serbian Ministry of Education, Science and Technological Development, project ID III 47010.

Narrating the state

> The establishment of a telling link between the conditions of the present and the situation of the past is an important tool of political legitimation. (Kapferer 2012:90)

Contesting the State consists of nine chapters, plus the Introduction. The papers were first presented at the conference in Ascona, and the chapters examine some of the 'classical' anthropological topics, but from very contemporary angles. Thus, T. S. M. Evens looks at the 'non-dualism' and identity formation among the Nuer, Overing explores egalitarianism in an Amazonian society (Piaroa), and Hobart the relation between Hindu epics and formation of the Indonesian state. Hart's essay presents a study of an exile returning to his native country (Greece),[2] and Shrestha, in a 'post-Frazerian' way, documents the death of the divine kingship in Nepal. Three chapters that deal with topics that were very prominent in the media and popular discourses in recent years include Taylor on cosmology and Rwandan concepts of the state, Dawod on Sadam Hussein's rise to power in Iraq, and Kapferer and Wijeyeratne on the uneasy transition from war to peace in Sri Lanka. Finally, Friedman's more theoretical concluding chapter (on cosmopolitan intellectuals and re-configuration of the state) nicely ties with the introduction, in which Kapferer and Taylor briefly outline forces in the production of the state.

The volume is exciting collection of case studies, combined with specific theoretical points (the editors begin with quoting Cassirer, and there are frequent references to philosophers and social theorists),[3] and it opens very interesting questions regarding power, authority, and indigenous concepts of them. Its main value is in demonstrating how anthropological research is relevant *here and now* – as well as showing how anthropology is a truly *comparative endeavour*. The contributors respond to contemporary challenges of globalization, while at the same time presenting critical views of different points of view, based on contributors' extensive fieldwork. The papers in *Contesting the State* are also elegantly organized around topics that allow them to converse with each other (like Evens and Overing, for example, on 'societies without a state'), even without making direct references to each other's papers.

The idea of looking into 'newly emerging ontologies,' such as power and control, will appeal to a wide range of scholars in social sciences and humanities, and should serve as an invitation to a thought-provoking dialogue, perhaps similar to the one inaugurated following the publication of *African Political Systems*. On the one hand, state as a political institution demonstrates capacity to change and adapt to new challenges. On the other, some of the more recent global developments (like 'neoliberalism') perhaps make states more congenial to difference, despite increasing internal fragmentation.

Myths and ethnicities

> Myth is a basic category of reference to the historical past. (Malinowski 1993:69)

Kapferer's book is a reprint of the 1988 volume, with the new Introduction, and five additional chapters/commentaries. Additional chapters provide a *dialogue* similar to the 'Comments and

---

[2] Although it is unfortunate that she does not mention Ristovic's study (2000), which dealt extensively with the topic of children refugees from Greece.
[3] With the important point that scholars like Foucault, for example, formulated their notions within the conceptual history of West European (in his case, French) socio-political context.

Reply' section following articles published in *Current Anthropology*, although less critical to the author (after all, this is Kapferer's book). However, they provide some kind of a book within a book, exploring from different angles (sometimes with refreshingly new insights) topics of nationalism and violence (like Bastin's comparative perspective, or Morris's re-evaluation of the sources for studying the ANZAC).

Kapferer's starting point is on the lines of what Cassirer called a move 'from form to function' (1923:11). Historically, nationalism was rejected by many social scientists as 'pre-modern' or destructive, and it was assumed that it will gradually dissipate, or retreat confronted with forces of modernisation.

> How nationalist discourse develops as a humanly destructive force is an empirical matter and demands an interrogation of nationalist arguments and how they became vital in political and social dynamics giving rise to the force and shape of their violence. (...) The perspectives of Gellner (1983) and Hobsbawm (1983), who exemplify such positions [objectivist and rationalist – A.B.], dismiss nationalist arguments as mere figments of the imagination or constructions and distortions of reality. Theirs are important contributions, however, they risk an overdetermination in a European and North American historical experience. Furthermore, they do not confront thoroughly enough either nationalist arguments or the discursive structures of their appeal. (Kapferer 2012:xiv)

The book is more than another approach to ethnicity and violence – it 'describes nationalism as an *ontology*; that is a doctrine about the essence of reality' (Eriksen 2010:129). War, birth, and death are all used as powerful symbols, but they gradually transcend the symbolic and enter 'reality.' In his understanding of interplay between symbols and everyday life, as well as insistence on religious aspects of nationalism, Kapferer appreciates Anderson's (1983) insistence on the importance of understanding nationalist constructions. However, he also notes:

> I conceived of *Legends* as an extension of Anderson's kind of approach, but my objective was to concentrate more on the diverse styles of nationalist imaginations than did Anderson, who in my view remained committed to a linear and too homogenized conception, one still honed within a Western historical perspective. (Kapferer 2012:xxii)

The relationship between myth and history is at the core of Kapferer's arguments. Both of these are different[4] forms of discourse. In his article 'The narrative turn', Paul Ricœur distinguished between two general types of narratives, historical and fictional.[5] Both of these types can be analysed in terms of the *common structure* (as done by structuralists), or their historicity (since they refer 'to the same fundamental feature of our individual and social existence' [Ricœur 1981:274]). The 'impossible logic' of narrative structures opens up another world. In Ricœur's words:

> Everything happens as if the free play of the imagination of mankind in its best storytellers had spontaneously created the intelligible forms on which our reflective judgement can in turn be applied, without having to impose upon itself the impossible task of constructing a

---

[4] Or not so different – see Ricœur 1987.
[5] The fictional narratives include 'myths, folklore, legends, novels, epics, tragedies, drama, films, comic strips, etc.' (Ricœur 1981:281).

> priori the matrix of all possible stories. If that is the case, we could then paraphrase Kant's famous formula about schematism and say: the narrative schematism 'is an art hidden in the human soul, and it will always be difficult to extract the true mechanism from nature in order to lay it open before our eyes'. (1981:287)

The very distinction between 'history' and 'fiction' is in itself fictional in many ways. Ricœur points to the role of the myth as *mimesis* (following the argument from Aristotle's *Poetics*), but this is a *creative imitation* (1981:292–293), not a mere reflection of some 'objective' reality. Through the process of this creative imitation, the world of narratives (Ricœur's 'the world of fiction') brings us '*to the heart of the real world of action*' (p. 296). In conclusion, it seems that 'fiction, by opening us to the unreal, leads us to what is essential in reality' (*ibid.*).

Myths are important for people's sense of identity, as they offer a 'safe heaven,' a place where individuals can feel that their sense of belonging to a group (whether it is an ethnic group or a nation) could be in their best interest. Myths also form an important part of national ideologies, and one of the main achievements of Kapferer's study is to show how different national ideologies (in this case, Sinhalese and Australian) can be structured along very similar lines.

Nationalism influences and shapes ideology by providing important symbolic markers that allow members of the society to focus their anxieties and experience a sense of unity (Billig 1995, Eriksen 2010, Jenkins 1994). It also helps members of a society to form what is sometimes called the 'ethnonational bond' (Connor 1993), or 'ethnonational mobilization' (Ivekovic 2000). This 'bond' then serves to create a feeling of belonging to a shared community. Despite potential fallacies in the process of reaching this unity, the experience is real, and so are its consequences – and thus it is very important to comprehend the mechanisms that shape the public opinion when it comes to particular cases (Kapferer 2012:90 ff).

Concluding remarks

> The world of human culture (...) could not arise until the darkness of myth was fought and overcome. (Cassirer 1946:297–298, *passim*)

Anthropological studies of ethnicity, nationalism, and the state have become increasingly popular in the last two decades. The end of 'Cold War,' dramatic political changes in the Balkans, former USSR, as well as in East Africa, provided significant insights into the works of political institutions. Globalized economies (which were, of course, present before, but we are today much more *aware* of them) made interdependencies of different political, social and cultural institutions more present in the media and in daily lives of people all around the planet. As Cassirer wrote, quoting Hegel: 'The state is no work of art; it exists in the world, and hence in the sphere of choice, accidence, and error. Hence the evil behaviour of its members can disfigure it in many ways' (1946:266). Of the books discussed here, *Contesting the State* represents a long overdue critical approach to debates on authority and power in contemporary world. *Legends of People, Myths of State* has had an interesting history since it was first published. Some of Kapferer's arguments (whether one likes them or not)[6] actually look much more convincing today, then two decades ago, when nationalism seemed like another fallacy that is bound to gradually

---

[6] For example, Spencer 1990a. On the other hand, Spencer 1990b is much more conciliatory, and seems to realize that the two of them actually address very different issues.

fade away. The civil war – which was not directly addressed in the book when it was first published – that began in Sri Lanka in 1983, ended in 2009, leaving at least 100,000 people dead and country economically devastated. There were also significant developments in the other case study of the book, Australia, with the political changes towards development of an 'egalitarian individualism' (addressed in the final chapter of the new edition),[7] as well as Prime Minister's historical public apology to members of the Aboriginal population (in February 2008). Perhaps some of these recent events better explain Kapferer's very pessimistic view of the state in general (primarily Australia, but Sri Lanka as well).

Nationalism did not whither away – it demonstrated amazing capacity of transformation and resilience. The same can be said of the states – the advent of global political institutions did not provide for any significant 'supra-national' identities. Anthropologists are in a unique position to observe and to comment on these developments, and these two books present an essential contribution to understanding ethnicity, violence, and myths justifying them. For states, just like any other social institutions, contain their own interpretations. One only needs to gain access to them.[8]

References

Abélès, Marc 1990: *Anthropologie de l'État*. Paris: Armand Colin.
Anderson, Benedict 1983: *Imagined Communities: Reflections on the Origin and Spread of Nationalism*. London: Verso.
Barth, Fredrik 1969: Introduction. In: Fredrik Barth (ed.), *Ethnic Groups and Boundaries: The Social Organisation of Culture Difference*. Bergen: Universitets Forlaget, pp. 9–37.
Billig, Michael 1995: *Banal Nationalism*. Newbury Park and London: Sage.
Bošković, Aleksandar; Suzana Ignjatović 2012: Understanding ethnic conflicts through rational choice: A review article. *Ethnos* 77(2):289–294.
Cassirer, Ernst 1923: *Philosophie der symbolischen Formen. Die Sprache*. Darmstadt: Wissenschaftliche Buchgesellschaft.
Cassirer, Ernst 1946: *The Myth of the State*. New Haven: Yale University Press.
Connor, Walker 1993: Beyond reason: The nature of the ethnonational bond. *Ethnic and Racial Studies* 16(3):373–389.
Eriksen, Thomas Hylland 2010: *Ethnicity & Nationalism: Anthropological Perspectives*. 3rd, revised edition. London: Pluto Press.
Fortes, Meyer; E. E. Evans-Pritchard (eds.) 1940: *African Political Systems*. London: Oxford University Press.
Friedman, Jonathan 1992: Myth, history, and political identity. *Cultural Anthropology* 7(2):194–210.
Geertz, Clifford 1972: Deep play: Notes on the Balinese cockfight. U: Clifford Geertz (prir.), *Myth, Symbol and Culture*. New York: W.W. Norton & Company, Inc, pp. 1–37.
Gellner, Ernest 1983: *Nations and Nationalism: New Perspectives on the Past*. Oxford: Blackwell.
Hobsbawm, Eric 1983: Introduction: inventing traditions. In: Eric Hobsbawm and Terence Ranger (eds.), *The Invention of Tradition*. Cambridge: Cambridge University Press, pp. 1–14.
Ivekovic, Ivan 2000: *Ethnic and Regional Conflicts in Yugoslavia and Transcaucasia: A Political Economy of Contemporary Ethnonational Mobilization*. Ravenna: Longo Editore.
Jenkins, Richard 1994: Rethinking ethnicity: identity, categorization and power. *Ethnic and Racial Studies* 17(2):197–223.

---

[7] But see also a brilliant vignette on Crocodile Dundee, Kapferer 2012:16–17.
[8] Cf. Geertz 1972:37.

Malinowski, Bronislaw 1993 [1904/5]: Observations on Friedrich Nietzche's *The Birth of Tragedy*. In: Robert J. Thornton and Peter Skalnik (eds.), *The Early Writings of Bronislaw Malinowski*. Cambridge: Cambridge University Press, pp. 67–88.

Ricœur, Paul 1981 [1979]: The narrative function. In: Paul Ricœur, *Hermeneutics & The Human Sciences*. Edited and translated by John B. Thompson. Cambridge and Paris: Cambridge University Press and Maison des Sciences de l'Homme, pp. 274–296.

Ricœur, Paul 1987: Myth and history. In *Encyclopedia of Religion* (Mircea Eliade, gen. ed.) New York: Macmillan. Vol. 10:273–282.

Rivers, W. H. R. 1914: *A History of Melanesian Society*. 2 Vols. Cambridge: Cambridge University Press.

Ristovic, Milan 2000: *A Long Journey Home: Greek Refugee Children in Yugoslavia, 1948–1960*. Translated by Aleksandar Boškovic. Thessaloniki: Institute of Balkan Studies.

Schlee, Günther 2008: *How Enemies are Made: Towards a Theory of Ethnic and Religious Conflicts*. New York and Oxford: Berghahn.

Spencer, Jonathan 1990a: Writing within: Anthropology, nationalism, and culture in Sri Lanka. *Current Anthropology* 31(3):283–300.

Spencer, Jonathan 1990b: Collective violence and everyday practice in Sri Lanka. *Modern Asian Studies* 24(3):603–623.

Aleksandar Bošković

REIMER

www.reimer-verlag.de

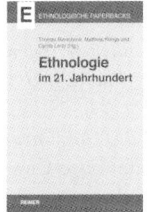

Thomas Bierschenk, Matthias Krings und Carola Lentz (Hg.)
Ethnologie im 21. Jahrhundert
288 Seiten
Broschiert / ISBN 978-3-496-02863-5

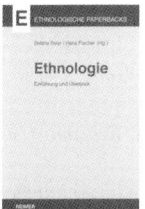

Bettina Beer, Hans Fischer (Hg.)
Ethnologie
Einführung und Überblick
476 Seiten mit 16 Abbildungen
Broschiert / ISBN 978-3-496-02844-4

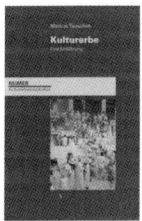

Markus Tauschek
Kulturerbe
Eine Einführung
212 Seiten mit 12 s/w-Abbildungen
Broschiert / ISBN 978-3-496-01484-3

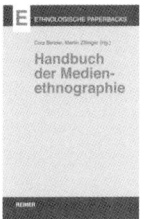

Cora Bender, Martin Zillinger (Hg.)
Handbuch der Medienethnographie
ca. 400 Seiten mit ca. 50 Abbildungen
Broschiert / ISBN 978-3-496-02849-9

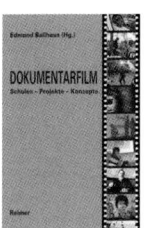

Edmund Ballhaus (Hg.)
Dokumentarfilm
Schulen – Projekte – Konzepte
420 Seiten
Broschiert / ISBN 978-3-496-02864-2

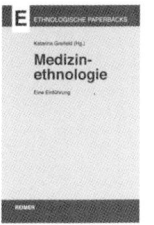

Katarina Greifeld (Hg.)
Medizinethnologie
Eine Einführung
204 Seiten mit 6 s/w-Abbildungen
Broschiert / ISBN 978-3-496-02859-8

REIMER

www.reimer-verlag.de

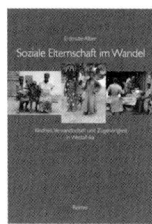

Erdmute Alber
Soziale Elternschaft im Wandel
Kindspflegschaft, Verwandtschaft und Zugehörigkeit in Westafrika
426 Seiten mit 19 Abbildungen, 21 Tabellen und 5 Grafiken
Broschiert / ISBN 978-3-496-02868-0

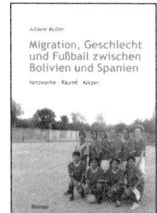

Juliane Müller
Migration, Geschlecht und Fußball zwischen Bolivien und Spanien
Netzwerke – Räume – Körper
224 Seiten mit 16 Farb-Abbildungen
Broschiert / ISBN 978-3-496-02846-8

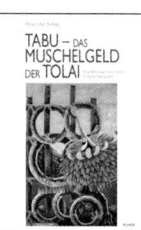

Alexander Solyga
Tabu – das Muschelgeld der Tolai
Eine Ethnologie des Geldes in Papua-Neuguinea
411 Seiten mit 18 Farbabbildungen, 4 Grafiken, 6 Tabellen
Broschiert / ISBN 978-3-496-02851-2

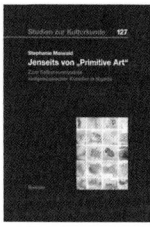

Stephanie Maiwald
Jenseits von »Primitive Art«
Zum Selbstverständnis zeitgenössischer Künstler in Nigeria
245 Seiten, mit 16 Farb- und 4 s/w-Abbildungen
Broschiert / ISBN 978-3-496-02867-3

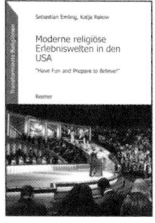

Sebastian Emling, Katja Rakow
Moderne religiöse Erlebniswelten in den USA
»Have Fun and Prepare to Believe!«
ca. 200 Seiten mit 10 Farbabbildungen
Broschiert / ISBN 978-3-496-02860-4

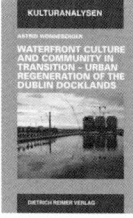

Astrid Wonneberger
Waterfront Culture and Community in Transition
Urban Regeneration of the Dublin Docklands
Englisch
397 Seiten mit 90 s/w-Abbildungen
Broschiert / ISBN 978-3-496-02861-1